Global Media Discourse

Global Media Discourse provides an accessible, lively introduction into how globalisation is changing the language and communicative practices of the media.

Featuring a wide range of exercises, examples and images, this textbook offers the student a practical way into analysing the discourses of the global media industrles. Building on a comprehensive introduction to the history and theory of global media communication, it draws case studies from films, global women's magazines, Vietnamese news reporting and computer war games. Finally this book investigates how global media communication is produced, looking at the formats, languages and images used in creating media materials, both globally and in localised forms.

Written in an accessible style, this book integrates a range of approaches, including political economy, discourse analysis and ethnography and will be of particular interest to students of media and communication studies, applied linguistics and (critical) discourse analysis.

David Machin is Lecturer in the Department of Media and Communication at the University of Leicester, UK. Among his previous publications are: *Introduction to Multimodal Analysis* (2007), *News Production: Theory and Practice* (2006) and *The Anglo-American Media Connection* (1999).

Theo van Leeuwen has worked as a television producer and director and is currently Dean for the Faculty of Humanities and Social Sciences at the University of Technology, Sydney, Australia. He has written many books and articles on multi-modality, discourse analysis and visual communication including: *Introducing Social Semiotics* (2004), A *Handbook of Visual Analysis* with Carey Jewitt (2001) and *Reading Images – A Grammar of Visual Design* with Gunther Kress (2006).

Global Media Discourse

A critical introduction

**David Machin and
Theo van Leeuwen**

Routledge
Taylor & Francis Group

LONDON AND NEW YORK

First published 2007
by Routledge
2 Park Square, Milton Park, Abingdon, Oxon OX14 4RN

Simultaneously published in the USA and Canada
by Routledge
711 Third Avenue, New York, NY 10017

Routledge is an imprint of the Taylor & Francis Group, an informa business

© 2007 David Machin & Theo van Leeuwen

Typeset in Bell Gothic by
Florence Production Ltd, Stoodleigh, Devon

British Library Cataloguing in Publication Data
A catalogue record for this book is available
from the British Library

Library of Congress Cataloging in Publication Data
Machin, David, Ph.D.
   Global media discourse: a critical introduction/David Machin
   and Theo van Leeuwen.
       p. cm.
     Includes bibliographical references.
   1. Communication, International.   2. Globalization.
   I. Van Leeuwen, Theo, 1947–   II. Title.
   P96.I5.M235 2007
   302.2–dc22   2006035956

ISBN10: 0–415–35945–7 (hbk)
ISBN10: 0–415–35946–5 (pbk)
ISBN10: 0–203–00747–6 (ebk)

ISBN13: 978–0–415–35945–0 (hbk)
ISBN13: 978–0–415–35946–7 (pbk)
ISBN13: 978–0–203–00747–1 (ebk)

Contents

Figures

Preface

This book is one of the outcomes of a five-year research programme on language and global communication carried out at Cardiff University's Centre for Language and Communication and funded by the Leverhulme Trust.

In this programme we studied how globalisation has changed language and communication in a range of fields including not just the media, but also health, tourism and Welsh language and culture. The programme created a wonderfully stimulating environment for our work. There were regular workshops in which we presented our work in progress to our colleagues, and we would like to express our enormous appreciation for their constant interest in, and engagement with, our work. Thank you, Hywel Bishop, Nik Coupland, Betsy Evans, Peter Garrett, Adam Jaworski, Sarah Lawson, Annabelle Mooney, Klas Prytz, Srikant Sarangi, Joanna Thornborrow, Gordon Tucker, Angela Williams and Virpi Ylänne. The programme also allowed us to invite guests to these workshops and we are grateful for comments and contributions by Peter Auer, Jan Blommaert, Brigitta Busch, Norman Fairclough, Monica Heller, Alastair Pennycook, Robert Phillipson and Tove Skuttnab-Kangas, Ben Rampton, Ron and Suzie Scollon, Abram de Swaan, Terry Threadgold and Jeremy Tunstall. Our project officer Lowri Griffith worked behind the scenes, not just to coordinate and organise the programme's activities, but also to imbue it with a sense of community and conviviality. Her work was enormously important to us all.

Initially we thought our research would involve a great deal of travel, but we ended up creating, instead, a global network of helpers and co-researchers who spent shorter or longer times with us in Cardiff and sent us media materials and interviews from many corners of the world. They included Janneke Fernhout, Michelle Lazar, Ping Shaw, Usama Suleiman, Sa Tran, Hans van Leeuwen, Emily Pettafor and Julia Zullo and we are also grateful to the many media workers who were willing to be interviewed.

As our work progressed, we tried it out on, and with, our undergraduate and postgraduate students at Cardiff University, and we have benefited a great deal from their questions and ideas. A special thanks goes to Lu Xing-Hua. We also presented our work in many different venues. We would like to single out in particular the annual meetings of the critical discourse analysis group, and we are grateful to Lilie Chouliaraki, Norman Fairclough, Phil Graham, Betsy Mitsikopoulou, Teun van Dijk, Ruth Wodak and others for their interest and encouragement.

Working together on this project has been one of the most productive and enjoyable ventures in our lives as researchers and university teachers. For Theo it finally achieved the kind of interdisciplinarity between political economy, discourse analysis and ethnography which he had always argued for, but never actually practised. For David it meant an encounter with detailed linguistic and multimodal discourse which has changed and enriched his work as a media researcher and teacher. Both of us aimed at developing an approach to media discourse that would appeal, not just to people already working in the relatively small field of media discourse, but also to the much bigger field of media studies generally. Both of us also wanted to make a book which would be accessible and speak, not just to specialists, but also to students and non-specialists, and we are grateful to our editors, Louise Semlyen and Nadia Seemungal, for having made this possible. We also thank Bethan Evans for help with obtaining image rights. Whether we have succeeded or not it is of course too early to tell.

David Machin and Theo van Leeuwen

Introduction

It is not hard to see that the media are becoming increasingly global. The same films screen all over the world. The same television programmes and the same news footage are shown everywhere, albeit sometimes in 'localised' versions. The same bestsellers and glossy magazines dominate the stands of newsagents and booksellers and the same music is heard the world over. Global culture industries now produce and distribute consciousness for us all.

At the same time, new forms of migration have brought more cultural diversity to the major cities of European nation states than they have seen for a long time. And alongside the mainstream global media that seek to reach out to everyone everywhere, there are no longer only national media, but also a diversity of other media, catering for ethnic communities, sometimes locally produced, sometimes globally distributed from their countries of origin, as for instance in the case of Bollywood.

Nation states have tried, and are still trying, to stem this tide, to preserve the unity of their national media and to keep out what they often see as threats against their beliefs and ways of life. The Netherlands, in the 1980s, quickly cabled the whole country and prohibited satellite dishes to try and halt the erosion of its traditional media system (De Swaan, 1991). China has blocked media sources such as CNN, NBC and the *Washington Post*, and still blocks the websites of the BBC and several other Western news and entertainment media. Other examples could be mentioned. In many cases resistance gradually weakened. Economic prosperity and global culture seem to go hand in hand, and cannot be bought separately. In other cases, we cannot be so sure. In Indonesia, the editor and the centrefold model of the first localised issue of *Playboy* were charged with indecency, after demonstrations against 'Western decadence'. This kind of resistance seems to be growing.

Critics of globalisation have argued that globalisation leads to unprecedented standardisation and cultural homogeneity. Some make comparisons with the natural environment. Like species, they argue, local cultures and languages are in danger of becoming extinct and, as a result, the world's cultural resources will dwindle. Innovation will become more difficult. The global media industries have responded by deliberately creating diversity, producing global media in 'local' languages and integrating 'local' content in various ways. We discuss several examples of such localisation in this book. Theorists, too, have responded by arguing that global media products are not necessarily everywhere 'read' in the same way. People from different cultures will interpret and experience them differently, they say, thereby 'indigenising' the global media (Appadurai, 1990), so that diversity is maintained after all, albeit in a less tangible form. We discuss such theories in Chapter 1. For the moment it is clear that we live in a period of transition. Two worlds coexist uneasily: the world of nation states, with their national languages and cultures, and the global world with its emerging global language and culture carried, not by nation states, but by global corporations and international organisations.

Another thing is also becoming clear – this new global culture is not universally accepted. It has not brought about a global village in which we can all live peacefully together. Other global cultures have emerged alongside, carried by transnational religions and dispersed ethnic groups. New cultural and political conflicts are emerging, and a new war – the 'war on terrorism'. Like the cold war, this war is ideologically driven. But the enemy is no longer an alliance of nation states. It is a globally dispersed cultural, political and religious movement. It is for this reason that we pay special attention to Arab-language media that seek to present an alternative version of this war.

Theorists of media globalisation tend to foreground either the evident increase in global homogeneity or these new diversities (which also include new chances for local minorities or regions whose languages and cultures were repressed by nation states). We discuss these issues in Chapter 2, and again in Chapter 7. Here we would like to stress that, in this book, we do not so much seek to give answers as to ask questions and offer tools for exploring these questions, in all their complexity. We look both at 'top-down' localisations of global media products, asking in which respects they are similar and in which respect different, both in form and content, and at 'local' media that are either produced for the global market or as alternatives to the dominant global media. How different are they from the global media products they seek to challenge or compete with?

In exploring questions of this kind, we focus on the global media products themselves, but not at the expense of their contexts of production, distribution and, especially, reception. Global media impact on the societies in which they are introduced and may clash with traditional ways of life. In a country like Vietnam this is happening right now. In a country like the Netherlands it started to happen more than 50 years ago. The Dutch writer Geert Mak described his first encounter with global media, at age 5, in the quiet and rather provincial Holland of the times:

> I try to remember the living room at the Westersingel, on an autumn evening in 1952. No sound other than the quiet ticking of the cosy stove, the only heater in the house. A single lamp lights up the dark oak dinner table, the chairs around it, the chest of drawers behind it, the rest of the room. Everything revolves around that light and that table.
>
> Suddenly there are footsteps outside, and through the letterbox comes something incredibly colourful and glossy: a comic strip magazine. It is the first Donald Duck, delivered door to door and free in half the country. Most of the pictures inside are in black and white but they nevertheless make a deep impression. A duck as a school teacher! And the nephews just pressing an icecream

to his forehead when he complains about a headache! Unheard of liberties, set in an only dimly known world of cars, refrigerators and televisions. A world which was neither Protestant nor Catholic nor Neutral, but in which people belonged to nothing. That too was unprecedented.

(Mak, 1999: 418)

As we will see when we discuss Disney in more detail, magazines like this did not arrive from nowhere. They were not carried like seeds on the wind. There were intentions behind their worldwide distribution, a mission to spread the virtues of the American way, 'a Marshall plan of ideas', as the American film producer Walter Wanger said in 1950 (quoted in Miller *et al.*, 2000: 25). And they were read in specific ways in a Holland where people did not yet have cars, refrigerators and televisions, where they clashed with traditional respect for authorities and with the Dutch 'pillar' system in which everyone belonged to a social 'pillar' with its own media, its own educational and political institutions, and so on.

This book is divided into three parts. The first part sets up the context. We present a history of media globalisation and an overview of the main themes of globalisation theory, and we apply these themes to specific case studies of media globalisation so as to keep in focus the complexities that tend to get backgrounded in all too broad theoretical statements (including theoretical statements about complexity).

The second part focuses on lifestyle and entertainment media in relation to three areas, covered in three separate chapters: identity and community; sex and work; and war. Chapter 3 proposes that global media engender different kinds of identity and community from those traditionally fostered in nation states. Chapter 4 deals specifically with the kind of identities that global media create for women. Our focus is on the magazine *Cosmopolitan*, which started in the early 1960s in the USA, as part of the 'second wave' of feminism, and which now appears in localised form in 48 languages around the world. *Cosmopolitan* has consistently, and globally, propagated its ideal of the 'fun, fearless female' – a woman who has a career and remains independent, although she is frequently involved in pleasure-seeking casual affairs. In many cultural contexts this ideal is just as revolutionary as the three little ducks' disrespect for authority was for the 5-year-old Geert Mak in 1952 Holland. For women it holds out the prospect of liberation from patriarchal relations; for the traditional, patriarchal societies in which they live it threatens the fabric that held them together. Chapter 5 explores how the 'war on terrorism' is represented in computer war games. The American computer game industry is now bigger than the Hollywood film industry. Many of the games it produces deal with war, are closely modelled on actual events (mostly in the Middle East), and are explicitly intended to aid the war against terrorism. Middle Eastern game designers have produced alternative war games, to propagate another view of the same events. We compare their games to American war games and talk to players from different cultural backgrounds to probe their awareness of the political dimensions of these games.

In Part III we look at the 'how' of global media communication. We will look at the 'formats' of media materials (celebrity profiles, 'hot tips' genres, and so on), arguing that they are not just neutral containers for 'localised' content, but carriers of culturally specific messages of their own. We look at language, exploring the influence of globalisation on journalistic English in Vietnam and the way in which the Dutch, Spanish and Chinese languages have adapted themselves to the conversational, tongue-in-cheek 'tone' of *Cosmopolitan* magazine. And finally, we look at the images that are produced for global consumption by global image banks such as Getty Creative Images.

Most of the examples we use in the book come from our own research over the past five years.[1] They represent only a small selection from the many examples we could also have chosen, and for this reason our book cannot provide definitive answers. We hope it will be useful as a guide towards further exploration. The questions we have added to the chapters aim to assist in that process.

Note

1   The project was part of a larger project entitled Language and Global Communication, carried out at Cardiff University 2001–2006, and funded by The Leverhulme Trust.

PART I

Contexts

In this first section we set up the context, presenting a short history of media globalisation and an overview of the main themes of globalisation theory.

Chapter 1 deals with the rise of global media. One of the major theoretical issues of globalisation is the homogenisation of world culture through Western media, and through the values and kinds of identity they promote. We look at examples of the earliest forms of global media and show how their rise to global dominance formed part of a US project that was at once economic and ideological. US news, movies, advertising and magazines created the template for today's global media, its industrialised and standardised processes, and its use of local features in order to make global media products successful. We also show how, right from the beginning, politics, culture and economics came together in the entertainment products that were shipped around the planet.

Chapter 2 is concerned with the question of what media globalisation is, and with the different ways that global media and global media formats and styles find their way into societies. While there are as many different stories about globalisation as there are societies, there are, nevertheless, some notable patterns. The chapter looks at these complexities, using two case studies: Dutch women's magazines and Arab comic strips. This allows us to avoid the kind of broad generalisations that often characterise theories of globalisation.

1 Histories of media globalisation

In this chapter we look at the history of media globalisation, singling out some key developments and exemplifying them with case histories. We start with the history of news agencies, the first truly global media enterprise.

The globalisation of news

Many of us tend to think of news as a natural phenomenon – a straightforward and self-evident process where professional journalists inform members of their societies about important issues. It seems natural that we should find newspapers all around the planet. Yet sociologists have shown us that what we call 'news' is quite an odd set of institutional practices that must be understood in terms of its social and historical development. And this context is a European and American one. News itself, and its associated practices, the organisations of its institutions, its formats and genre, have their origins particularly in European and American culture. And central to the global spread of news as a genre and also in terms of content has been the news agency – the first global medium.

Early nineteenth-century newspapers were an important vehicle of political communication. They did not yet separate 'fact' and 'comment'. They openly took sides in political issues and carried editorials on the front page in which they conducted debates with 'correspondents' that could last for days. Today, editorials are sometimes still called 'leading articles', but they are no longer on the front page, and their writers no longer conduct debates with letter writers, while 'correspondents' are now professional journalists, rather than readers. News agencies started in the middle of the nineteenth century to supply these newspapers with news items from across the world. Information became a commodity, presented in a neutral style to be saleable to editors of different political persuasion. In developing such a neutral style, news agencies would pioneer a 'journalism of information' (Boyd-Barrett et al., 1998: 7) that would eventually take over from the earlier journalism of argument and political debate, although this happened much more slowly on the continent. They would also spearhead the importance of the urgency and topicality of the news, setting great store on speed of delivery. In this they were helped by the new technology of the telegraph.

The first agencies started in the late 1840s in Germany (Wolff), France (Havas) and the UK (Reuters). Other national agencies followed, but the three major agencies managed to monopolise the flow of news and form a cartel that divided up the world in the same way as empire-building nation states in that same period divided up the world to form their colonial empires. In this arrangement the big three agencies had monopoly access to the national agencies in their territories, and these national agencies in turn (and, therefore, also the newspapers that relied on them) could only buy news from the global agency that had the monopoly in their territory.

Three aspects in the development of news agencies are particularly important for understanding the development of global media communication generally:

- the close links they forged between news and the global financial market;
- the 'journalism of information' they developed, with its standardised formats and routine devices for guaranteeing facticity and credibility; and
- the way in which they catered both to national, often propagandistic, interests, and to international, often market-oriented interests.

We discuss these in turn.

News and the market

From the beginning the news agencies provided not only news to the press, but also business intelligence to financial brokers and businessmen. Reuters, Wolff and Havas had all worked in banking before they started their news agencies, and they established their agencies close to, or in, the stock exchanges of London, Berlin and Paris. They saw news as a commodity, supplying traders with the opening and closing prices of the stock exchanges as fast as they could, to provide them with the up-to-date information they needed to be ahead of their competitors.

Today's news agencies have not changed in this respect. They operate on the principle that 'almost anything that passes as news in print, broadcasting and electronic media is likely to have some financial implication for someone' and that the best stories 'move markets' (Boyd-Barrett, 1998: 62). Boyd-Barrett (ibid., 72) quotes a Reuters quality controller praising a journalist: 'Our story weakened the dollar and the Bank of Japan intervened in its support . . . Our competitors were left chasing reactions in support . . . We beat the competition hands down. Great stuff.' Companies such as Reuters, now joined by newcomers like Bloomberg, Dow Jones and Knight Ridder, also provide 'financial desktop products' such as interactive dealing services, automated matching systems for futures contracts, and information management tools. More than 90 per cent of Reuters' revenue now comes from financial services.

Many people still think of politics, culture and economics as separate domains. In global media communication they come together. We are now familiar with the ways in which marketing permeates culture and politics. The news agencies already pioneered this more than 150 years ago, in a different age.

Standardisation

To sell to editors of different political persuasion, news had to become politically neutral, pure information, pure fact. This approach, which today is common in newspapers the world over, was gradually developed and globally propagated by the major news agencies. In a 1915 jubilee brochure, Reuters already wrote of 'compressing news into minute globules' (Palmer, 1998: 184). These 'globules' condensed news stories to their absolute essence, and at the same time used standard devices to guarantee facticity, for instance an insistence on including specific times and places and on mentioning sources for anything even remotely open to interpretation. Michael Palmer (1998) has described how Reuters imposed its standards on early twentieth-century Russia, where it had started to work with a new local news agency, Vestnik, in 1904. Regularly, Reuters chided Vestnik for filing stories which consisted 'mainly of argumentative statements which appear to have a semi-official character and to be intended to influence public opinion in this country' (ibid., 182). 'We must not be judgemental or editorialise', they wrote. 'Stick to the facts.' And: 'One of your dispatches yesterday began with "The mess persists . . .". If such be the case, mere factual reporting should suffice. Facts without comments please.' (ibid., 182). Vestnik, on the other hand, felt that many of Reuters' reports were not factual, but 'speculated about events'. 'We abstained from communicating to you these rumours until they found realisation', they wrote. 'If, however, you are willing to receive from us private and totally unconfirmed rumours, we are quite prepared to supply you with them just to please you' (ibid., 182).

In the course of the twentieth century, standardisation increased further. In the 1980s the chief editors of news agencies began to publish voluminous handbooks to prescribe company style in minute detail and they also started quality control units to reinforce their prescriptions day by day, as in this quote, where a journalist is reminded of the principles of the 'lead paragraph':

> Those first 20 or 30 words make or break the story . . . Many media subscribers scanning wire services directories on a computer screen will decide whether to use a Reuters' story rather than an AP or AFP story on the basis solely of the headline and first paragraph . . . The lead paragraph should . . . stand as a self-contained story, complete with source if the subject is contentious . . . .
>
> (ibid., 187)

Today such standardisation is second nature to working journalists the world over. When we discuss a Vietnamese newspaper in Chapter 7, we see that what went on in Russia in 1904, the process of adapting local approaches to a global 'journalism of information', was still going on, just a few years ago, in Hanoi.

International and national aspects

The rise of the news agencies took place in the second half of the nineteenth century, the heyday of nationalism in Europe. Nation states all started their own news agencies, and the national interests these agencies sought to protect sometimes clashed with the interests of the international agencies on which they depended. Schulze-Schneider

(1998) has documented the case of Spain, where the national agency Fabra had been controlled by Havas from its inception in 1865. When Spain fought its war in Cuba in 1898, the world press was on Cuba's side and Havas ignored the news Fabra provided. Fabra then protested and Havas eventually compromised by agreeing to distribute official Spanish statements. Later, the propagandistic role of news agencies intensified. In 1939, after the Civil War, EFE, a new Spanish agency, was started, as an instrument of the Franco regime. It made no secret of its propagandistic intentions: 'News agencies are a powerful instrument in the task of distribution of news and influence abroad' (ibid., 120). The Nazis had already nationalised Wolff in 1933, merging it with its competitor Telegrafisches Union, and viewing it as a key tool of National-Socialist propaganda (Wilke, 1998). America and Britain also enlisted their media in the war effort.

In the 1960s, the newly independent African countries set up their own news agencies, as well as a pan-African TV exchange. Similar agencies and exchanges were established in other parts of the world: Eurovision, Arabvision, Asiavision, Caribvision. They adopted some of the values of the 'journalism of information', but had other interests as well. The charter of Arabvision, for instance, states that the material it will distribute 'shall reflect the interests of the Arab man, deepen his belief in the unity of objectives and destiny of the Arab nation, develop common trends in the Arab homeland by disseminating information on its message and potentialities, while stressing and supporting the causes of the struggle' (quoted in Hjarvard, 1998: 212). Western journalists constantly criticise these agencies and exchanges for being under the control of governments. The majority of the political news items supplied by Asiavision from any country, complained one journalist, 'are about the activities of the government, with a heavy dose of official visits and ceremonies. Coverage of opposition activities is rare, and in the case of some members completely absent' (ibid., 215).

Under Communism, the news agencies of Eastern European countries were also government-controlled. After the fall of the Berlin Wall in 1989, the major Western agencies moved in, further diminishing the remaining influence of local agencies. A company like Reuters now derives 25 per cent of its revenue from the former Communist countries in Eastern Europe. The Baltic states and the new states of the former Yugoslavia, however, have founded new, fervently nationalistic state media.

On the surface, most countries' news and information media are still national. They support their countries' national ethos and protect national interests. But below that – invisible to most newspaper readers, radio listeners and television viewers – there has been a gradual increase in the influence of the global media producers and their market-driven interests. National news agencies had never found it easy to reach out beyond their own territory and today they are in decline in many parts of the world. The exchanges that seek to provide alternatives to the agenda of the global agencies also find it difficult to keep their heads above water. The view that only private ownership and an open market can guarantee free, unbiased information is gaining ground everywhere.

The cartel of European news agencies collapsed in 1934, when the United Press Association (UPA) refused to join the cartel and began its own global operations. The other major American agency, Associated Press (AP) followed. From this moment, the major news agencies began to compete with each other, and the USA, rather than Europe, became the major player. The new global agencies that started in the late twentieth century were all American: Bloomberg, Knight Ridder, Dow Jones.

It is sometimes said, particularly by 'local' broadcasters, that news agencies only supply 'raw material', which they then 'localise' and 'domesticate'. Broadcasters often refer to agency material as 'protection' or 'insurance policy' and take credit for stories they have not themselves generated (Patterson, 1998: 85). Careful content research has shown, however, that agency video material is most often used in virtually unchanged form (ibid., 85). A famous case was the 1984 famine in Ethiopia, which the BBC claimed to have brought to the attention of the world when it had in fact been filmed by a Reuters' correspondent: 'The power of exchange systems and TV news agencies . . . is much greater than the public generally knows or feels' (Malik, 1992: 88).

Newer news outlets in poorer countries will be set up to run directly from material provided from the big agencies. Many will not have the facilities for extra levels of editing or presentation. So giant media corporations like Reuters and Worldwide Television News will send packages of more or less identical clips and pre-prepared scripts around the world for easy, cheap, immediate use (Patterson, 1998; Machin and Niblock, 2006).

The globalisation of American media

From the 1920s onwards, America began to take the lead, not only in the provision of news, but also in other media, so much so that, in the 1970s, a study of the political economy of the mass media could be called *The Media Are American* (Tunstall, 1977). Hollywood was the first breakthrough. Until 1918, most movies and movie equipment were produced in Europe. France even exported a dozen films a week to the USA (Miller *et al.*, 2000). But in 1918 Congress passed an Act that would allow the Motion Picture Export Association (MPEA) to set export prices and impose conditions on overseas sales that were not allowed at home, such as blind bidding and block booking. As a result foreign sales soon became a significant part of the film industry's revenue. After the Second World War, America was in a position to impose quotas in Europe and gradually push local production to the margins, especially now that the Hollywood giants have become part of large conglomerates that not only produce the films, but also own multiplex cinemas, video retail outlets and cable/satellite channels everywhere in the world. By the mid-1990s America controlled about 85 per cent of the world's film market and even in France, which has been the only European country to retain a strong home production industry, French-language films now account for only 30 per cent of their home box office revenue (Robinson, 1995: 245).

When television came along, the USA was already well ahead of the game. All of the main television formats – news, soaps, drama, game shows and advertising – were invented in America. After the Second World War, the state-controlled public service television channels that most other countries had established gradually weakened and, one by one, gave in to the pressure of establishing commercial broadcasting. The arrival of satellite broadcasting hastened the process. Satellite TV changed what audiences expected from television, and even the strictest government-controlled television channels had to shift towards more entertainment-based programming, as for instance in India and Egypt.

In the 1980s, satellite broadcasters, like other global corporations, began to see profit in localisation. CNN established Spanish and Hindi services, for instance, and MTV established production centres in Italy, Germany, the UK, India, Taiwan and Singapore. Hong Kong's STAR TV, which, in 1991, had launched a satellite covering 38 nations and capturing a potential audience of 2.7 billion, soon discovered that 'Indians do not like watching serials in Mandarin and that the Chinese react equally negatively to South Indian Malayalam songs' (*Financial Times*, 17 November 1995) and started diversifying its programming. For this reason, some media theorists have argued that globalisation leads to heterogenisation rather than homogenisation (for example, Sinclair *et al.*, 1996), and that we now live in a world characterised by 'regional realignments and fracturings, national and ethnic separatisms, and in parallel, a proliferation of overlapping and criss-crossing media vectors which undermine a unified and singular notion of the global' (Ang, 1994: 325).

It is true that satellite TV allowed other exporters of television programmes to enter the market, for instance Brazil in Latin America and Egypt in the Middle East. But it is also true that local as well as global television producers everywhere use American genres and formats as their 'best practice models' and 'adopt Western broadcasting structures (commercialisation, management hierarchies, broadcasting schedules, etc.' (Butcher, 2003: 16), and, everywhere, depend on advertising. The new world of the privatisation of television is ultimately driven by the $400 billion global advertising industry, which, itself, has also seen an unprecedented concentration of ownership, as global corporations seek global deals to ensure global brands. The same logic of commercialisation now drives the content of news. With the need to feed shareholders, outlets increasingly have fewer and fewer staff and must think carefully about addressing groups favoured by advertisers (Machin and Niblock, 2006).

The music industry should perhaps be mentioned as well. It, too, started in the USA, where the format of the 'single' was pioneered. Today, a small number of record companies, owned by large media conglomerates such as AOL Time Warner, Bertelsmann and Sony, control about 90 per cent of world record sales. Global music corporations have also moved towards localisation. David Flack, Creative Director of MTV Asia, even sees himself as building other peoples' national identities:

Localisation is actually helping build national identity. I've made it a personal rule not to commission anything outside of a country for that country. If we're doing a show for Indonesia, the title sequence and all the rest has to be generated by people from that country, otherwise it's not going to be relevant to them . . . English is a kind of hip factor, but it's good to be talking in the local language.

(quoted in Graddol, 1998: 47)

Of course we should not forget that this idea of 'nation' and of 'national identity' is itself a European one, which has also been sent and adopted around the planet, mainly as the European colonial powers conquered and invaded and began to divide up the world in their own image.

In music, too, media theorists have argued the case for increasing diversity and heterogeneity, as local versions of global music genres, such as hip hop, emerge in many different countries. But while it is true that the new genre of 'world music' has found worldwide distribution, it occupies only a modest amount of space in the big record stores. And while it is true that global music is not only globally listened to, but also globally (re)produced and to some degree made local, 'indigenised', it is also true that it is based on formats that were developed in the USA and that are promoted by the big transnational record labels.

Three themes are particularly important for an understanding of America's rise to media hegemony:

- ❶ the missionary zeal that informed it;
- ❷ the link between entertainment and politics on which it was founded; and
- ❸ again, the emphasis on standardisation.

We discuss these themes in turn, using two case studies as examples, *Reader's Digest* and Disney. As it happens both were prime targets of a classic critique of American global media on which we touch in Chapter 2, the work of Dorfman and Mattelart (Dorfman, 1983; Dorfman and Mattelart, 1984).

The missionary spirit of American media globalisation

Already in the 1920s, the then Commerce Secretary, Herbert Hoover, had praised Hollywood as 'a powerful influence on behalf of American goods' as well as on behalf of 'intellectual ideals and national ideals' (quoted in Miller *et al.*, 2000: 26). Later, film producer Walter Wanger would speak of America's post-war movie export as 'A Marshall Plan of ideas' (Miller *et al.*, 2000: 25). The combination of profit motive and idealism is typical and would continue to characterise American media globalisation. Often profit was foregone for the sake of ensuring worldwide access to the media that spread the American way of life, as in the case of the free distribution of *Donald Duck* in the Netherlands. In *The Media are American*, Tunstall (1977) showed how, in the late 1970s, the same television series sold to different countries for very different prices. Where, for example, the UK was charged $3,500–5,000 for a half-hour episode of a TV series, and West Germany $4,900–5,300, Uganda was charged $25–30 for the same episode, and Bulgaria $65–100 (Tunstall, 1977: 301–3).

Reader's Digest is a particularly telling example of this missionary spirit. Founded in 1922, it condensed, every month, 31 articles selected from magazines such as *Literary Digest, Women's Home Companion, Vanity Fair*, etc. Its breakthrough came in the early 1930s when it added 'Art of Living' articles with titles such as 'Is Honesty The Best Policy?', 'How To Regulate Your Weight', 'The Shortest Route To The Top', and started experimenting with forms of reader participation in which readers could send in anecdotes and jokes as well as personal experiences ('The Night I Met Einstein'; 'Larry couldn't walk, he could barely talk, but what a gift of the spirit he brought to others').

A journalist who worked on the magazine described its founding editor, DeWitt Wallace, as a somewhat naive idealist bent on spreading 'good American values' ('family, church, community') across the world, and valuing the idea of 'service' above profits (Canning, 1996: 140), which did not stop him from becoming a multi-millionaire. 'Readers everywhere', he said, 'will join in emphasizing the need for extending the interpretative influence of *Reader's Digest* throughout those countries where a clear conception of the United States of today will promote an alliance of interests for the cause of peace tomorrow' (Wood, 1958: 169).

DeWitt Wallace's global mission was astonishingly successful. It started with a UK version in 1938. A Spanish-language edition was launched two years later, followed by a Portuguese edition in 1942, a Swedish edition in 1943, and an Arab-language edition in 1943. By 1958 the magazine was published in 13 languages, counting 30 different editions for 100 countries. It had offices in New York, London, Paris, Copenhagen, Havana, Helsinki, Quebec, Madrid, Milan, Oslo, Rio de Janeiro, Stockholm, Stuttgart, Sydney, Toronto and Tokyo. Its European circulation had reached 2,800,000 and its worldwide circulation 8,800,000.

The global spread of Disney had started a little earlier. By 1937 Disney comic strips, comic books and story books appeared in 27 languages. Hitler had originally banned 'Michael Maus' because it had mocked German uniforms, but later allowed him back in. In Soviet Russia, Mickey had been banned as 'a typical example of the meekness of the proletariat under Capitalism', then reinterpreted as a social satire because it showed capitalists as mice and pigs, and finally banned again. In Japan, Mickey was the most popular figure after the Emperor (Schickel, 1968: 167). By 1966 Disney estimated that in that one year 240,000,000 people had seen a Disney movie, 100,000,000 watched a Disney TV show, 800,000,000 read Disney books or magazines, and 150,000,000 had read a Disney comic story.

Disney, too, saw his work as spreading good, clean American values. A study by Michael Real (1977) demonstrated that, by and large, American audiences saw it that way as well. Disney stood for positive values such as happiness, friendliness, honesty, innocence, industriousness and cleanliness. Wasko *et al.* (2001) repeated the study some 20 years later, in 17 countries, including Australia, Brazil, Denmark, France, Greece, Japan, Korea, Mexico, Norway and South Africa. Their results showed that something had changed. Attitudes towards Disney, and towards American commercial culture generally, had become more ambivalent. Yes, Disney was still associated with positive values everywhere, seen as presenting a 'cheerful, bright, hopeful and dreamful' America, as a 20-year-old Japanese student put it (ibid., 51). But it also stood for 'consumerism, individualism and excess', as a 21-year-old Mexican student said (ibid., 51), and there was much critique of the stereotyped ways in which Disney products depict the rest of the world, and of their racism and sexism. This study is discussed in more detail in Chapter 2.

Regulation and the free market

For much of the past 100 years, the media have been regulated at a national level. Such regulation has prevented newspapers, television and other media from being owned and controlled by a small number of people, who would thereby gain too much control over what people see, hear and read. It has ensured the media pluralism, the plurality of views, that is considered an essential aspect of public communication in democratic societies. More recently, however, another argument has gained ascendance: the view that democracy is best served by free ownership of the mass media, rather than state intervention and red tape. Free ownership alone would ensure that audiences get what they want. This line of free-market thinking has now become enshrined in the philosophy of the institutions that control the world's media market – the World Trade Organization and the World Bank (over both of which the USA has no small amount of control). And as a result the media have everywhere opened up to privatisation, commercialisation and globalisation.

After the Second World War, the USA, having overtaken its former competitors Britain and France, pushed for a loosening of trade restrictions in order to sell its products around the world. It used its military power and economic aid to get governments to act favourably to US aims, and as a result could expand its transnational industries (petroleum, pharmaceuticals, cars, etc.) across the face of the globe. It was also able to put in place the GATT agreement, whereby a number of countries agreed to reduce tariffs on trade in manufactured goods, and to use the International Monetary Fund (IMF) to push other countries to reduce tariffs in return for loans and aid through the World Bank. The IMF and the World Bank were established under the Bretton Woods Agreement of 1944 to aid international economic stability and growth. Both were set up as lending agencies to help countries in trouble with balance of payments and also to finance rebuilding after the Second World War. Of course, this was in the interest of economically stronger nations, and money was primarily given to projects run by large Western corporations.

In the 1980s, GATT shifted its attention to the service sector, meaning that foreign investments would be allowed in areas such as water and administration. But GATT had no formal rules, was based on mutual agreements and mainly addressed trade in manufactured goods. In 1995 it was therefore replaced by the World Trade Organization (WTO), which took on a much broader view of trade that included telecommunications, mass media, services, insurance, etc., and which also acquired the power of sanctions. The door was now open for the established media conglomerates and their portfolios of advertiser-driven content to exploit the new markets.

In the 1990s, the USA introduced important changes in media regulation. US government policy had always supported the profitable expansion of US media at home and abroad. Each segment of the US media had its own regulatory box. But, pushed by media lobbying, the Telecommunications Act of 1996 changed all this by abolishing the boundaries between the different media, and allowing companies to make acquisitions and mergers across a range of media. The Act also removed caps on numbers of outlets, such as the number of radio stations that could be owned by a single company. The spirit of the Act was then exported to other countries, starting with Europe and Latin America. Since the mid-1990s there has, therefore, been a massive wave of commercialisation of the mass media across the planet, leading to the reduction of many localised differences. National governments were obliged to relinquish control over their media if they wanted to participate in world trade. Many commentators declared that the era of media globalisation had truly begun. Meanwhile the WTO and the World Bank set out to establish a media system better able to serve the global market economy, and everywhere former public media were sold off to private interests.

This regulatory environment led to the creation of massive media conglomerates such as Viacom, Disney and News Corporation, able to produce movies, show them around the world in their own cinemas and on their own television channels, promote them on other media and rent them out in their global chain of video rental stores. Such conglomerates also have chains of radio stations, newspapers, magazines and book publishing companies. After deregulation, all the major US networks were bought up by these conglomerates – ABC by Disney, CBS by Viacom, and NBC by General Electric. As a result, we can now find ourselves watching an action movie where an American hero fights against evil terrorists, followed by a news item on the fight against terrorism produced by the same corporation.

Such corporations are billion dollar a year organisations and some of them are among the biggest companies in the world (McChesney, 2004: 21). They are closely tied to investment banking and to industrial capital with interests across a range of other industries (Wasko, 1982; Herman and Chomsky, 1998). Large financial groups tend to own large chunks of them (Snoddy, 1996). Not surprisingly, many argue that such corporations are unlikely to be critical of free-market policies and of capitalism, as they are crucially dependent on the global advertising industry, which in turn is dominated by a handful of US and British corporations (for example, Hollingsworth, 1986; Kellner, 1990). As more new countries enter the global trade networks, these large corporations move in, simply introducing their own products, buying up local media, or creating trading relationships with existing large media organisations to bring them into the global system.

Entertainment and politics

The link between entertainment and propaganda goes back at least as far as the 1930s when Goebbels (1948: 122) wrote that 'argument is no longer effective' and looked towards popular song, humour and movies as key media of propaganda: 'With films we can make politics too. It is a good expedient in the struggle for the soul of our people' (quoted in Bramstedt, 1965: 278). The American popular media have consistently spread, not just good, clean family values, but also political messages. We, again, use *Reader's Digest* and Disney as examples. Our discussion of computer war games, in Chapter 5, provides a more extended and more recent example.

The first foreign-language editions of *Reader's Digest* were started in the service of war propaganda. The Spanish edition was launched in 1940 to support the US war propaganda effort in South America and carried a four-page insert featuring the Stars and Stripes together with the flags of the 20 Latin American states. The price was halved to make the magazine affordable to all. The next two editions, the Swedish and the Arab ones, were both requested by the Office of War Information. In the late 1960s and early 1970s the magazine had close connections with the Nixon government. Articles such as 'From Hanoi – With Thanks' (January 1970) were prepared with help from Nixon's State Department and showed how anti-war demonstrators were 'giving comfort and aid to the enemy' (Canning, 1996: 140). In the 1980s the magazine became a CIA mouthpiece and strongly supported the conservative policies of the Reagan government. Canning (1996: 316) lists some telling headlines:

1992	'We're Spending Too Much On Schools'
	'Don't Buy These Environmental Myths'
	'Worker's Compensation: License to Steal'
1993	'Get Tough With Killer Kids'
	'Why Welfare For Illegal Aliens'
	'*Must* Our Prisons Be Resorts?'

'In a single issue', Canning writes (ibid., 317), 'Reader's Digest repudiated the homeless ("until they summon the will to help themselves, all the help in the world is so much wasted effort"), starving Africans ("The overwhelming responsibility ... lies with the people of Africa. No amount of money can do the job they must do for themselves"), AIDS victims ("HIV remains overwhelmingly confined to gays and drugs users ... unless you are a member of these groups, there is no reason to fear"), Union members ("from coast to coast, tax payers are asked to fund bloated, wasteful labor contracts"). All in a single issue.' But David Ogilvy, advertising guru and founder of the Ogilvy and Mather's advertising agency, praised the *Digest*: 'The magazine exports the best in American life ... In my opinion the *Digest* is doing as much as the United States Information Agency to win the battle for men's minds' (quoted in Schiller, 1976: 6).

Disney, too, participated in the Second World War propaganda effort and Disney cartoons contained many references to political events, for instance to war demonstrations.

Dorfman and Mattelart, in their book *How to Read Donald Duck* (1983), included an image, for which they were later taken to court by Disney (we were unable to obtain permissions to use them here), where Donald Duck shows that anti-Vietnam war protesters are hypocrites. The demonstrations are portrayed as a social disease. Donald Duck also appeared with a character called 'Wan Beeg Rath' who was a Vietcong soldier. In these stories the soldiers would be in favour of the King saying things like 'why they keep these silly revolutions going forever'.

As Dorfman and Mattelart have pointed out (Dorfman, 1983; Dorfman and Mattelart, 1984), Disney's most profound political effect lies in the humorous and seemingly innocent way in which he constantly reaffirms American superiority and hegemony by depicting the rest of the world in terms of comical, backward stereotypes, not unlike those used in an earlier age to justify colonialism:

> Just as Disney plunders all folklore, fairy tales, and nineteenth and twentieth-century children's literature, reshaping it in his average North American image, so he proceeds with world geography. He feels no obligation to avoid the caricature, and rebaptizes every country as if it were a can on a shelf, an object of infinite fun, always good for a laugh: Azteclano, Chiliburgeria, Brutopia, Volcanovia, Inca Blinca, Hondorica and San Bananidor in Latin America . . . Siambodia, Unsteadystan and South Miseryland in East Asia – a disheartening panorama of the majority of mankind as viewed by a minority that happens to have a monopoly on the concoction of postcards and package tours.
>
> (Dorfman, 1983: 24)

A consistent finding of Wasko *et al.*'s (2001) study of attitudes towards Disney across the world is that Disney is fairly uncritically accepted and enjoyed until people come face to face with stereotypes of their own countries, their own stories, their own traditions. Only then does the arrogance implicit in Disney's attitude to the world suddenly hit home.

Standardisation

It was in America that cultural production was turned into an 'industry', and 'industries' tend to produce standardised products. Critics like Adorno had already drawn attention to this before the Second World War, for instance in relation to the standardised formats of American popular song (Adorno, 1978 [1938]), but since then the standardisation of information and entertainment has progressed a good deal further. *Reader's Digest* and Disney are used as examples.

★ ENGLISH ★ FRENCH ★ SPANISH ★ PORTUGUESE

★ DANISH ★ NORWEGIAN ★ ARABIC ★ FINNISH

THIRTEEN DIFFERENT LANGUAGES

Figure 1.1 Local versions of *Reader's Digest*

Already in the 1930s *Reader's Digest* had developed very precise guidelines for the look and style of the magazine, and these were imposed on all local editions. They all had to be called (in the local language of course) either 'Selections from Reader's Digest' or 'The Best from Reader's Digest' and they all had to look exactly the same, with the same masthead, picture panel and list of contents. Only the Japanese edition was a little smaller (Figure 1.1). The same technical requirements of length, structure, readability and, of course, point of view had to be adhered to the world over. To achieve this, local editors selected by *Reader's Digest*'s Director International, and supervised locally for the first few months of their tenure, worked under strict control from the magazine's headquarters in Pleasantville. Advance copies of the US edition would be sent to the local editors who then selected from these offerings and sent their selections back to the USA for comments. Translation was local, and sometimes included some cultural adaptation: sexuality had to be watched in the Arab edition, articles on birth control avoided in Catholic countries, and so on. Yet overall, DeWitt Wallace was convinced that 'people around the world would respond to the same amalgam of humour, intimate biography and thrilling narrative, expose and art-of-living material which arouses the interest of Digest readers in the United States' (quoted in Wood, 1958: 177).

Disney products were, in the main, not localised, although they were of course translated or dubbed, usually by local companies who were closely supervised by Disney. The Brazilian edition was an exception, because a local company had been able to buy the rights to publish *O Pato Donald* and adapt the American comics to some degree. The Brazilian Mickey celebrates carnival, for instance, and characters from the American South become Brazilian *caipiras* telling Brazilian folk stories. *Miki*, the Egyptian version of Mickey Mouse, is another exception. It had Mickey celebrating Ramadan, or wearing Egyptian dress and carrying worry beads (Douglas and Malti-Douglas, 1994).

Disney also pioneered the merchandising of his characters, making it possible to wear the Disney brand as a badge of identity. The result can be seen in Disney shops the world over. Silvia Molina y Vedia (2001) interviewed 17–21-year-old Mexican students about Disney. Many denied interest in Disney or even expressed their dislike of Disney products. And yet they would wear Disney socks, Disney T-shirts, Disney backpack patches, and so on:

> When asked how it was possible to deny all contact with Disney and at the same time, habitually use such objects, all responded with an initial moment of confusion. Some were surprised and said they hadn't noticed. Others said that it didn't really have anything to do with Disney, but was merely fashionable or simply 'looked nice'. A few others were at a loss what to say and walked away, while some laughed and avoided further comment.
>
> (Molina y Vedia, 2001: 216)

Other media globalisations

We do not want to give the impression that the flow of information and entertainment was entirely one-way. Countries other than America have occasionally succeeded in marketing their media products globally, and there have been, and still are, alternatives to the American dominance over the world's mainstream media. In the 1970s there was a major move to try and create a 'new world information and communication order' (NWICO). It led to a 1983 UNESCO report that covered all the issues – the monopoly of the news agencies as well as the one-way traffic in media entertainment and the spread of advertising, which the report described as propagating materialistic values (MacBride and Roach, 2000). But America withdrew from UNESCO in the same year that the report was published, and in the ensuing climate of deregulation and privatisation the movement lost its impetus. The same happened to the Inter Press Service (IPS), an alternative international information provider set up by Christian Democratic parties in Europe and Latin America 'to give a voice to those who traditionally have been marginalized by mainstream media' (quoted in Giffard, 1998: 193). After the end of the Cold War, however, the developing world lost its strategic importance for the West, and much of the money that used to flow to developing world countries was redirected to Eastern Europe. The IPS budget went down from $15 million to $5 million, staffing levels were cut severely and production went down (ibid., 198). Kivikuro (1998) tells a similar story about the decline of the Tanzanian news agency Shihate.

The global flow of entertainment media, meanwhile, has become more complex. American media products are no longer always made in America. Many Disney films, for instance, are produced in Australia (Nightingale, 1998), mainly using Australian technical know-how, while artistic control remains in the USA. Like other countries, Australia nevertheless manages, from time to time, to export its own global media products, for instance the television series *Neighbours* and some of its movies, and a few Australian actors have become Hollywood stars. Other examples could be mentioned, for instance the television programme *Big Brother*, which originated in the Netherlands and is owned by the Dutch company Endemol, or the success of Japanese comic strips. Most local products, however, do not travel well and increasingly rely on government subsidy. And many do not survive. Kaitatzi-Whitlock and Terzis (1998: 136), for instance, have described how, in the 1930s, Mickey Mouse 'came to rival Karagiozis, the wily, sulky and self-derogatory anti-hero of traditional Greek shadow theatre, and ever since then, the odds have been against Karagiozls'. In the Netherlands, in the late 1960s, a Dutch-language version of *Sesame Street* displaced *De Fabeltjeskrant,* a very popular children's television programme based on traditional Dutch puppet theatre techniques. In Korea, too, local producers could not resist Disney and either disappeared or merged (Seung Hyun Kim and Kyung Sook Lee, 1998).

Finally, we should again mention the global cultural industries that cater for dispersed ethnic groups, for instance Bollywood. Some of these industries have very large global audiences, although they do not reach out beyond their own ethnic groups in the way that the American media do. Nevertheless, they have contributed to the multicultural diversity of modern cities, and new generations have started to pioneer new cultural forms that mix American commercialised culture with traditions from their own ethnic heritage, such as in the area of popular music (cf. Mitchell, 1996). And we should still bear in mind that many of these alternative media industries still rely on formats that were invented in the USA. As we argue in Part III of this book, formats themselves are not value neutral but shape the ideas that they contain.

Questions

1   Look at one or two recent issues of the *National Geographic*. Can you find examples of standardisation? Can you find evidence of political propaganda, and if so, is it mixed up in some way with elements of entertainment?
2   Collect some local or localised advertisements drawing on the national identity of your country for its text and/or imagery. What is local about them and what global?
3   Compare articles about the same issue (preferably an action by some 'local' government) from two newspapers, a local and a localised global one (for example, the Singapore *Straits Times* and the Asian edition of *Time* magazine). How are they different?
4   Interview members of the same family from three generations (your own family or another) in relation to a particular example of global media, for instance magazines. What magazines were they reading when they were in their teens? Try to draw some conclusions. Is there evidence of increasing globalisation in your country? If so, how do your interviewees feel about this?

2 Theories of media globalisation

Homogenisation

This chapter looks more closely at two key themes of globalisation theory. On the first, the theme of homogeneity and diversity, we have already touched. Does globalisation lead to increased cultural homogeneity, does it engender new forms of diversity – or does it do both? The second is the question of what globalisation is, and when it began. Is it a distinct feature of modernity, or even of postmodernity? Or has it existed for as long as there have been trade routes, cultural exchanges, empires and major religions that stretched across the known worlds of the time?

The problem with the debate about homogeneity and diversity is, it is not a neutral issue. The claim that globalisation homogenises culture is usually part of an explicit critique of globalisation, even if it is not always clear in the name of who or what globalisation is criticised – what interests are at stake for the critics, and what alternatives, if any, they have in mind. And the claim that globalisation does *not* have to lead to increased homogeneity, in turn, is usually part of a critique of those critics, and, therefore, if not a defence of globalisation, then at least a view which is *not* explicitly critical of globalisation and the global culture industry.

The case for cultural homogenisation is often associated with another more specific idea, the idea of 'cultural imperialism', the idea that 'globalisation is really another name for the dominant role of the United States', as Henry Kissinger once put it (quoted in Miller *et al.,* 2000: 17). Well-known theories of cultural imperialism include Schiller (1971, 1976), Dorfman (1983), Dorfman and Mattelart (1984), and Herman and Chomsky (2002). The term 'imperialism' suggests an empire which conquers territories by force and then 'pacifies' them. In a literal sense this did not happen in the case of American 'cultural imperialism', or at least, the force that was used was economic force, the power to set prices and quotas, and the power of superior technologies, superior budgets and superior technical skills (cf. Tunstall, 1977; Tunstall and Machin, 1999). Yet, as Schiller (1971) has pointed out, and as we see in the discussion on computer war games in Chapter 5, there is a close connection between America's military-industrial complex and its commercialised culture, and America used quite aggressive tactics in building its cultural empire, for instance in forcing commercial broadcasting on countries that wanted to keep it out (beaming advertisements into the UK and the Low Countries from pirate radio stations in the North Sea). The American communications system, Schiller has said, 'utilises the communication media for its defence and entrenchment wherever it exists already and for expansion to locales where it hopes to become active'

(1971: 3). As we have seen in Chapter 1, ~~in the second half of the twentieth century~~ ~~American media did indeed 'conquer' many parts of the world, not only by exporting~~ ~~their own media products but also by infiltrating themselves into local media~~ ~~everywhere, changing them from the inside out.~~ As Tunstall has said (1977: 17):

> In most of the world's countries the media are only there at all, on the present scale, as a result of imports in which the American media (with some British support) predominate. One major influence of American imported media lies in the styles and patterns which most other countries in the world have adopted and copied. This influence includes the very definition of what a *newspaper*, or a *feature film*, or a *television set* is.

This empire did not just happen. It was a deliberate and explicit project. From the 1920s onwards, but especially ~~since the Second World War, American media~~ ~~have quite deliberately sought cultural world domination.~~ Schiller (1971: 3) quotes *Life* editor Luce, who said, in 1941, 'We must accept wholeheartedly our duty and our opportunity as the most powerful and vital nation in the world and in consequence exert upon the world the full impact of our influence ... it now becomes our time to be the powerhouse from which the ideals spread across the world.' But today, global commercialised culture is no longer uniquely American, or rather, America is no longer just in America, it is everywhere, and it interacts everywhere with local cultures and local values.

The question is, why should this be bad? Why should it be criticised? Is it not possible to argue, as so many Americans have done, that we are finally moving towards a universal culture and, therefore, towards peace, towards a global village in which we are all free to say and do what we want, towards 'the end of history'? To answer this question, media theorists rarely point to the obvious: that peace has evidently not yet arrived, that American values and the American way of life are not universally accepted, and that ideological differences continue to cause conflict around the globe. Two aspects of American global media practices have often been singled out, particularly in critiques which, implicitly or explicitly, defended European national media and high culture: standardisation and simplification.

Standardisation implies a tightening of the rules, whether as a result of imposing more, and stricter, rules (for example, the style guides of modern news agencies) or as a result of technological restrictions on what is possible (for example, the standard 'landscape' format of film and television screens), and standardisation has indeed been a key feature of America's 'industrialisation' of creative production. Adorno's critique of American popular songs (1978 [1938]) is a classic example. In these songs, he said, 'the familiarity of a piece has become a surrogate for the quality ascribed to it' (ibid., 271) and 'the forms are so strictly standardised, down to the number of beats and the exact duration, that no specific form appears in any particular piece' (ibid., 289). Many have critiqued Adorno's views as an 'elitist' defence of high culture. They sometimes forget that he wrote in Germany in the

1930s, where Goebbels had waged a campaign against high art, and declared many works of high culture to be *entartet* ('degenerate'). 'We are loaded down with far too much tradition and piety', he had said. 'Look at the Americans, they have only a few Negro songs, but they present them so topically that they conquer the whole world with them' (Goebbels, 1948: 151).

It is true that Adorno belonged to a cultural elite, but it was no longer a powerful elite, quite the contrary. For critics there is always something at stake, always something to be defended. For Jack Lang, the French Minister of Culture who in 1983 called the American television series *Dallas* 'the symbol of American cultural imperialism' (quoted in Ang, 1985: 2), it was French culture and the French language. For Adorno it was high culture and the power of artists and intellectuals to make a real difference to the world. The cultures defended by such critics have great achievements behind them, but they are declining, slowly but surely. The cultures that are replacing them, or absorbing them, may as yet be crude by comparison. But they are irresistibly on the rise.

Adorno also attacked American popular music for its simplification. Simplification is not the same as standardisation, because it does not necessarily derive from industrial processes of creative production. 'Contemporary listening', Adorno said, 'has regressed, arrested at the infantile stage' (ibid., 86). This should again be seen in the light of the period in which he wrote, a period in which Goebbels had declared simplification a virtue: 'Influencing public opinion will be achieved only by the man who is able to reduce problems to the simplest terms and who has the courage to keep forever repeating them despite the objections of the intellectuals' (Goebbels, 1948: 22). No wonder that Adorno was appalled when he came across quite similar views in American commercialised culture, after his escape from the Nazis to New York.

Simplification is also an important aspect of Dorfman and Mattelart's critique of Disney and *Reader's Digest*. American media, Dorfman wrote, 'infantilise the reader':

> Disney, the superheroes and the *Digest* all propose to their readers, in one way or another, a rejuvenation of the tired adult world, the possibility of conserving some form of innocence as one grows up. Not only the characters, but those who absorb them are offered a fountain of eternal youth ... The adult-as-spoiled-child of Donald Duck, or the innocent-in-the-body-of-the-infinite-adult in Superman, or the reader as Adam-with-all-the-knowledge-of-Faust in the *Digest* – all complement and answer the needs of a subservient and passive consumer ... and all are products of the United States of America whose global preeminence ... has coincided with this century's technological leap in mass communication and left the US in a very special position to use its media art to engender its most lasting and popular symbols.
>
> (Dorfman, 1983: 200–1)

The idea of homogeneity, finally, is, in the context of globalisation theory, closely associated with the idea that cultural differences are disappearing as a result of globalisation. Yet, homogenisation was equally important in the formation of national cultures, albeit on a smaller scale and, there too, it oppressed local ('regional') cultures and languages ('dialects'). Attempts to keep nation states culturally homogeneous, at their worst resulting in 'ethnic cleansing', are at least as problematic as global homogenisation, if not more so. And while it has clearly been involved in a project of cultural homogenisation, based on a belief in the universal appeal of the American way of life, American commercialised culture has by now already moved beyond this stage. The term 'glocalisation' entered the vocabulary of theorists only in the 1990s, but it was originally 1980s' business jargon for the global distribution of products to increasingly differentiated local markets (Robertson, 1995: 20).

In later chapters we ask how far such 'differentiation' goes; whether it really reintroduces cultural difference or is only a surface phenomenon. For now, we need to return to the values at stake in the question of American cultural imperialism and the global commercialised culture that has overtaken it. For critics like Dorfman and Mattelart cultural homogenisation is bad when it pretends to be universal but isn't. When it pretends to stand for universal human values, but doesn't. When it excludes people, because they do not have enough money to be part of this global culture, or because they want to stick to different values, or because they want to make different kinds of cultural products. Writing from a Latin American point of view, they argued that Disney, while apparently universal ('Duckburg is everywhere and nowhere', Dorfman and Mattelart, 1984: 16), in fact reduced everything that does not adhere to American values and the American way of life to insignificant and demeaning caricatures:

> Who can deny that the Peruvian in Inca-Blinca is somnolent, sells pottery, sits on his haunches, eats hot peppers, has a thousand-year-old culture, all the dislocated prejudices proclaimed by the tourist posters themselves? Disney does not invent these caricatures, he only exploits them to the utmost ... The only means that the Mexican has of knowing Peru is through caricature, while Peru is incapable of being anything else, and is unable to rise above this prototypical situation, imprisoned, as it is made to seem, within its own exoticism.
>
> (Dorfman and Mattelart, 1984: 54)

Diversity

A critique of the critics of cultural imperialism emerged in the early 1980s, initially centring on the American television series *Dallas* (for example, Ang, 1985; Katz and Liebes, 1986). In the late 1970s, Tunstall had declared that 'the high tide of American media exports has passed' and that '*I Love Lucy*, *Peyton Place* and *Mission Impossible* no longer rule the global village quite as masterfully as in the 1960s' (1977: 18). But *Dallas*, the saga of a Texan oil family, surpassed them all, and became a new focus for the critique of American cultural imperialism, as in the reaction of Jack Lang, the French Minister of Culture, which we have already quoted. But not everybody agreed. A new generation of media theorists had grown up with American television and liked it, as Ang, for instance, quite openly admits (1985: 12). They did not recognise themselves in the image of the passive and infantilised victim of mass media manipulation that some of the critics of American cultural imperialism had drawn. Katz and Liebes (1986), for instance, set out to show that viewers in different cultural contexts understand and experience the same programmes in different ways. They conducted focus groups about *Dallas* with culturally different groups in Israel (Russian immigrants, Israeli Arabs, Moroccan immigrants and kibbutzniks) and concluded that they understood the programme differently, that they all enjoyed the programme and could yet be critical of it, and that they used the programme as 'raw material' for the 'interactive negotiation' of meaning. A snippet from one of these focus groups, the kibbutz group (ibid., 194):

Sarah:　　When I see them I pity them.
Amaliah:　I live better than they do.
Sarah:　　And I tell myself how terrible it would be if I was one of them.
Amaliah:　With all that they have money, my life style is higher than theirs.

Perhaps it is predictable that kibbutzniks, who have chosen a communal lifestyle, need to distance themselves from the wealthy lifestyle of *Dallas,* at least in public. But that does not mean that they could not secretly feel attracted to it at the same time. Advertising and many media stories work that way — they allow us to laugh at them, or to dismiss them as unreal, while at the same time getting their message across. Fairytales work that way as well, as Bettelheim (1976) has shown. Their distance from everyday reality allows deep-seated fears and desires to be addressed more effectively.

   Katz and Liebes claim that *Dallas* and other American programmes appeal to audiences across the world because they have 'primordial', universal themes. In this they are perhaps closer to *Reader's Digest* editor DeWitt Wallace's views about the universality of the *Digest*'s contents than they might have realised. They also argue that programmes like *Dallas* are deliberately ambiguous, deliberately open to different interpretations. The reading of a programme like *Dallas* is a 'process of negotiation between the story on the screen and the culture of the viewers' (Katz and Liebes, 1986: 187). In sum, like other theorists of the time, they shifted from an emphasis on production to an emphasis on consumption, and from an emphasis on the diversity of culturally different media products to an emphasis on the diversity of culturally different opinions *about* media products. Although this approach is still very common in media and cultural studies, it is now in the process of being overtaken. New critics are emerging, this time not from the USA or Northern Europe but from other parts of the world, this time not writing in defence of European national culture and high culture, but in defence of other cultures and other views that clash in other ways with the values of global commercialised culture and its definitions of freedom.

The study of Disney on which we have already touched (Wasko *et al.,* 2001), brings this out in unexpected ways. Like the *Dallas* studies, it focuses on audiences, but these audiences are from yet another generation. They are young students from the late 1990s – and from across the world. They have grown up with Disney and understand his message very well, yet they are at times ambivalent about Disney, or even critical. Brazilian students, for instance, dislike Disney's way of representing Latin America and are sceptical about the Disney ideology, yet a visit to Disneyland in Florida is a 'rite de passage' (Reis, 1998). Mexican students, Greek students and Korean students admit they liked Disney as children, but grew to become more critical. But there is a curious exception to this. In the Northern European countries included (especially Norway, Sweden and Denmark) this critical attitude is absent. Here students reject the suggestion that their countries are 'Americanised'. 'I never thought of Disney as American', says a Norwegian student, 'when I was a kid I always thought of them as Norwegian, I guess Donald could have been a Norwegian duck' (Wasko *et al.,* 1998: 56). In Denmark, too, Disney is fondly remembered: 'Donald Duck suits Danish mentality. He seems so Danish and not American' (Drotner, 1998: 102). In Sweden Disney is associated with Christmas in what is seen as a very local tradition:

> Since the 1960s the most popular television program of the year is an hour of Walt Disney cartoons shown in the afternoon on Christmas Eve. Attempts to change the content or the timing of this event have always met with storms of protest. Most Swedes have structured their celebrations around this media event – to miss the Disney show and the sing-along with the Swedish voice-over to Jimmy Cricket's 'When You Wish Upon A Star' is to miss a sacred (and very Swedish) Christmas tradition.
>
> (Löfgren, 1996: 103)

Elsewhere, on the other hand, young audiences *do* accept that they have been 'Americanised' – and worry about it. A 20-year-old female Korean student, for instance, says:

> The United States has been a fantasy land for me. My younger sister likes American-made products very much. Before I entered University I also liked them. Now, I realise that I have been mindlessly yearning for the United States. I know that I have been unconsciously Americanized.
>
> (Seung Hyun Kim and Kyung Sook Lee, 1998: 195)

And a 20-year-old male Australian student:

> My culture is so saturated with American product these days that it's hard to tell whether Disney is uniquely American or not. Call me a cynic. I call me observing the friggin' obvious. It's America . . . but then, aren't we all?
>
> (Nightingale, 2001: 78)

And much as they admit having enjoyed Disney as children, they are now more critical, especially of the way Disney represents their own countries and cultures, and of Disney's 'unbearably arrogant' merchandising and marketing (Guyot, 1998: 122).

The globalisation process

The term 'globalisation' is relatively new. But how new is the phenomenon to which it refers? Robertson (1990) describes globalisation as a long-term process that started in the fifteenth century and went through a number of phases. In the early fifteenth century, nation states began to establish themselves in Europe, while at the same time the world was opened up through exploration and trade. This Robertson calls the 'germinal stage' of globalisation (early fifteenth to mid-eighteenth century). The 'incipient' stage of globalisation (mid-eighteenth century to 1870s) saw the consolidation of homogeneous, unitary nation states, yet also the beginnings of international agreements and international legislation. In other words, the 'national' and the 'international' developed side by side, and in relation to each other. In the 'take-off' stage (1870s to mid-1920s), nation states intensified the processes of regulating their single national languages and repressing minority languages, and of inventing national traditions and histories, to ensure that nationality would become a core aspect of people's identities. And yet it was also a period of increasing global communication – through new, faster forms of transport and communication, the establishment of a common calendar and a common system of time zones, and through international exhibitions, sports events and prizes such as the Nobel prize. The next stage, Robertson characterises as a 'struggle for hegemony' (mid-1920s to late 1960s). The independence of nations was still a key theme, and newly independent, decolonised nations everywhere began to develop their own national institutions, yet the relations between all these independent nations became closer, first through the League of Nations, then through the United Nations. The most recent stage Robertson calls an 'uncertain phase'. On the one hand the intensity of global trade and global communication increases and many new global institutions are created; on the other hand the oldest and richest nations become more pre-occupied with maintaining their national homogeneity in a time of increasing immigration, and in the face of alternative globalisations, such as radical Islam.

Throughout this history, the 'particular' and the 'universal', as Robertson puts it (we could also say the 'national' and the 'international', or the 'local' and the 'global') are closely interrelated, though not always in the same ways. On the one hand, the particular was universalised. As nations 'particularised', they did so on the basis of a 'universal' model of what a nation is, just as, today, indigenous peoples follow universal models when they seek to rediscover their very particular roots. On the other hand, the universal was also particularised. As the world 'universalised', people began to hanker for the 'the particular, the "reinvention of differences"' (Wallerstein, 1984: 167), and, as Geertz has noted (1986: 115), while previously such differences were mostly established *between* societies, now they increasingly existed also within.

Robertson's historical mapping of globalisation is restricted to modern times, making globalisation more or less synonymous with Westernisation (cf. Nederveen Pieterse, 1995). This could be criticised as neglecting earlier political, economical and/or cultural attempts (often quite successful) to unify the different societies of the known world in a single whole. Already in the second century BC, the historian Polybius had said, commenting on the rise of the Roman Empire: 'Formerly the things which happened in the world had no connection amongst themselves . . . but since then all events are united in a common bundle' (quoted in Robertson, 1992a: 54). The cultural hegemony of the Catholic Church in medieval Europe is another example. And then we have not even mentioned the empires in other parts of the world, whose histories have not been taught in Western schools. How broad should we take 'globalisation' to be? Do the cultures of powerful groups always seek to impose themselves on other cultures, whether by changing them or enclosing them in ghettos of some kind (for example, changing them into exotic tourist attractions)?

Other commentators on globalisation bring the beginnings of globalisation even closer to the present time. For Giddens (1990) globalisation is one of the consequences of modernity and he, therefore, dates it from the 1800s, while Tomlinson (1991) sees globalisation as 'what comes after imperialism', situating its beginnings in the 1960s – as do Jameson (1984), who links globalisation with late capitalism, and Harvey (1989), who links it with the postmodern condition of time–space compression and flexible accumulation. The remainder of this chapter looks at these questions through two case histories of media globalisation. While our account owes a lot to Robertson, it also shows that you cannot be too global about globalisation, and that the globalisation process happens differently in different contexts.

The first case is that of women's magazines in the Netherlands. It may well be that this account will also apply to post-Second World War media globalisation in other Western European countries, but without having been able to study that in detail we cannot be sure. The second case is that of comic strips in the Middle East, which reveal a very different story. We do not argue here that there are as many histories as there are countries or regions. But we try to show that specific circumstances lead to specific histories, and only in so far as countries or regions have common circumstances, will there be similarities in their response to globalisation. Former Communist countries in Europe, for instance, will have a different history again from the two we have selected here.

Dutch women's magazines in the twentieth century[1]

In the late nineteenth century the Dutch developed a social and political system in which groups with different religious or political views – Catholic, Orthodox Protestant, Liberal Protestant, Socialist, Neutral – created entirely separate life worlds, with their own political parties, unions, schools, media, universities, and so on. Only the elites, the leaders of these *zuilen* ('pillars') would ever meet and interact across the divide. This system resulted from the so-called *schoolstrijd* ('struggle over schools'). The Catholics, recently emancipated after having been second-rate citizens (and having their religion proscribed) for several centuries, had sought the right to run their own schools, against new laws, that imposed the same rules on all primary schools and withdrew subsidy from non-state schools. The neo-orthodox Protestants, reacting against nineteenth-century Liberal hegemony, had followed suit. This eventually led to the system of societal 'pillars', of 'sovereignty in one's own circle', as Abraham Kuyper, one of its architects, had put it (Romein and Romein, 1937: 171).

Germinal stage (1930s–60s)

It is in this context that a range of Dutch women's magazines were created in the early 1930s. Magazines such as *Libelle, Margriet* and *Beatrijs* catered for women from specific *zuilen*, and addressed them as housewives and, especially, mothers, providing doctor's advice, parental advice, patterns for sewing children's clothes, tips for removing stains, and so on (cf. Figure 2.1).

Although one magazine, *Elegance* (started in 1937), aimed at 'the modern woman', included beauty, fashion, sports and culture, in most magazines these were not included. Nor were sexuality and love, although a Malthusian Society was propagating birth control, and had opened a clinic in 1931, under protest from the still very powerful churches (Vegt, 2004).

Typically Dutch as these magazines may have been, their 'illustrated' format and their emphasis on display advertisements were, nevertheless, modelled on American examples, even if they also incorporated traits of the older medium of the annual women's 'Spectator' or 'Almanac'. The first modern advertising agencies had started in the USA in the 1920s and they had quickly come to the conclusion that women were the 'purchase managers' of the household. As a result advertising became the economic base of women's magazines, and allowed them to acquire the high production values that would do justice to the lavish new display advertisements.

Two points are important to note. First of all, although these magazines were to quite some extent modelled on American examples, they were *initiated* by Dutch publishers who themselves imported and adapted selected characteristics of American magazine formats. And second, the reading public had no opportunity to see the models on which their magazines were based. As far as they were concerned, they were Dutch magazines and the editors liked to keep it that way. They were keen to play down the role of advertising, which, they felt, would distract from the moral tone and the practical-informational mission of the magazines (Wassenaar, 1976: 32).

After the Second World War (when all Dutch women's magazines had been closed down by the German occupiers), these 'pillarised' magazines continued as before, if anything with an even greater emphasis on women as mothers who were modest, caring, reliable and thrifty. A widely read book of the period, written by psychologist F.J. Buytendijk, and simply called *De Vrouw* ('Woman'), defined the essence of

Figure 2.1 Cover of *Margriet* 1945

woman's nature as 'zorgend bij de dingen zijn' ('caringly tending to things'). This renewed emphasis on women's traditional role was a reaction against a post-war moral panic in which it was widely held that many girls had thrown themselves into the arms of the American liberators, resulting in divorce, extramarital births and sexually transmitted diseases (Röling, 1995). The *zuilen* combined forces in combating this loosening of sexual morality, using their women's magazines as a key vehicle for reasserting traditional values.

Internationalisation (1960s–70s)

In the 1960s, Dutch society changed rapidly. Post-war scarcity had continued to be felt throughout the 1950s, but now people's income rose and many households acquired a refrigerator, a washing machine, a television, a motor car, etc., for the first time. More young people stayed in education, including women, and Holland began to import workers from Turkey and Morocco to fill low-skilled jobs. Young people began to rebel against traditional values, including traditional sexual morality. The Malthusian movement, renamed NVSH ('Dutch Association for Sexual Reformation'), until then a small avant-garde movement, quadrupled its membership, making contraception more widely accepted and available, especially after the pill was introduced in 1963, and it used its magazine as a forum for open discussion of sexual matters. Amidst all this, the traditional *zuilen* society collapsed and their elites rapidly lost power and influence.

Influenced by American feminism, a Dutch 'second wave' feminism started, in the late 1960s, with the publication of Joke Kool-Smit's (1967) 'Het onbehagen van de vrouw' ('Women's discontent') in the literary magazine *De Gids*, two years after Friedan's (1965) book *The Feminine Mystique*. The movement would be active throughout the 1970s. In particular a group calling themselves the *Dolle Minas* ('Crazy Minas') staged many, often playful, demonstrations to claim the right to education, equal pay and abortion, in all of which Holland was lagging behind most other European countries. The feminist monthly *Opzij* started in 1972, produced by volunteers, and focusing on articles on politics, labour, law, social security, education and urban planning.

The traditional Dutch women's magazines, meanwhile, lost their connection with the *zuilen*. The Catholic women's magazine *Beatrijs* quietly merged with *Libelle* in the late 1960s and the Protestant *Prinses* disappeared altogether. The remaining magazines continued to focus on the traditional women's roles of mother and wife, now adding the need to be and remain beautiful. Hesitant explorations into areas such as sexuality by *Libelle* and *Margriet* in the early 1970s led to a reduction in subscribers and in advertising revenue and were hastily reversed (Wassenaar, 1976: 57). A new Dutch glossy, *Avenue*, a locally produced (and somewhat more 'high culture') forerunner of magazines like *Cosmopolitan*, *Elle* and *Marie Claire*, would remain a trendsetter for some time until it eventually lost out to Dutch localisations of the foreign glossies from which it had, in part, been inspired.

In sum, the magazines that had started in the 1930s consolidated and continued along traditional lines, catering for older women, though no longer divided along the lines of the *zuilen*. Two 'elite' magazines appeared: *Avenue* targeting the fashion conscious, culturally interested reader, and *Opzij* the politically motivated, feminist reader. Both were strongly influenced by foreign models, but conceived of, and produced, in the Netherlands, by local cultural elites who mediated and adapted trends from abroad for the local public.

Top-down globalisation (1980s)

The 1980s saw the introduction of Dutch versions of foreign glossy magazines such as *Cosmopolitan, Elle* and *Marie Claire*. Elsewhere (Machin and van Leeuwen, 2003, 2004, 2005a) we have described how the founder of *Cosmopolitan*, Helen Gurley-Brown, laid down the ground rules that would be followed in all versions of the magazine (currently 48). They centred on the figure of the 'fun, fearless female' who has a career, a varied love life and, apparently, plenty of money, but no parents, husband, children, or indeed any other family. As in the case of *Reader's Digest*, localised versions are closely supervised by the magazine's head office. Local editors go to New York for an induction in the *Cosmo* values and style, and have to adopt an identical agenda (focusing on fashion, beauty, love, sexuality and career) and identical presentation formats and styles, but can adapt the content according to local circumstances and preferences. According to Viola Robbemondt, editor of the Dutch version (in an interview with Janneke Fernhout),

> the magazine follows the American format and structure exactly, but with our own angles that correspond to Dutch culture ... Typically Dutch, for instance, is that we write more about travel than the American version, and that the emphasis in articles on sex is on feelings, not on the act itself or on pleasing men.

These magazines are *localised* rather than local. Their agenda, format and style are imposed by Hearst in New York, and it is only the 'angle' which is adjusted to suit Dutch preferences, as perceived by local editorial staff. The 'local' franchise holder, incidentally, is in fact a Finnish company publishing magazines in Finland, the Netherlands, Belgium, the Czech Republic, Slovakia, Hungary, Romania, Croatia and Sweden. During the 1980s, the circulation of such magazines rose steadily, at the expense of the Dutch glossy *Avenue*, which eventually folded in 1994. *Opzij*, meanwhile, though still a serious magazine, and still calling itself a 'feminist monthly', is now presented as an expensive glossy, contains many more advertisements, and has moved from an 'outside' to an 'inside' perspective (Hermes, 1995: 96) focusing on love relationships, the body, psychotherapy, experiences and feelings', and selling many more copies than it did in its more militant days (82,927 in 2003, as against 104,676 for *Cosmopolitan*, 86,325 for *Elle*, and 86,325 for *Marie Claire*).

Traditional Dutch magazines such as *Libelle* and *Margriet* continued alongside, gradually losing circulation, but still well ahead of the glossies (2003 circulation figures were 621,068 for *Libelle* and 423,631 for *Margriet*).

Bottom-up globalisation (1990s–present)

The 1990s saw what some have called a 'third wave' of feminism. As Angela McRobbie has characterised it (1999: 126):

> To many young women official feminism is something that belongs to their mother's generation. They have to develop their own language for dealing with sexual inequality, and if they do this through a raunchy language of 'shagging, snogging and having a good time', then perhaps the role this plays is not unlike the sexually explicit manifestoes of early feminist pioneers like Germaine Greer and Sheila Rowbotham. The key difference is that this language is now found in the mainstream of commercial culture – not out there in the margins of the political underground.

The Dutch writer Cels (1999), documenting the growth of 'girl power' in the Netherlands, showed that young Dutch women interested in 'girl power' directly access (mostly) American media, especially songs, zines and websites. Such 'girl power' magazines as there are did not start as commercial ventures, but are homespun enterprises, although some eventually became print magazines (for example, *Bust*), and others fully-fledged e-magazines, for instance the *Postfeminist Monthly*, *Minx Magazine* and *Growl*. In other words, these media are no longer in Dutch and they are no longer mediated by Dutch cultural elites, feminist or otherwise, but directly accessed (and interacted with) on the internet, and given shape 'locally' in dress styles, behaviour, and so on.

In 2003, *Cosmo* and *Elle* brought out new magazines in an attempt to cater for this market (*Elle Girl* and *Cosmo Girl*, both starting in 2003) and, though it is too early to say how successful these magazines will be, it seems as if commercially produced magazines are now reacting rather than leading. Maybe Angela McRobbie is not entirely correct when she says that girl power 'is now found in the mainstream of commercial culture'.

In terms of Robertson's 'interpenetrations' of the 'particular' and the 'universal', the history of Dutch women's magazines shows a quite fundamental reversal. Initially Dutch women's magazines 'particularised' a 'universal' model, adapting it to the local situation, and presenting it as fully Dutch. Objectively the global already impinged on magazine readers, but they were not yet aware of it. Consciousness remained local. In a later stage, the situation was reversed. Global magazines were localised, not by the Dutch cultural elite itself, but from centres of cultural power such as New York and Paris. This defeated at least one Dutch attempt to produce their own glossy, and it is still difficult to decide whether *Avenue* should be seen as a forerunner of the foreign magazines, paving the way for their success, or as a victim of their more powerful resources. In a third stage, some new and significant women's media are, it seems, no longer localised at all. Mostly American songs, magazines and websites are directly accessed by local young women, in English, and without any mediation from Dutch cultural elites. But these media are of course taken up locally, in interactive and individualistic ways, and where this option is taken up, traditional women's magazines will no longer lead, and can only follow, and try to remain in profit by diversifying.

Arab comic strips

The story of comic strips in the Middle East is very different. Instead of a story in which local versions gradually prepare the way for 'top-down' globalisations and, eventually, a direct accessing of American media, this story *starts* with the introduction of top-down globalisation, and leads gradually to the development of indigenous media.[2]

Top-down globalisation (1950s–60s)

As we have seen, Disney introduced Arab-language comics in the early 1950s, and European comics such as *Tin Tin* were introduced at the same time, especially in the French colonies of North Africa. *Miki*, the Egyptian version of Mickey Mouse, was distributed across the Arab world, and contained both Egyptian-originated and translated content (Douglas and Malti-Douglas, 1994: 10). Some of the stories were locally produced, for instance 'The Adventures of Ramses in Paris' (1972), in which a statue of Ramses comes alive, dons modern clothes, and takes the train to Luxor to be reunited with his family. There he is told of the theft of the mummy of Tut Ankh Amon. He travels to Paris to try and retrieve it, but is captured by the police and returned to Egypt, where he becomes a lifeless statue again, reflecting, in the final frame of the comic: 'There is nothing better than Egypt.' 'The Adventures of Ramses in Paris' may use a global format of storytelling, but the story it tells is Egyptian – a story of Western archaeological theft, of Egypt's nostalgia for its glorious past and its problems in successfully competing with its former colonisers – although at the base of this still lies a European model of nation and of invented national heritage and mythology.

Indigenisation (1970s–80s)

As the Arab world became oil-rich, a flourishing art of indigenous comic strips emerged. It differed in significant ways from Western comics. First of all, there was no opposition here between 'high-brow' and 'low-brow'. Arab comics were produced by highly respected visual artists and serious writers and journalists, people who travelled and worked across the Arab nations and had a pan-Arabic outlook.

Visual style was often Western-influenced, especially in North Africa, where French artists were sometimes engaged. Second, while popular Middle Eastern films and TV programmes used local dialects, comics used high Arabic, a cultured, literary language understood across the Arab world. Finally, comics were for the most part produced (and censored) by governments, as educational material for children.

The most common themes were pan-Arab solidarity, anti-imperialism, anti-Zionism, the glory of Arab history and the Arab heritage, and respect for Islam, as 'heritage' and as a source of morality. A political biography of Saddam Hussein called *The Long Days* (1977) tells of his stoic manliness, as he removes a bullet from his leg without wincing; his closeness to Arab tradition, as he converses with Bedouins, dressed in Saudi Arabian dress; and his flight across the desert, after a Baath attack on dictator Qasim had failed. At the end, an open window and a flight of birds overhead symbolised 'the new day' of his ascent to power.

Islamisation (1990s–now)

While Dutch women's magazines became secularised and Americanised as a result of globalisation, Arab comics went in the opposite direction and became both more religious and less 'American' in form and content. From the 1970s onwards, more and more Islamic comic strips were produced, initially for the most part by the religious wings of government ministries, for example the Egyptian High Council of Islamic Affairs, but, from the late 1980s onwards, also by non-governmental organisations, some with connections to Islamic oppositional groups, for instance the Egyptian *Al-Muslim al-Saghîr* ('The Little Muslim').

Some of these Islamised comics are quite political. In one, a group of children are heroes in the Intifada, collecting dynamite to be used against the Israelis. In the end they do not need to do the deed themselves as the Israelis accidentally (or rather, thanks to the intervention of Providence) blow themselves up. In another, morality and patriotism go hand in hand as a little girl finds a box with a letter from a soldier to his mother and takes the box to the mother. Other stories are straightforward moral instruction, for instance 'A Day in the Life of the Muslim Child' (1988) recounts a day devoted to prayer and good deeds and has its dialogue balloons mostly filled with pious greetings and blessings. Descriptive labels such as 'He gets up to perform the dawn prayer' and 'He helps his mother at home' are included at the bottom of the frames. But, as Douglas and Malti-Douglas note (1994: 89), the frame that reads 'He likes sport' is unexpectedly aggressive: it shows the hero dressed in karate outfit and working out with a punch bag. And the other worshippers in the mosque frame are strangely ghostly. These are just a few examples from the very wide range of genres and styles of comics that thrive in the Arab world – and the Arab world is not restricted to the Middle East. 'Wherever there are Arabs, there are Arab strips', say Douglas and Malti-Douglas (1994: 198) and Arab comics have also documented the trials and tribulations of immigrants, sometimes in quite radical ways. 'L'Oud' by Farid Boujellal (1983) shows a man looking wistfully at a photograph of his wife fully veiled. The frame pulls back to reveal that there are photographs of naked women pinned to the wall behind him.

Clearly in different historical, political and cultural contexts, globalisation happens in different ways. The loss of national identity is not a universal phenomenon – some countries have only just acquired it, are just in the process of inventing it, or have regained it. In the case of Middle Eastern comic strips there has been an active process of indigenisation, not because American global media are read and interpreted in different ways, but because comic strips are actually produced here that differ from their American and European models in form as well as content.

Questions

1 Read Dorfman's essay on *Reader's Digest* (Dorfman, 1983: 135–73). What are his principal points of critique?

2 Not only theorists criticise 'cultural imperialism'. In *Watching Dallas* (1985: 86–96), Ien Ang discusses the views of *Dallas* viewers who dislike the programme. What are their arguments? What is Ang's view of these arguments?

3 Interview two people from different generations or nationalities or ethnic backgrounds. Ask them which television series they watch, and if this includes American series, whether they prefer American or local series (or, alternatively, local series vs. series from their country or origin) and why. Try to explain any differences between their answers.

4 Make a collection of short media writings you consider standardised (for example, news in brief, plot summaries of television programmes, very short CD reviews). What is standardised about them? Does it matter? Interview a journalist who writes this kind of material and ask him or her how they learned to write it, whether they think it is standardised and, if so, whether it matters.

Notes

1 Much of the research for this section was conducted by Janneke Fernhout (cf. Fernhout, 2004).

2 This section relies for the most part on Douglas and Malti-Douglas (1994).

PART II
Discourses

Humans have always communicated by telling stories, not just for entertainment, but also, as anthropologists and psychologists have pointed out, to explore and share values, to evaluate different kinds of events and people, and to develop agreed upon or contested models of the world, and of our place in it. Society, Burke (1944) has said, is like a conversation where people join in, say their piece, and leave. Global media models of the world and its peoples are one voice in that conversation. They not only entertain, they also transmit views about the way the world works, about how people behave or should behave, and about the problems we encounter and the solutions that are available for dealing with them. Like stories told around the campfire, they promote and criticise some identities and kinds of social organisation and celebrate others. In doing so they reflect the interests of the storyteller. The three chapters in this section are about stories of this kind, and about the people, places and events in them.

The first, Chapter 3, proposes that global media engender different kinds of identity and community from those traditionally fostered in nation states. Just as earlier identities were promoted in the interest of the ruling classes of nation states, so these new kinds of identity serve the interests of global consumer capitalism. And people themselves play an active role in producing them.

Chapter 4 deals specifically with the kind of identities that global media create for women. Our focus is on the global magazine *Cosmopolitan*, which propagates its ideal of the 'fun, fearless female' in 50 different versions around the world. We ask: What is different in these versions? What kinds of models of the world do they transmit? What kinds of behaviour do they problematise and what kinds of behaviour do they endorse? But we are also interested in what stays the same, and what is, therefore, presented as universally valid, valid for all women, whatever their nationality.

Chapter 5 explores how the 'war on terrorism' is represented in computer war games. The American computer game industry is now bigger than the Hollywood film industry. Many of the games it produces deal with war, are closely modelled on actual events (mostly in the Middle East) and are explicitly intended to aid the war against terrorism. They seek to define that war, and warfare generally, and they promote particular kinds of behaviour and particular kinds of solutions to global problems. Middle Eastern game designers have produced alternative war games, in an attempt to propagate another view of the same events. The second part of Chapter 5 explores the degree to which they have succeeded in doing so.

3 Discourses of identity and community

Two models of identity

In Chapter 2 we saw that nation states have sought to build homogeneous cultures and make nationality a core aspect of people's identities, so that people would *feel* Dutch, or Swedish, or British and incorporate nationality in their very being. More recently, globalised commercial culture has created new identities that are no longer connected to a specific nation or place of origin. Here is an example of 'identity talk', an extract from a research interview with two 37-year-old English women. They were asked to describe their identity to a male interviewer, and they did so confidently. As one of them said: 'I know who I am and what I want.' (Names have been changed.)

Sandy: I am a confident person. I think that this is difficult for men.
Interviewer: What do you mean by confident?
Sandy: Well, me and my friends, we are just confident and independent. I guess we just really know ourselves. We are independent. Men don't know what to do with this.
Interviewer: What do you mean?
Sandy: Well my friends just do anything they want, when they want.
Interviewer: Like what?
Sandy: Well anything. They go to parties, they like dancing. I really like cars.
Linda: They have whatever boyfriends they want. The men have been doing it for years and now we can do exactly the same. I have a friend who just picks guys up. She knows just what she wants.
Interviewer: Are they independent in terms of political thinking?
Sandy: I just don't bother with politics, you have to get on with life, not be so heavy. Live a bit. You have to get out some.
Linda: Well, I think it's about really knowing yourself. You have to know who you are. I think my boyfriend has difficulty with that. I just say to him I am independent and I am proud of that. I just know who I am and what I want.

How do these two women describe their identity? First of all in terms of gender, of female identity, positively contrasted to male identity. Being a woman is fundamental to their view of who they are. Second, they nominate identity traits that are 'psychological' and individual rather than social, 'personality traits' such as 'confident' and 'independent'. And third, they mention their preferred leisure time activities such as 'going to parties' and 'picking up guys' and consumer goods such as 'cars'. Note that there are many other potential aspects of identity that they do *not* mention, for instance nationality, race, class background, family relationships (being someone's daughter, wife, lover, mother, aunt, etc.), job, income level, education, religion, political convictions, and so on. As it happens, both women work in a child nursery. Their income is low, they do not have a fixed contract and they live in rented accommodation. But in the interview they do not choose to see that as part of 'who they are'.

The interview was part of our research on the magazine *Cosmopolitan*, and this allowed us to notice that these women's views of their identity are highly compatible with the model of the 'fun, fearless female' identity propagated by this magazine. As we already noted, the *Cosmo* 'fun, fearless woman' is essentially on her own. She may have friends and colleagues, but she does not have parents or children, and the few husbands that appear in the magazine are usually a hindrance rather than a help. Nor does she have political or religious beliefs or forms of community and solidarity; yet she is part of a global sisterhood of 'fun, fearless women' whose main preoccupations are the pursuit of romantic adventure and sexual pleasure, of health and beauty, of consumer goods and pleasurable activities, and of career success, although the latter varies across different versions. The 'career' sections in the Indian version of *Cosmopolitan*, for instance, address their readers as though they are company directors, managers or self-employed designers, actors, etc., while the career sections in European versions address their readers as though they are employees, usually in offices (Machin and van Leeuwen, 2004).

Such media are of course read differently in different cultural contexts, yet the agenda they set is the same everywhere. In the Netherlands,[1] we interviewed middle-aged (45–51) and young (22–5) women. Both groups distanced themselves from *Cosmopolitan*, just as Katz and Liebes' interviewees distanced themselves from *Dallas*. The older women found the magazine superficial and thought it had too many advertisements. But their descriptions of the values and priorities of the younger generation could have been lifted straight out of *Cosmo*: fun, independence, travel, self-confidence, adventure (names have been changed):

Anja:	Well, they are not my values, but I don't think there's anything wrong with it, enjoying your freedom a little bit . . .
Olga:	Yes, if I had that age, I would do it myself.
Joke:	Yes, there's nothing wrong with it.

The younger women also distanced themselves from the magazine. They found the women portrayed in *Cosmopolitan* a little too glamorous, 'too perfect'. The Dutch pride themselves on their pragmatic, down-to-earth attitude. 'Just act normal, that's crazy enough', they say. *Cosmopolitan* editor Viola Robbemondt is aware of this and said that she had to take care to avoid that the Dutch edition would be 'too polished' (Fernhout, 2004: 33). When the women were asked about their own values, they nominated values such as 'honesty', 'love', 'social contacts', 'equality' and 'tolerance'. But when they were asked about the values of young Dutch women generally, they nominated values that were much more like those of *Cosmopolitan*'s 'fun, fearless female', values like 'independence', 'equality', 'having different experiences' and 'enjoying life', and they grudgingly admitted the attractiveness of the *Cosmo* lifestyle (names have been changed):

Saskia:	I would like to be smart, and enterprising, and sexy.
Heidi:	A bit of everything [laughs].
Saskia:	Yes, well, I think so.
Yvon:	I think so.
Marieke:	Yes.
Saskia:	There's nothing I don't want to have but it is all so enormous. I'd like to be cool in real life.

In other parts of the world, however, people distance themselves more radically from the values of *Cosmopolitan*, as in this interview with two Taiwanese women in their mid-20s (names have been changed):

Pei-Fen:	You can see it from the way they look. They all have jobs and are very beautiful.
Interviewer:	Is this something you would like to be?
Tsai-Yun:	I don't think it's real. The women in *Cosmo* have everything. Real women cannot be so confident. You can't become like that. Not in real life.
Interviewer:	But you might like it?
Pei-Fen:	No, it's not possible.
Tsai-Yun:	In Taiwan we respect our partner. We want to work together. We are not interested in sex in this way.
Interviewer:	You think younger women these days are not interested in sex in this way, then? They want to wait for the right partner?
Pei-Fen:	No, some of the students have sex now. They don't want to wait. They want to have boyfriends. This is from the influence of Western images.
Interviewer:	Is it a bad thing?
Tsai-Yun:	Yes, it is bad for relationships as there is no respect. It is all superficial. I think we want to find a man where there can be respect and where there can be a family. Cosmopolitan is always about sex.

The remainder of this chapter focuses on the two major sets of identity categories, or 'models of identity', that are now available in contemporary society, often in uneasy tension with each other, a tension which, we feel, is insufficiently acknowledged in the literature. One is imposed by nation states, reinforced in national news media, education systems and other national institutions, and defines people primarily as citizens. The other serves the interests of global corporations, is disseminated through marketing practices and global media, and defines people primarily as consumers. The two models are discourses, ways of talking about identity that are expressed by specific sets of linguistic, visual and other semiotic resources. But they also have a history and they inform, and are informed by, practices that have material consequences, both in macro contexts such as the policies and practices of nation states and global corporations, and in the micro practices all citizens/consumers have to engage with in their daily lives.

We discuss the two models in turn, and conclude by relating them to some of the theoretical positions in the now very extensive literature on identity. This literature rightly criticises the essentialism that is fundamental to our first model. But it also celebrates our second model as an alternative which allows identities to be individual, flexible and complex, and it does so without taking into account the origins of this model, and its continuing, and quite fundamental links with corporate ideologies and practices.

Identity and the power of the nation state

This section begins by introducing 'social actor analysis' (van Leeuwen, 1996), a set of discourse-analytical concepts that can help us investigate the words and expressions available to speakers of English for answering the question, 'Who are you?' (or: 'Who are we?', 'Who is he/she?', 'Who are they?'). Such expressions often categorise people, and there are two ways in which this can be done. One is 'functionalisation', defining people's identity 'in terms of an activity, in terms of something [people] do, for instance an occupation or a role' (ibid., 54). To express this, English allows us to turn verbs that denote activities into nouns, into fixed categories, by adding suffixes such as *-er, -ant, -ent, -ian*, etc. (for example, 'asylum seeker', 'immigrant', 'insurgent', 'guardian', etc.) or to make nouns from other nouns that denote a place or tool closely associated with an activity, through suffixes such as *-ist, -eer*, etc. (for example, 'pianist', 'mountaineer'). The other is 'identification', defining people's identity, 'not in terms of what they do, but in terms of what they, more or less permanently, or unavoidably, are' (ibid., 54). Three types of 'identification' can be distinguished: 'classification', 'relational identification' and 'physical identification'.

In the case of 'classification', people's identity is defined 'in terms of the major categories by means of which a given society or institution differentiates between classes of people' (ibid., 54). Such categories are historically and culturally variable. What in one period or culture is constructed as 'doing', as a more or less impermanent and changeable role, may in another be constructed as 'being', as a more or less fixed and unchangeable identity. An example is Foucault's description of the way homosexuality changed from 'the practice of sodomy' into 'a kind of interior androgyny, a hermaphrodism of the soul'. As Foucault said, 'The sodomite had been a temporary aberration; the homosexual was now a species' (Foucault, 1981: 42). Such changes may occur slowly, appearing at first as new ideas, before they are incorporated into practices, but they always respond to the needs and interests of the institutions which introduce and promote them. We always have to ask whose interests they serve, and how they can do this.

'Relational identification' defines identity in terms of people's relations to each other (for example, kinship, work, friendship, networks). Limited, and culturally specific, sets of nouns denote such relations: 'friend', 'aunt', 'colleague', etc. In English they typically come with possessive pronouns ('my friend', 'his mother'), genitives ('the child's mother') or other means of denoting both parties of the relationship. Relational identity plays an increasingly marginal role in Western society, but anthropologists have shown that in many societies it is the single most important form of 'classification'. Von Sturmer (1981), for instance, has described how Australian Aborigines, when they first meet, 'search for relations whom they share and then establish relationships on that basis' (ibid., 13). This clearly differs from first meetings in Western societies where the opening questions tend to be 'What do you do?' and 'Where are you from?' In the past, however, relational identification was more prominent in British society. In Jane Austen's novels characters are constantly asked about their connections. In *Pride and Prejudice*, for instance, Lizzie is asked by Catherine De Burgh, 'Your father may be a gentleman, but who are your connections? Who are your aunts and uncles?'

In the case of 'physical identification', finally, identity is constructed in terms of physical characteristics. This is realised by a limited and specific repertoire of nouns denoting the physical characteristics (for example, skin colour, hair colour) of specific groups of people, for instance women and blacks ('blonde', 'redhead', 'black').

Let us now look how these resources are used in a specific context, a University Appointees Payroll Details form that has to be filled in as part of applying for a job.

Three types of categorisation are used here, in diffuse and complex co-articulations:

1   the 'physical identifications' of certain 'races';
2   classifications which constitute 'ethnic' groups, on the basis of provenance; and
3   classifications on the basis of citizenship ('British', and perhaps also 'Irish').

Looking at the specific categorisations, and the way in which they combine, we can make a number of observations:

•   Much as it may have been discredited by writers about racist practices in the colonial era, the form maintains the distinction between 'pure' and 'mixed' race.
•   Going by the criterion of 'physical identification', the form recognises only two races, 'white' and 'black'. Other 'races' are no longer defined in this way. With respect to 'Asians', for instance, there has been a redefinition, a shift of emphasis

Black or black British
Black African
Black Caribbean
Any other black background
Chinese or other ethnic group
Chinese
Any other ethnic group
White
British
Irish
Other white
Asian or Asian British
Indian
Bangladeshi
Pakistani
Any other Asian background
Mixed race
White & black Caribbean
White & black African
White & Asian
Any other mixed race

from 'physical' to 'cultural' difference that coincided with the rapid economic development of a number of important 'Asian' states (although the term 'Asian' still appears under the heading of 'mixed race'). Asians are no longer 'yellow'.

- The form explicitly recognises only one or two specific nationalities, 'British', and perhaps 'Irish', even though these nationalities are listed as sub-groups of (the white) 'race'. 'Non-whites' from ex-colonies can be 'British', albeit in a diluted, qualified form, but others cannot, even though many immigrants and descendants from immigrants from other places have been given British citizenship.

- Anyone who is not 'British', or hailing from an ex-colony, or Chinese, is an 'other': apart from its complex and sometimes confused co-articulations of race, provenance and nationality, the form also sets up a fine-grained pecking order among the groups it lists.

Classifications of this kind are designed in the service of specific needs and interests, in this case the needs of nation states (and key national institutions such as education) and their current preoccupation with formulating and propagating a coherent sense of 'nationality', despite the diversity that has resulted from new patterns of immigration. National identity has become complex and multi-layered, engendering all kind of hybrid forms which, however, all turn around just two key factors. The first is 'race', which here plays an undiminished role, however much racism has been debated and critiqued in the national media. The second is a shared history, in this case the history of the British Empire, which allows 'black British' and 'Asian British' people the status of citizens, albeit it in a qualified way that sets them apart from 'true' citizens.

Note the absence of 'functionalisation'. If 'functionalisation' had been the dominant mode of categorising people, it might have been easier to see that people from all these racial, 'ethnic' and national categories *do* the same kind of things, even if they 'are' not the same. They go to school, set up households, purchase goods and services, work, pay taxes, etc. But this is not the case. The nation state and its institutions classify people in terms of what they 'are'. And these classifications are kept as permanent records. However long members of any of these intricately classified groups live in the UK, they will always have to reaffirm their identity in these terms, and will always have to reaffirm their difference. They will see this mirrored in the classifications used by the media, which continue to quote, for instance, 'Asian community leaders' and 'Muslim spokespeople', as though all the members of these groups think and feel the same. And they will have to reaffirm these identities also in the private sphere. At the very least, they will continue to be asked: 'Where are you from?', even if they have lived in the UK all their lives.

One of us grew up in the Netherlands, but has not lived there for over 30 years. When meeting new people, they notice his Dutch accent and immediately ask: 'Where are you from?' If he answers 'London', the question is repeated impatiently, 'No, where are you really from?' The other author comes from the north of England, where his family always associated 'Britain' with the south and with London, and fought on the streets with what they called the 'British police' during the miners' strike. As a result, he does not identify with Britain as a political entity. Yet he has no choice but to continue to tick the category 'white British'. The form of identity we have discussed here is one we can neither choose nor change, and the further it is removed from the privileged category of 'white British', the more we will feel the consequences of its power, both in the public and the private sphere.

So far we have focused on linguistic representations of identity, but it should be noted that identity is represented – and 'presented' – in many other ways. Images can also realise 'racist' and 'ethnic' stereotypes (van Leeuwen, 2000a). They may for instance use 'biological categorisation', realised by standardised exaggerations of physical features that connote the usually negative associations which the members of a particular group evoke to those for whom the representation is primarily intended. Such categorisations have a history. The stereotyped black, for instance, has exaggeratedly white teeth and eyes. In the USA this signifier developed out of comparisons with raccoons (hence the derogatory slang word 'coons' for 'blacks'), animals of the night with a reputation of being sly thieves. Initially the comparison was explicit, with pictures that contained both a raccoon and a little black boy and exaggerated the supposed visual similarities. Later it could be recognised as a stereotyped part of black physiognomy without any form of explicit comparison, for instance in 'black minstrel' imagery (ibid., 347). Such stereotypes continue to be used, especially in advertisements, cartoons, toys, and so on (Nederveen Pieterse, 1992).

'Cultural categorisation', on the other hand, is signified by means of standard attributes such as items of dress and hairstyles. These do not have to be exaggerated or caricatured. Their mere presence is enough. Again, a shift from 'racial' to cultural difference can be noted, at least on the surface. Many of the debates now centre on the signifiers of cultural difference, for instance the head coverings of Muslim women. Yet, as we have seen, this does not mean that racism has disappeared.

Identity and corporate power

Let us now look at another example, an article in the G2 Supplement of *The Guardian* (12 March 2004), which explains how a particular marketing expert describes the identity of people as consumers in terms of quite different kinds of social groupings. We include 3 of his 11 categories: 'Symbols of success' (representing 9.6 per cent of the population), 'Ties of community' (representing 16 per cent) and 'Urban intelligence' (representing 7.2 per cent).

'Symbols of success'
Their incomes have risen into upper income tax ranges, they have substantial equity and are most likely to be white British. They typically live in posh areas such as Kensington or Edinburgh's New Town, work as senior managers for large corporations, or have respected roles in professional practices. You only call them Smug Ponces because you're jealous. Likely to shop at: Waitrose, M&S, Sainsbury's, Tesco.

'Ties of Community'
This group lives in very established, rather old-fashioned communities. Traditionally they marry young, work in manual jobs and have strong social support networks with friends and relations living nearby. There is a sub-type of this group called Coronation Street, but not all Lee and Noreens live in back-to-back terraces or keep pigeons. Likely to shop at: Morrisons, Asda, Kwik Save.

'Urban Intelligence'
Young, well educated, liberal, childless and well off. They are mindful of career uncertainties but are often involved in high risk investments such as the buy-to-let market. Not all of them read *The Guardian*; many are in lifestyle thrall to Sarah Beeney. Likely to shop at Sainsbury's.

How do these classifications differ from those of our previous example?

- They are unsystematic. Despite the way they mix race, provenance and nationality, the classifications in our previous example involved clear binary opposites: specific versus unspecific identities ('others'), 'mixed' versus 'pure' races, 'white' versus 'black'. It would be possible to represent them in the form of a taxonomy: there are two kinds of white people, for instance, those with a named nationality and those without (the 'other whites'); then, lower down, there are two kinds of named nationality ('British' and 'Irish'), and so on. But the classifications of consumer identities we cited above cannot be represented in this way, because they define identity in terms of clusters of features, rather than in terms of single designations.
- Although it does use a number of traditional demographic categories, including race and nationality (and age), our second model does not do so systematically (for instance, race and nationality are only used as one of the co-categorisations in the case of 'Symbols of success'), and it prefers categorisations which can change as people climb the social ladder: income, property, place of residence. It also includes a new, and even more easily changeable set of identity features, co-defining identity on the basis of what people think, their 'outlook' ('liberal', 'old-fashioned', etc.), on the basis of their 'independence' from people who might 'tie them down' (husbands or wives, children, relatives living close by), on the basis of the newspapers or magazines they read and the hobbies they pursue, and, above all, on the basis of their consumer behaviour.
- The identity features used by the model include functionalisations as well as categorisations. People are defined, not only on the basis of 'who they are', but also, and above all, on the basis of 'what they do': their job, their leisure time activities, and of course their patterns of consumption. 'Ethnic' provenance matters less here. So long as you are a good consumer it is no longer important whether you are Asian, Chinese, Irish, or any kind of 'other'.

'Lifestyle' identities of this kind emerged as corporations looked for new ways of creating market demand. Arnold Mitchell (1978) referred to them, not as 'demographics' but as 'psychographics', clusters of 'behaviours', 'attitudes' and consumption patterns, for instance the 'Actualiser', who is sceptical of advertising, has considerable financial resources, and reads newspapers every day; the 'Experiencer', who follows fashion, buys on impulse, and listens to music a lot; or the 'Striver', who is status oriented and spends a great deal of money on leisure-time activities and on him- or herself, and so on. Sociologists such as Chaney (1996) have described such lifestyles as forms of identity that are less fixed than traditional identities and can be more freely chosen: 'People use lifestyles in everyday life to identify and explain wider complexes of identity and affiliation' (ibid., 12), and he, too, stresses their link with consumer goods. Lifestyle identities, he says, are fundamentally based on appearances. They allow attitudes, values and preferences to be signified by styles of dress and adornment, interior decoration, and so on.

Such styles – of dress, hairstyle, speech and other aspects of self-presentation – have of course always signified identity. But in the past they signified different kinds of identity, based on class, gender, age and other stable social categories. They could tell you where someone came from and they indexed their gender, age, social class, profession or trade, and so on. Today this form of social style has much diminished. Women may wear the same clothes as men, children the same clothes as adults, and young people on the streets of Tokyo do not dress so very differently from young people on the streets of Madrid. People now express different things with the way they dress, wear their hair, speak, and so on. They use self-presentation to convey lifestyle identities rather than traditional, given, social identities, although some groups still adhere, or even return to, forms of dress and self-presentation that express traditional identities and categories such as provenance, gender, age and religion.

Lifestyle combines individual and social style. On the one hand, it is an individual style, a style through which people express who they are as unique individuals rather than as social types. On the other hand, it is a social style, because the lifestyle choices of individuals inevitably align them with others who share their taste, their preferred leisure activities and interests, and their outlook on life. For this reason these groups have been thought of as 'interpretive communities' (Fish, 1980; Radway, 1987).

Sociolinguists have described 'speech communities' as communities that 'share rules for the conduct and interpretation of speech, and rules for the interpretation of at least one linguistic variety' (Hymes, 1972: 53–4). If we extend this to non-linguistic modes of communication, such as beauty and fashion, the readers of *Cosmopolitan* can be said to form such an interpretive community. They share an involvement with the same modalities and genres of linguistic and non-linguistic communication, and the same constructions of reality. And although this involvement may at first sight appear passive, the involvement of an 'audience', it is in fact actively articulated, through patterns of consumption, through fashion accessories, and through forms of bodily *hexis* and social behaviour. This makes it possible for women to recognise, anywhere in the world, and across linguistic boundaries, other women as also adhering to (or at least attracted to) the values and lifestyles propagated in *Cosmopolitan*. But one question arises. Should the producers and distributors of *Cosmopolitan* be included in this community? If we do that, the *Cosmopolitan* community is no longer just an 'interpretive community' of equals sharing the same taste, the same ideas and the same lifestyle, and we can see that these tastes and ideas and lifestyles are designed by a hierarchically organised institution with a head office that regulates the work of local editorial teams and shapes the magazine in deliberate and strategic ways. Perhaps that fact needs to be incorporated in any description and theory of lifestyle communities.

The means we use to express lifestyle are heterogeneous and rest primarily on connotation, on signs that are already loaded with cultural meaning, yet not subject to prescription or tradition. More specifically, they rest on *composites of connotation*. A well-cut, expensive white shirt (connotations: elegance, a touch of formality, etc.) may be combined with drill trousers with a camouflage motif (connotations: jungle adventures, toughness, the resourcefulness of a commando, etc.) and sports shoes (connotations: affinity with healthy living, exercise and sport, now also with rap music). Such composites are often picked up from the media, from fashion spreads, or from style icons and role models, such as David Beckham around 2000–5. Beckham's identity, as portrayed in the media, combines aspects of the rebel and the model citizen. Though often initially portrayed as a troublemaker, he nevertheless also speaks up for disadvantaged children, campaigns against racism and stands for clean living, family values and the new masculinity – he is happy to change nappies and 'not scared of his feminine side' (Beckham, 2000: 95). The pictures of him that circulate in the public domain emphasise different aspects of this complex identity at different times. But they always portray his identity through his appearance, through the way he is dressed, wears his hair and poses, and also through the setting in which he is photographed. In one photo he wears a bandana (connotation: rebel), black clothes of fashionable loose cut (connotation: fashionable, bit of an 'artist') and sports shoes (connotation: sport, rap), and poses against a background of well-to-do respectability (London's Belgravia, we think).

Such contradictions are typical of the way lifestyle models are portrayed. They allow us to think and talk of ourselves as individuals, yet also fit in with the social scheme of things. And unlike traditional identity markers, they change with fashion, which means you have to pay constant attention to the media to stay up to date with the most recent lifestyle signifiers. Clearly, consumption and consumer goods are crucial for the expression of lifestyle identities. Lifestyle provides identities for 'people for whom occupational and economic roles no longer provide a coherent set of values and for whom identity has come to be generated in the consumption rather than in the production realm' (Zablocki and Kanter, 1976: 270).

It may be true that 'people use lifestyles', as Zablocki and Kanter say, but such formulations make it easy to forget that lifestyles also use people. They are created and propagated to serve the interests and needs of powerful social institutions, in this case large corporations; and these institutions, like the nation state, keep records of people's identities through marketing surveys, and through the information consumers wittingly or unwittingly provide every time they use their credit cards and loyalty cards for purchases. This information, like the classifications required by the nation state, has material consequences, as it is instrumental in deciding what goods and services will be provided, and for whom.

Returning now to our original example, we can now see the role of the 'lifestyle' model of identity in the way the two interviewed women talked about 'independence'. They focused, not on traditional identity categories or on their dependence on the patriarchal practices that still prevent women from receiving equal pay and equal access to many professions, but on 'independence' as an 'attitude' embodied in consumer goods such as cars, and lived out in leisure-time activities such as clubbing and having casual affairs – exactly as in the *Cosmopolitan* discourse of the 'fun, fearless woman'. At times the identification with this kind of independence, and with the devaluation of relational identification it entails (for example, the devaluation of the 'relational' identity of 'wife' and 'mother'), seems only skin-deep:

> *Interviewer:* So you are happy to have casual relationships?
> *Linda:* I would like to fall in love and have family. I haven't met the right guy.
> *Sandy:* It's hard in the clubs and pubs. Most guys are just after a shag really.
> *Linda:* Or they are just boring. You want someone who can have a laugh but is also pretty sensitive. Lots of guys are scared of us I think.
> *Sandy:* We just end up having a laugh together. We have a drink, take the piss out of some guys.

A few other aspects of 'consumer identity' need to be pointed out. To do so, we will use a final example, an article in *Cosmopolitan* (November 2003) which introduced 'Joseph Cohen, author of The Penis Book', who can tell 'what kind of a man he is by the size and shape of his penis'. He describes five types of man, the 'Peanut', the 'Banana', the 'Baggy Jacket', the 'Well Hung' and 'Mr Average'. Here are some extracts from his characterisation of the 'Baggy Jacket' (i.e. man whose penis has a loose foreskin):

> He is very laid back. He likes to be in a job where he can be as relaxed as his foreskin is . . . He isn't a fussy lover and has plenty of ideas if the lady is willing . . . But if you're looking for a laugh-a-minute kind of man, Cohen suggests you look elsewhere. 'He is going to leave you feeling pretty empty in your heart and mind. He'll never suggest a restaurant or a weekend getaway destination', he says. 'But on the plus-side, he's always up for some hot sex.'

This excerpt illustrates a number of further points:

* Lifestyle classifications, especially in magazines, but also elsewhere, are often presented in the tongue-in-cheek, 'over the top', humorous way that also characterises many advertisements and, indeed, increasingly many of the texts that corporations distribute to their consumers or clients, for instance, the brochures through which banks offer insurance policies. On the one hand, the

message is received. Men are reduced to their penis and to the skill with which they use it to provide women with pleasure. All else follows from this. On the other hand, the message can also be dismissed, laughed away: 'It's only a joke, a bit of fun.'

- The article is also an example of 'physical identification'. Reflection on the vocabulary of physical identification ('blonde', 'black', 'disabled', 'hulk', etc.) quickly reveals that it focuses on people who are deemed inferior, stigmatised, or otherwise held in low regard. The science that linked physical features to identities has been discredited precisely because it led to the racist theories that have legitimised colonialism and, eventually, the Nazi genocides. Here it returns as a joke. But, as we have already mentioned in relation to visual categorisation, it is, today, precisely in entertainment contexts (for example, Disney) that degrading, racist and sexist stereotypes of 'physical identity' continue to flourish.
- Finally, 'pop psychological' classifications of this kind describe identity in entirely individualist terms. Neither 'Baggy Jackets', nor 'Strivers' can be said to form a social group. These classifications encourage people to think of themselves, not in terms of the groups with which they may have some form of solidarity and community, but as isolated individuals, whose actions are either determined by fate (astrology, the colour of your skin, the shape of your penis), or active individual agency; and whose identity is to a large extent defined by the kind of 'personality traits' ('confident', 'independent', 'fun loving', 'shy', 'laid back') that were developed for the purpose of personality tests by psychologists such as Eysenck and have now become ubiquitous in the lifestyle media that constantly interpret people's taste in matters such as colour, interior decoration, etc., as expressions of their unique personalities, rather than (also) of the habitus of one or more social groups.

The power of classification

There is now an extensive literature on identity. Sociologists, anthropologists, linguists and, to a lesser degree, social psychologists, have observed that identity is dependent on context, which is adaptive, and in flux throughout our lives. In this they have built on the work of Simmel (for example, 1971), Tönnies (2001) and Durkheim (2002) who studied what happens to people's identity when they move from traditional rural communities to urban environments that are characterised by change and anonymity and require people to play different roles throughout the day.

Derrida (for example, 1990) has observed that Western thought has had the tendency to isolate features and build them into systems of binary opposites in which one side is always given higher status, marginalising the other, as on the 'diversity' form discussed above ('white' versus 'black'; 'citizen' versus 'non-citizen'; etc.). This can make diversity and complexity invisible. Many contemporary writers on identity, similarly, critique singular, essentialist constructions of identity, and stress complexity. In their view, the elements of identity are not only potentially infinite

(Weeks, 1990), they combine: gender is combined with social class, and so on. A person's identity is:

> a heterogeneous set made up of all the names or identities given or taken up by her. But in a lifelong process, identity is endlessly created anew, according to various social constraints, social interactions, encounters, and wishes that may happen to be very subjective and unique
>
> (Le Page and Tabouret-Keller, 1985: 316)

In a similar vein, Mercer (1990: 65) has argued that 'essentialist notions of identity and objectivity surface in the vortex of this bewildering experience of difference because of the absence of a common idea of what diversity really means', and that the 'official discourse of anti-racism failed precisely because it imposed a one-dimensional view' (ibid., 97). Again, Homi Bhabha (1990) has critiqued the Western tendency to essentialise other cultures and ascribe static identities to them, and Hall (1989) has discussed how the Caribbean diaspora rediscovered Africa and used this to construct a narrative that could make Caribbean identity whole, arguing that this hides difference and obscures how people change as they collect experience. Such accounts critique our first model of identity, together with the practices it has engendered, for instance the tendency to have one black or Asian representative on a committee as if there was something essential about blacks or Asians that could be represented by a single representative – a tendency which can make members of such groups who do not subscribe to such an identity feel guilty, or cause them to be marginalised, thus leading to fragmented identities (Parmar, 1990). We agree with these critiques. They link classification systems to powerful social practices and their effects on subjects in precisely the way we have argued for. But many of the writers we have discussed go a step further, asserting, and sometimes even celebrating, our second model of identity, as one that offers the alternative – unique, individual, flexible, complex identities – and they do so without taking into account the origins of this model in the work of 1970s' marketing experts, and the way in which it serves the interests of large corporations and informs their policies and practices. In our view, this link needs, at the very least, to be explicitly discussed and problematised. If people, in interviews such as those that we have quoted here, use the 'lifestyle model' as a resource for describing themselves, then this is not so different from the way others may use the essentialist categories imposed by the nation state and its institutions to describe themselves. Both can be 'owned' in the same way – and both can lead to fragmented identities, to contradictions, for instance the contradiction between identifying with the idea of 'independence' and yet also longing for 'Mr Right' and for 'having a family'.

This tendency is particularly noticeable in work that links identity to media reception. The same period that spawned the theories we have just discussed also spawned the new emphasis on reception in media and cultural studies discussed in Chapter 2 (Morley, 1981; and Radway, 1987 are further key references). The initial aim was to relate differences in reception to traditional identity categories, for instance in Katz and Liebes (Russian immigrants, Moroccan immigrants, etc.). But this was soon abandoned for an approach in which reception was related to people's individual identities and histories (Radway, 1988). It was an approach with clear predecessors in 1950s' and 1960s' American mass communication theory (cf. for example, Berlo (1960), who coined the slogan 'meanings are in people') – and again, origins and affinities of this kind, and their implications, are not acknowledged or discussed.

Historically, there is a pattern here. As marketing experts and large corporations began to emphasise production over consumption, so did theorists of identity and meaning. As they abandoned singular, stable demographic identities in favour of complex, flexible and individual identities, so did theorists of identity. As they championed the consumer's power of choice, so did theorists of identity. We do not want to argue here that these theorists are wrong. As we said, they have contributed a necessary and wholly convincing critique of the essentialist identity model. The greater emphasis on functionalisation, on choice, and on identity as a cluster of features does have positive potential. But this does not diminish the fact that the 'lifestyle' model is just as much produced and imposed by a powerful social institution as the older model, even if it propagates a different kind of identity and communicates it very differently.

We would also like to argue for a different kind of complexity, a complexity in which several 'regimes' of identity, driven by different needs and interests, operate side by side, and can be combined in different ways – those constructed by and for nation states and, though less powerfully so, nation-less ethnic groups, and those constructed by, and in the interest of, large, global corporations. The question, therefore, is not what identity *is*, in some absolute, essentialist sense, but in how nation states and global corporations (re)*construct* identity in different ways, and what people do with this when they construct their own identities, often by mixing elements from the models described here. And, finally, we should remember that whatever agency, whatever scope for initiative, people have in constructing their identities, it is constrained to different degrees both by the socially constructed and imposed models of identity we have described, and by the institutions that maintain them. While 'lifestyle identity' may have some genuine advantages over essentialist forms of identity, there is also a drawback: just *how* agentive people can be within this model, how much they will, or will not be constrained by it, depends to a great extent on their financial resources.

Questions

1   Ask two people of different age and/or nationality and/or ethnic background to describe themselves (a) in the form of a contact advertisement, and (b) for the purposes of a short job application letter. In terms of 'social actor' analysis, how do the two self-descriptions differ, and what would account for the differences?

2   Interview two people of different age and/or nationality and/or ethnic background, and ask them which groups they belong to. Are any of these groups 'interpretive communities'? What would account for any differences between the answers of your two interviewees?

3   Collect (or make) pictures of people who wear dreadlocks as part of a 'composite of connotations'. What connotations do you think the dreadlocks would have for them? What are the connotations of other aspects of their self-presentation (for example, dress)? What kind of lifestyles are signified?

4   Collect diversity questionnaires of the kind discussed in this chapter from two different institutions. What kind of categories of people do the forms recognise? What would account for the differences?

Note

1   The Dutch interviews and focus groups were conducted by Janneke Fernhout (cf. Fernhout, 2004).

4 Discourses of sex and work

Stories and discourses

Anthropologists (for example, Lévi-Strauss, 1967) and psychologists (for example, Jerome Bruner, 1990) agree that storytelling is a fundamental part of social life, whether in small groups such as the family or the workplace, or in larger groups such as the tribe and the nation. Everywhere people tell stories to help them understand their experiences and shape their lives. This does not mean that there is always a simple and straightforward link between story and life. Stories that are important for our lives in the here and now may be set in distant times and distant lands, particularly when they touch on problematic motives. Bettelheim (1976) has explained fairytales in this way. Hansel and Gretel, for instance, are abandoned by their parents, sent out into the wilderness where they will face all kinds of dangers. 'The child at school age', explains Bettelheim (1976: 166), 'often cannot yet believe that he will ever be able to meet the world without his parents.' The story of Hansel and Gretel can help the child 'to learn to trust that some day he will master the dangers of the world, even in the exaggerated form in which his fears depict them'.

Lévi-Strauss, in describing the myths of the Tsimshian Indians, a people of the North-west Canadian coast, points out that the world described in these stories does not always reflect reality. In the story *Asdiwal*, Asdiwal marries and goes to live in the village of his new wife, and the same happens with other marriages in the story even though it was actually the other way round in Tsimshian society: women went to live in the village of their new husbands. As Lévi-Strauss says, the myth 'does not seek to depict what is real, but to justify the shortcomings of reality to show that they are *untenable*' (1967: 30). Many human interest and crime stories in the media are like that. They remind us of the importance of society's rules and customs by showing the consequences of deviating from them. The same applies to many movie stories. In *Thelma and Louise* (Scott Ridley, 1991), for instance, two women decide to escape from their unsatisfactory relationships with men, and embark on a journey together. Louise then kills a man who threatens to rape Thelma and the two find themselves pursued by police. The film empathises with the women and their feelings, yet, in the end, depicts their actions as untenable, as leading to disaster.

Cosmopolitan is a contemporary medium of storytelling for women. The stories it tells about sex, work, health and beauty are not unique to the magazine, and circulate also in many other ways – in the writings of feminists like Camille Paglia (1992, 1994), in television series like *Sex and the City*, in women's everyday conversations, and so on. Other stories about sexuality circulate at the same time, embodying a different approach to the same topics. This can be confusing. People may hold different, incompatible views at the same time, without being able to resolve the contradictions, as we saw in Chapter 3 where the same woman could, one moment, speak of herself as a fun-loving, independent pleasure-seeker, and the next moment as passively waiting for Mr Right and hoping to start a family.

In this chapter we try to describe the stories *Cosmopolitan* tells women about sex and work. They are important stories, not least because they create very close relations between sex and work, representing sex as a kind of work, and work as something in which libido can be invested. In *Cosmopolitan*, sex and work involve the same problems, the same risks, the same insecurities, the same threats to women's independence and control over their lives, and they need to be tackled with the same kind of strategies. As Deborah Cameron has expressed it (2000: 9):

> Advice on all kinds of personal relationships urges us to treat them as if they were business projects. We are told to 'set goals' and 'negotiate contracts' with family members and friends. We are urged to 'work on' our individual selves with a view to becoming happier, better adjusted and more successful. This acquires a certain edge as other developments within enterprise culture shift responsibilities from the state to the individual.

Although *Cosmopolitan* is not the only vehicle for disseminating these stories, it is a very important one, because of its global circulation. It exerts its influence even where it has not yet established a local franchise, for instance in Vietnam, where the Communist government does not allow foreign ownership of magazines. Figure 4.1 shows the first article on making sex more satisfying ever to appear in a Vietnamese women's magazine. It is illustrated with images from commercial image banks showing Western couples lying in bed, wrapped in sheets and bathed in warm, glowing light. When asked why she featured the article, the editor, who had a pile of past issues of *Cosmopolitan* in her office, said that advertisers favour these kinds of articles and these kinds of images. And in the age of *Doi Moi*, Vietnam's market reform, advertising and promotion have become important for Vietnam's economy.

Discourse as the recontextualisation of social practices

Cosmopolitan stories about sex and work are based on a particular view of sex and work that we will, following Michel Foucault (1972), call a 'discourse'. A discourse of sex or of work (and, as we have said, several of each exist at the same time) can find its expression in many different ways – in academic writing, in stories, in advice columns, in everyday conversation, and so on. But it is always essentially the same set of ideas about sex or work that is being expressed, however different the form. Discourses can therefore be defined as:

> socially constructed knowledges of (some aspect of) reality ... developed in specific social contexts and in ways which are appropriate to the interests of

Figure 4.1 Sex in a Vietnamese women's magazine (*Woman's World*, September 2002)

social actors in these contexts, whether these are very broad contexts ('Western Europe') or not (a particular family), explicitly institutionalised contexts (newspapers) or not (dinner table conversations).

(Kress and van Leeuwen, 2001: 4)

Discourses of sex such as we discuss here have come about as part of the emergence of global corporate culture. As we saw, Vietnam adopted them because they attract advertisers. Lifestyle identity is good for business. Naomi Klein (1999: 114) quotes Ann Powers who has said of 'girl power' that

at this intersection between the conventional feminine and the evolving Girl, what's springing up is not a revolution but a mall ... A genuine movement devolves into a giant shopping spree, where girls are encouraged to purchase whatever identity fits them best off the rack.

In this section we first of all outline the key elements of our approach to 'discourse'.

Discourses represent social practices

In our view, knowledge is ultimately based on social practice, on shared concrete experiences. At first sight, this might seem an overstatement. Knowing about the weather, for instance, would seem to have its basis in natural events rather than social actions. Yet, weather reports and other weather discourses, too, ultimately derive from practice, in this case the practices of meteorologists – practices of observation, of recording, and of performing mathematical and linguistic operations on these recordings. As these practices are recontextualised (Bernstein, 1990), and moved from the context of the weather bureau to the context of the newspaper, for instance, they are 'objectivated', shorn of any reference to what meteorologists do, and rephrased in terms of what the weather does. 'Even in the most abstract and theoretical aspects of human thought and verbal usage, the real understanding of words ultimately derives from active experience of those aspects of reality to which the words belong' (Malinowski 1935: 58).

Discourses transform social practices

This means that discourses also, and at the same time, *transform* social practices, on the basis of the interests at stake in the given context. Weather reports, for instance, acquire their legitimation as scientific, and hence reliable, by means of objectivation, by means of transforming something meteorologists do into something that nature does. We are not saying, of course, that nature does not do anything, only that our knowledge of it will always be mediated through human social practices.

For the purposes of analysis, we consider every practice to incorporate and integrate the following elements:

- participants, in different participant roles;
- their activities and reactions to the activities and/or other elements of the practice;
- the times and places of the practice or parts of it;
- the dress and grooming required; and
- the tools and materials required.

Discourses selectively represent and transform these elements according to the interests of the context. To give an example of selective representation, in a novel representing a love relationship there will usually be less detail with regard to dress and grooming than in a *Cosmopolitan* representation of such a relationship, the reason being that novels carry no advertisements, whereas magazines like *Cosmopolitan* are characterised by a close interlinking of editorial and advertising content. As far as transformation is concerned, while an 'outsider' discourse (for example, an expert discourse of love relations) will be characterised by an abstract knowledge of the participants, realised by abstract terms such as 'partners', an 'insider' discourse (for example, in a 'confession' genre) will be characterised by a specific, concrete knowledge of the participants, realised, for instance, by reference to specific individuals (cf. van Leeuwen, 1995, 1996).

Discourses legitimate social practices

Discourses not only constitute (selective and transformed) versions of social practices, they also legitimate (or de-legitimate, critique) the practices which they recontextualise. Purposes, evaluations and reasons for practices and/or elements of practices are discursively constructed and discursively linked to the practices or elements which they legitimate (cf. for example, van Leeuwen and Wodak, 1999; van Leeuwen, 2000b) – and the same practice may be linked to quite different purposes, evaluations and legitimations in different contexts. The 'purpose' of a love relationship, for instance, may be constructed as 'pleasure' or, in a socio-biological vein, as selecting the best genes for procreation, to mention just two possibilities. Some discourses will take such purposes for granted, but involve detailed knowledge of the practice itself. Others will involve very little knowledge of the recontextualised practice or practices and concentrate on purposes, their evaluations and legitimations. In texts based on these discourses the practices themselves may only be realised through a handful of nominalised verbs.

Discourse schemas

If 'discourse' is understood as 'socially constructed knowledge', and if *knowing* is based on *doing*, then the 'activity sequence' (Martin, 1992) must be the key to discourse analysis. In this sense discourse analysis is essentially similar to a 'Proppian' narrative analysis (Propp, 1968), that is, a narrative analysis that deals with the narrated events, rather than with the events of the telling of the story. But there are also some significant differences from Proppian narrative analysis.

First of all, the analysis not only applies to narratives, but to all genres. It is not an analysis of the form of the text, but the analysis of the form of the knowledge that underlies the text – and, needless to say, a given text may combine several such knowledges, hence draw on several discourses. The discourse analysis of, say, a highly abstract theoretical text must, therefore, unpack the nominalisations and abstractions of that text, and reconstitute its links with the activities which it ultimately recontextualises, however attenuated that link may sometimes be. Second, while Proppian analysis does not deal with the relation between the story and the world, our approach to discourse entails that even fairytales and other stories that use a fantasy modality recontextualise actual social practices. This has of course been recognised in many other approaches to narrative (Lévi-Strauss, 1967; Bettelheim, 1979; Wright, 1975), and Proppian analysis has also been used for the analysis of non-fictional texts in media and film studies (for example, Nichols, 1981; Bell, 1982).

A discourse analysis of this kind can be performed at different levels of abstraction. A relatively high level of abstraction yields what we will call here *discourse schemas,* the socio-cognitive schemas that allow practices to be transformed into discourses about practices. Such schemas constitute interpretative frameworks, historically and socioculturally specific frameworks for understanding social practices. In the case of literature they have, for instance, included 'conflict-resolution' schemas, 'quest' schemas, and so on. As these were only studied in relation to literature, they have been conflated with genres. But from our perspective schemas such as 'conflict-resolution' and the 'quest' can also be applied to non-narrative genres, and to other semiotic modes. Much psychological literature, for instance, is based on 'conflict and resolution', and it has also been argued that, in music, the sonata form rests on a similar schema (cf. van Leeuwen, 1999).

This chapter focuses specifically on one particular discourse schema. To bring it into focus, compare the following two texts from the Dutch *Cosmopolitan* of November 2001. Both are taken from an article entitled '*Goed Kwaad – Woede is positief (als je weet hoe je er mee om moet gaan)*'. The first part of the article's title is an untranslatable pun. *Kwaad* means both 'angry' and 'evil'. *Goed* means 'good' but is also an intensifier, so that *goed kwaad* means both 'good (and) evil' and 'very angry'. The subtitle translates as, 'Anger is positive, if you know how to deal with it.' The first of the two texts below is a case story, set apart by a layout box; the second is from the journalist's report of the views of 'Cosmo's own psychologist', Lilien Macknack:

Liesbet (30): My partner often works late, as he has a very demanding job. I myself work from home. I used to start looking at the clock at five. At six he would be home. A minute too late and I would be furious. I would throw his dinner in the bin, lock the front door at five past six, go to bed alone at ten and throw his duvet down the stairs. After many angry outbursts I realised the true reason of my anger. It was always me who had to clean up the mess in the house. I am also busy. I felt he didn't take my work seriously. Now he helps clean up in the evenings. And when I start my day in a clean house, I don't mind it so much if he's late.

Liliën: You mention two extremes, and as so often, the middle road is best. The solution is to express your anger immediately or as soon as possible. In that way you rid yourself of it and the message hits home. An example: you have a shared job and your colleague always leaves your shared desk in a mess. You don't say anything, but you are extremely irritated. Your anger mounts up. Suddenly you can't repress it anymore and there is an enormous outburst. Result: the message does not hit home because your reaction is excessive. And afterwards you will feel even worse. If you had acted in time, your colleague would have understood you and you would have felt better.

There are many differences between these two texts; generic differences, for instance (the first is a 'case story', the second a piece of expert counselling), and differences in content (the first deals with a personal relationship, the second with a work relationship). Yet both are based on the same activity sequence: something upsetting happens, the upset person represses her anger, with bad consequences for her equilibrium, and then eventually bursts out in anger anyway, which only makes matters worse. Finally, she talks it over with the person concerned, and in this way solves her problem. In the first text this final stage becomes the resolution of a conflict narrative. In the second text it is expressed through the addition of purposes and evaluations ('the solution is . . .'; 'your reaction is excessive . . .'), and, rather than telling a story, the text has an expository structure: it first offers a solution, then states its benefits, and finally illustrates the point with an example. But the activity sequence is the same in both cases. This activity sequence is already relatively abstract, as it can be applied to a range of problems and situations, but making it even more abstract shows that it instantiates a discourse schema that applies not just to this particular 'anger management' discourse, but also to many others. A discourse *schema*, therefore, takes the form of a more abstract activity sequence, as shown below (the asterisk signifies a 'wrong solution' leading to a 'problematic outcome'):

Initial problem (various)
⇓
*Solution (suppress anger)
⇓
Problematic outcome (physical and/or mental well-being affected)
⇓
*Solution (excessive outburst of anger)
⇓
Problematic outcome (problems continued and aggravated)
⇓
Solution (self-expression and communication)
⇓
Final outcome (problem solved)

Clearly this schema can be used narratively, to tell a story in which various solutions are tried out in turn and found wanting, until the 'right' solution is finally hit upon. But it can equally underlie more abstract texts which, for instance, evaluate different possible solutions without any sense of chronology. We have found it to be the dominant schema in *Cosmopolitan*, although it is by no means the only one – profiles of women, for instance, often have a biographical, 'conversion story' schema, in which a single motif or aspiration forms the foundation of the whole of a women's life. In this chapter, however, we concentrate on the 'problem–solution' discourse schema. We use it to investigate, first of all, what kinds of problems and what kinds of solutions occur in *Cosmopolitan*'s different versions, and second, to ask why it is dominant, how it understands the practices it represents, and how this serves the interests that underlie the magazine's approach.

Problems

In this section we look at the kinds of 'initial problems' that feature in articles based on the 'problem–solution' discourse schema discussed in the previous section. Our analysis is based on 40 articles (many of them containing a range of problems and solutions) from the November 2001 issues of eight versions of *Cosmopolitan* – the Indian, Taiwanese, Spanish, UK, Dutch, Finnish, Greek and German versions. We distinguish five categories. As shown, they are, for the most part, presented as personal problems, unrelated to social and political issues.

Unreliable partners

In the world of *Cosmopolitan*, our fellow human beings are essentially unreliable, especially those closest to us – our colleagues, friends and lovers. As already mentioned, parents, children or relatives do not exist in this world, although husbands occasionally occur in the Asian versions. As a result of their essential unreliability and selfishness, colleagues at work and partners in love constantly pose problems. They plot against you behind your back, they take advantage of you, they double-cross you. Here are two examples of the way this category of problem gets formulated in the magazines, the first from an article about revenge in the German version, the second from an article titled 'Having Affairs on the Side' in the Dutch version (as mentioned above, all examples in this and the next section are from November 2001 issues):

> You share your desk, but not your ideas about fairness and teamwork. Your charming colleague always pushes the routine jobs towards you while he plays the creative soul.

> Wendela (31): When I was 8 months pregnant I found out that my boyfriend had been leading a double life for months. When he wasn't with me or at work he was with girlfriend number 2.

Risky encounters

Encounters with new people, whether new colleagues at work, or men making advances, are always problematic, always fraught with risk. A wary attitude is called for. The examples below are from an article titled 'Slow-Mo Love' in the Indian version and a series of tips on the careers page of the Taiwanese version (the second example includes the solution, namely rejection):

> I met Jugraj at an IT exhibition in 1995. He immediately started asking me out, which I found rather pushy.

> Chatty colleagues will hinder your work. When they move in your direction stand up to show that you're terribly busy and they will shut up automatically.

Institutional obstacles

Cosmo women face many institutional obstacles in a male-dominated world. They may have difficulty in gaining access to certain places or activities, or in getting promotion, or in achieving other forms of success in their endeavours. Although this is in principle an issue of social and cultural gender inequality, it is usually formulated as a personal problem, and the social and political issues behind it are rarely dealt with explicitly. Here are two examples, one from the 'Studies and Career' pages of the Finnish version, and one from an article in the Indian version entitled, 'How to Get Treated Like a VIP: Why stand in line when you can be waited on hand and foot':

> Do your ideas go unnoticed because no one listens to you? *Cosmo* tells you how to get your ideas taken seriously.

> Have you ever stopped to think why one aspiring club-hopper is made to wait outside the town's swankiest soirees before she gets the nod while another has the entire club's staff dedicated to making her night out a divine experience?

Lack of confidence

The problems faced by *Cosmo* women, however, are not only caused by external factors. They also stem from women's own insecurity and lack of confidence, whether at work or in relation to their bodies or sexual competence. The first of the two examples below is from an article titled 'Go Home When You are Sick' in the Finnish version, the second comes from the Indian *Cosmopolitan*:

> More and more young women come to work even when they are sick . . . because they don't want to be considered weak.

You've heard time and again the secret of sensational sex is simple: if you feel good about yourself, you'll be a great lover. But the fact remains that some days . . . it just doesn't work when you think your bottom is a bag of porridge and your legs make a cocktail stick shapely.

Sexual dissatisfaction

Achieving sexual satisfaction on your own terms is of central importance to *Cosmo* women. Not achieving it, whether because of insecurity or for other reasons, is therefore a key problem. The examples below are from the Spanish and Indian versions:

I am so good at giving men fellatio that they simply don't want to make love to me because invariably they 'finish' before I have time to gain any pleasure.

It's the inevitable question hovering over any first-time close encounter: will the big O make a show? Climaxing with someone new isn't always easy, but if you're turned on, there is no reason you can't both peak.

Clearly the world of *Cosmopolitan* is a world fraught with risk and insecurity in which women have ultimately only themselves to rely on if they are to achieve what they want: independence, success, freedom and sexual satisfaction.

Solutions

In this section we analyse the kinds of solutions *Cosmopolitan* offers to the problems discussed above, taking our examples from the same selection of 40 articles from eight versions of the magazine we used in the previous section.

Acquiring skills

Learning new skills is a frequently proposed solution. Such skills might, for instance, relate to self-presentation and the deliberate exploitation of female attractiveness through dress and grooming, and even seductive behaviour, or to being 'well organised' (for example, simple secretarial skills). Here are two examples, one from the Finnish version (a solution for the problem of lack of confidence at work) and one from the UK version (a solution for the problem of not achieving sexual satisfaction):

Do you need to sound assured and confident? People with a low voice are usually considered reliable. If you lower your pitch artificially, you end up with a dull, nasal sound. You can hum your voice range up and down a few times a day. Eventually you will have a more varied pitch.

Helen can remember what inspired her to add vocals to her sexual repertoire. 'I probably learned it before I even had sex, from watching films where women always seem to be loud during sex scenes. I guess I thought that's what I was supposed to do too. The sounds I make help turn me on – and I know they turn men on – and once I'm aroused, I can't even control what comes out of my mouth.'

Rejection

As we have seen, people form a potential risk and should not be trusted too easily. One approach to dealing with this problem is, quite simply, rejection. As we shall see, it occurs especially often in the Asian versions of the magazine that we have studied. The first of the two examples below is from the Indian, the second from the Taiwanese *Cosmopolitan*:

My fear of getting hurt stopped me and I withdrew from him.

She resolutely cut off the relationship with her husband, went back to work, and brought herself happiness again.

Communication

A frequent solution for the problem of 'unreliable partners' is communication, 'talking things over'. *Cosmopolitan* rarely goes into detail as to what form this might take, perhaps because it would be difficult to formulate this within the confines of the typical *Cosmopolitan* genres, such as the 'hot tips' genre (see Chapter 6). The examples below are from the UK and Dutch versions of the magazine:

They'll need to . . . learn new ways to relate to each other or putting intensity back into sex. They'll also need to develop communication skills to resolve conflict, so they can cope with the difficulties within the relationship.

One day I finally confronted her and told her I couldn't do her work on top of my own. The funny thing was, she reacted very well to that.

Pleasing people

Another approach to the problem of unreliable partners (especially men) is pleasing them, whether through flattery, seductive behaviour, or otherwise. In the first example below, the Greek version of the magazine uses this approach as a solution for lack of confidence at work. It is of course also a frequent solution for sexual problems, as in the second example, from the Indian version:

Find out which is your boss's favourite snack or sweet and offer him one. While he is enjoying it, you can gently start talking about work.

Meg, 27, shares her secret for fishing his wishes: 'When I was with my boyfriend for the first time, I asked playfully, "Hatin' it? Lovin' it?" He laughed and totally opened up after that.'

Taking control

The solution of taking control, taking the initiative, almost invariably relates only to sexual problems, as in these examples from the Taiwanese and UK versions of the magazine:

To pay for sex is the last thought that would cross my mind. But a few days ago, on my way back home, the idea suddenly jumped into my mind. Then I bought a newspaper in a convenience store and found a phone number in the classified adverts.

Nick: Hearing Cassie tell me what she wanted was a big turn-on.

All these solutions are offered as strategic solutions, involving planning and preparation, and the acquisition of repertoires of possible behaviours. This in turn means taking control, taking an active role. But it could be argued that control remains rather limited. At work women may learn to keep the boss happy, or to keep on top of things by learning some mundane practical skill such as 'desk tidying'. Elsewhere they may become adept at a range of survival tricks from the pop psychology school on how to outmanoeuvre people, while control over men remains largely restricted to sex. Whatever they are counselled to do, the possibility of support from other people is not envisaged. In the world of *Cosmopolitan* there is no solidarity with fellow human beings, no counsel from religious and cultural traditions, and there are no structural and political solutions by means of whatever form of collective action. It is all up to the individual, who must, alone, face the world, using survival strategies in which traditional 'female wiles' continue to play a key role, despite the feminist origins of the magazine. This 'survival of the fittest' and 'winner takes all' approach is the essential *message* of the discourse schema, its meaning, the way it interprets the social practices of work and the personal relationships it recontextualises. And it is clearly an approach that suits the interests of the global neo-capitalist order of which *Cosmopolitan* forms part.

Outcomes

To complete this account, two points can be made with regard to the 'outcome' element of the discourse schema. First, outcomes always relate to initial problems – the lack is remedied, women become confident, achieve sexual satisfaction, and so on. Second, *wrong* solutions lead to the opposite of preferred solutions (for example, 'repression' instead of 'self-expression'), and hence to problematic outcomes which, in turn, require new solutions, as in the Taiwanese example below, where trust is the wrong solution to the problem of risky encounters:

> My friend is a 30-something now and didn't go to work after she was married. In the beginning, she thought she had married Mr Right, but after more than one year she found her husband was not loyal to her. In the end, Jenny resolutely cut off the relationship with her husband, went back to work and brought herself happiness again.

This would be analysed as follows, with asterisks marking 'wrong solutions', and with the classifications of the problems and solutions which we have introduced in this chapter indicated in brackets:

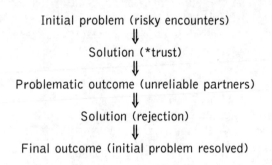

Initial problem (risky encounters)
⇓
Solution (*trust)
⇓
Problematic outcome (unreliable partners)
⇓
Solution (rejection)
⇓
Final outcome (initial problem resolved)

It is of course primarily these 'wrong solutions' which make the discourse schema recursive and allow it to expand beyond the three minimally necessary elements of problems, solutions and outcomes.

Global schemas and local discourses

The 'problem–solution' discourse schema we have described here is a global model for the representation of social practices and, we argue, a model fit for the spirit of strategic communication that pervades global commercialised culture. But, being an abstract model, an interpretive framework, it can nevertheless accommodate local accents, for instance in the form of different, more culturally specific problems and solutions, and hence also outcomes. In other words, while all versions of the magazine use this discourse schema as their dominant mode of constructing the world of the *Cosmopolitan* woman (and, in problem–solution genres, for tutoring her in the ways of this world), the types of problem and solution may be differently distributed among the versions. To illustrate this point, we give two examples, the first one relating to interpersonal relations at work, the second to taking control in sexual matters.

Going by the sample of 40 articles from eight versions that we have studied here, the problems of 'unreliable partners' and 'risky encounters' are global. They occur in all the versions analysed, and, in every case, in relation to both work and personal relationships. But the solutions differ. In the Indian and Taiwanese versions 'communication' is the *wrong* solution, and 'rejection' is preferred, as, for instance, in the following two instances, both again from November 2001 issues. In the first example, from the Indian *Cosmopolitan*, making friends too quickly leads to problems that can only be solved by rejection. In the second example, from the Taiwanese version, the same kind of solution is advocated by a corporate training consultant:

Ayesha Wahi was only 21 when she landed her first job. Though she was anxious about her new workplace, her fears were quickly put to rest when she met newcomer Shalini Gupta. 'Beings friends with her came easy, as she was relaxed and lots of fun,' she says. But what started as casual female bonding grew into vile professional jealousy when Wahi was promoted over Gupta. Her jealous co-worker started bad-mouthing her and spreading so many nasty rumours that Wahi eventually quit her job.

What is it that makes us behave like warriors at work? It is a dog-eat-dog battlefield where you have to be sharp about telling friend from foe. 'Friendship at work hinders professionalism as there is an emotional involvement with your so-called friend,' says corporate training consultant Renu Mattoo. Get wise about work mates with our genius workplan.

In northern European versions, on the other hand, 'communication' is the preferred solution and almost always leads to positive outcomes. The first of the two examples below comes from an article about friendship at work from the German version, the second from the already quoted article on anger management in the Dutch *Cosmopolitan*:

Suzanne Metzger, 26, and Nadine Knebel, 25, work in a multimedia agency. Susanne is an account director and Nadine's immediate superior. They became friends when they worked together on a project with many night shifts. The closer they became personally, the more work conflicts they had. 'Discussions about work decisions often became quite emotional,' says Nadine. 'But now we have it under control, because we have clearly worked out our areas and responsibilities.'

Sandra (24): In my previous job I had a colleague who always asked me to do her work, as she was so busy. I would do it, but I became increasingly fed up with her, and with myself. I hated myself for letting it happen all the time. And she took more and more advantage of me. Often I already started fretting about it the night before. One day I confronted her and told her I couldn't do her work on top of my own, because I had plenty of work myself.

The funny thing was, she reacted very well to this. My sense of victory was overwhelming. I have become much more daring now, and that makes me feel really good about myself.

Our second example relates to taking control in sexual matters. In the already quoted article 'Cosmo Confession: I bought a man' from the Taiwanese *Cosmopolitan*, taking control sexually has an ambivalent outcome and does not diminish the woman's lack of confidence and sexual satisfaction as much as she had thought. Towards the end, the woman confesses:

When he asked me if I had an orgasm I lied and answered 'yes', as I was worried that if I said no he might have taken a more aggressive step which would have definitely been too much for me. I don't regret doing it although it is better to have sex for love's sake.

In the UK version, on the other hand, the solution of 'taking control' always works, as in this example:

Amelia says:'We tried a fantastic chair-sitting position – I loved being in control.'
Howie says: 'The chair position was great as Amelia could take control.'

Such examples suggest that there is, on the one hand, a global socio-cognitive schema for interpreting the problems and vicissitudes that can arise in women's lives, and, within this framework, a global stock of problems and solutions, clearly limited, and closely linked to a specific account of what women want: freedom, independence, access, confidence, sexual satisfaction. On the other hand, this schema does allow for cultural difference. As we have seen, in the Asian versions there is no trust, only survival of the fittest and 'dog-eats-dog', whereas in the European versions 'communication' can solve all problems, whether at work or at home. Again, in the Spanish and Greek issues analysed, the theme of pleasing men, whether they are partners or bosses, is more foregrounded than in northern European versions (in the UK version, for instance, it is at best a by-product of pleasing oneself). These local accents are, nevertheless, congruent with the global schema – they stay well within the same, common definitions of what constitutes problems and solutions. The essential global message, the underlying philosophy of life, lies in the semantic organisation of the discourses which the schema provides.

Conclusion

In this chapter, we have first introduced the notion of 'discourse schema', understood as an interpretive schema for the recontextualisation of social practices. It is likely that, in a given culture, there exists only a handful of such discourse schemas.

Second, we have identified and described one specific discourse schema, the 'problem–solution' schema. This schema plays a key role in *Cosmopolitan* magazine, but it is clearly not restricted to that context only. It interprets social practices as goal-oriented and strategic, even in matters of the emotions (for example, anger, or love) and it can apply to a wide range of more specific discourses (for example, discourses of work, of personal relationship, of anger management, and so on).

Third, we have shown that such discourses can, in turn, have 'local accents'. These local accents, however, are essentially a surface phenomenon. They do not affect the underlying semantic structuring of the discourses and, therefore, do not realise cultural difference in a deeper sense.

Finally, we have argued that such discourse schemas serve the interests of specific social institutions. The discourses discussed recontextualise the social identities and practices of women as strategies for obtaining or maintaining certain life goals such as independence, freedom, career success and sexual satisfaction, and for overcoming the obstacles to the achievement of these goals. In many societies women's independence is limited, and their chances of achieving career success and sexual satisfaction curtailed. As a result, women in these societies have something to gain from the introduction of the *Cosmo* ethos. In return, global capital has much to gain from their allegiance to these new forms of identity, as they rely so fundamentally on consumer goods for their expression.

It is in this context that *Cosmopolitan* seeks to create the 'community' of its readers, envisaging them on the one hand as thrown back on to their own resources, and living without a true sense of belonging in a world of risky and unstable relationships; yet, on the other hand, also as a community bound by its allegiance to the values and lifestyles portrayed in the magazine and similar discourses – values and lifestyles which women need not necessarily live in every detail – signifying them by means of dress, fashion accessories and form of bodily *hexis* is often sufficient. Attractive, glamorous and well-dressed, *Cosmopolitan* women take the risks of modern life in their stride and invest their libido as much in work as in relationships. Although the magazine constantly reminds them of their vulnerability, their loneliness and the restrictions imposed by their gender, they continue to strike the pose of the 'fun, fearless female'. After all, every problem has its simple, strategic solution.

Questions

1   Study the problems and solutions in a global men's magazine. How do they differ from the ones described in this chapter?

2   Apply the problem–solution schema introduced in this chapter to short *Cosmopolitan* articles on beauty.

3   Find two quite different texts about divorce, or, more generally, 'splitting up', for example texts from different cultural or religious backgrounds, a movie versus a children's book, or a magazine article versus a Family Court brochure. Compare them in terms of the participants, actions, emotional reactions and settings they

include. What kind of reasons for leaving one's partner count as valid or invalid in each?

4   Compare the solutions to the same kind of problem in magazines from two different periods or countries or socio-cultural groups.

Note

1   A version of part of this chapter was published in Machin and van Leeuwen (2003).

5 Discourses of war

Computer war games: entertainment and propaganda[1]

In 2001, the American computer game industry finally overtook Hollywood, growing by an astounding 43 per cent to $9.4 billion, and becoming the latest major American contribution to global media culture. Like other American media, it combines entertainment and propaganda. This is most evident in the case of computer war games, many of which are made in close collaboration with the American military and based on actual conflicts in which America has been involved, particularly in the Middle East.

Mark Long, Director of Zombie Productions, which created the *Delta Force* games for the software development company Novalogic, told us in an interview that his company works closely with former Delta and Special Forces for details of the games, and 'has even generated terrain maps from declassified Department of Defense Predator UAV imagery'. Novalogic works with the military in other contexts as well. Its subsidiary Novalogic Systems creates military simulations for both air and land manoeuvres, works with the US Army's Training and Doctrine Command Analysis Center, and has close relations with Lockheed Martin Aeronautical systems, making flight simulations for its military aircraft. Percentages of game profits are donated to the Special Operations Warrior foundation, which provides scholarships for the children of army personnel killed on duty.

Similar close links exist between Hollywood and the military. Ridley Scott, the director of the *Black Hawk Down* movie, also discussed in this chapter, told CNN that the Pentagon proved 'very, very, very user-friendly' over the film, as long as 'what you are actually trying to do is present the military in the right and proper light'. The result, he said, was an 'almost page by page process of negotiation' with Pentagon officials over the screenplay (Peterson, 2002).

Games like *Black Hawk Down* are sold the world over, often in pirated copies, especially in countries like China and Vietnam, and, of course, also in the Middle East, so that players in Lebanon, Jordan and other Middle East countries may get to 'kill' Islamic terrorists operating in their own country. Perhaps it is no surprise that Arab game designers see this as propaganda, and decided to produce their own computer games, so as to present a different perspective on events. In Lebanon, in 2001, the Hezbollah undertook the design of *Special Force*, a computer game inspired by *Delta Force* that would allow players to fight as one of a group of Islamic resistance fighters, killing Israeli commandos and infiltrating Israeli lines to return the Israeli-diverted water supply to southern Lebanese villages. The makers of the game wanted to 'contest the view of Arabs and Muslims being portrayed as terrorists in western games and introduce the resistance to young people' (Karouny, 2003). Helped by its War Information Department, Hezbollah took two years to produce the game. As its designers said to us, the game showed the 'integrity of the resistance and the fight against the occupation' and allowed each player to be a 'partner in victory'.

As a result of its games and other media activities, Hezbollah became lionised in the Arab world as a model of resistance against the 'new Western colonialism' (Dallal, 2001), gaining respect especially from young Arabs around the world. The game itself was an impressive success, not least because there were many odds to overcome. Since the US conglomerates control both the distribution networks and the software licensing, its designers had to 'invent an Arab gaming industry from scratch'. International game developers, publishers and distributors all rejected the game, and for their distribution the designers had to rely on the internet and on promotion through other Hezbollah media.

In this chapter we investigate the discourses of war that underlie these games, focusing first on *Black Hawk Down* and then comparing *Special Forces*, the Hezbollah game, to the American game *Delta Force*. But to appreciate how the game and the movie of *Black Hawk Down* represent the 1992 American invasion of Somalia, we shall sketch in some background first.

The USA and Somalia

At the end of the 1970s a Moscow-supported anti-US military coup in Ethiopia had removed the US-friendly emperor Selassie, declaring the country a Marxist-Leninist State. US President Carter responded by cutting aid to Ethiopia and supporting the deeply authoritarian Barre regime in neighbouring Somalia. From the late 1970s to 1991, under US patronage, thousands of Somali civilians died in a range of civil rights abuses. There was a death penalty for belonging to any political organisation.

In the early 1980s Barre invaded Ogaden, an Ethiopian territory inhabited by ethnic Somalis. The USA initially said it would stop providing arms unless Barre withdrew from Ogaden. But when Moscow intervened, pushing Barre's army back over the border, along with several hundred thousands of ethnic Somali refugees, the Reagan administration rushed more arms to Mogadishu. Between 1980 and 1989 the USA gave Somalia some $400 million worth of military aid along with another $200 million in cash arms sales funded with Saudi Arabian assistance.

Barre's attempts to gain complete control of the country were ruthless. Aid agencies accused him of genocide on clans opposing his rule (in Somalia everyone belongs to one of five clans). As well as using arms, his forces poisoned wells, slaughtered farm animals, and carpet-bombed urban areas. Around 60,000 people were killed at this time (Africa Watch, 1990; Schraeder, 1990). By the early 1990s the fighting had escalated into a civil war, with civilians being massacred in the streets and looting the only form of livelihood. There was no food, but automatic weapons and grenade launchers were everywhere. A UNICEF report (UNICEF, 1989) revealed that, in these times of starvation and poverty, Barre was spending about one fifth of his government's expenditure on the military. The country was heading for disaster. Unfortunately for Somalia the Cold War had ended and America was building up to the Gulf War. Somalia was no longer of strategic interest to them, and they pulled out. The next year, up to six million people died in the famine. It has been widely argued that had the USA not funded Barre's regime, this situation would not have come about (Shalom, 1993).

Although Congress was initially reluctant to provide more aid (Lewis, 1992), later that year the USA did back the UN and sent relief specialists. To do so they needed the support of the warring factions. This they found in the US-friendly Ali Mahdi who had started the wave of conflict by trying to push his rival Mohammed Farah Aidid out of Mogadishu (Post *et al.,* 1992; Perlez, 1992a, 1992b). The plan was to send troops to drop food supplies from helicopters. But the Red Cross, which had provided most of the relief during the famine, was against this. They had already liaised with clan leaders to create food distribution networks and were concerned that the presence of the military would create further instability (Perlez, 1992c). The USA started to carry out the airlifts, nevertheless. The Red Cross, meanwhile, continued to work with the clan leaders, even though the US military presence caused further massive movements of population and, many felt, made things much worse – there is evidence that things were a good deal more peaceful in unoccupied areas (Maren, 1994). It was at this time, with the worst of the famine already over (Perlez, 1992d), that Bush decided to send troops to Somalia.

When the US Seals arrived, under the spotlights of a pre-planned media circus, the Red Cross urged them to at least get to the affected areas as quickly as possible, as delays could cause further casualties. However, the Marines made a dramatic and needless amphibious landing and did not get to the worst areas until a week after their arrival (Waller, 1992). Footage showing them giving out food was taken earlier in areas where there were fewer problems (Shalom, 1993). Arguably, 'Operation Restore Hope' had only served to disrupt some of the stability created by agreements between the clans and the Red Cross, and to create panic among clan leaders who felt that the USA was against them, especially Aidid, whose importance was probably overrated by the USA (Sciolino, 1993).

'Operation Restore Hope' showed that quick-fix solutions, both in terms of airlifting food and military occupation, cannot replace complex long-term work. Today Somalia remains in disarray. According to aid agencies, half a million people are short of food, and hundreds of thousands are displaced. But, according to Médécins Sans Frontières, international aid has dropped 90 per cent since the 1990s.

Documentary anchorage

Both the game and the movie of *Black Hawk Down* have documentary style intro-ductions that anchor them to the actual US invasion in Somalia described above.

The game opens with a short film, using newsreel footage and a factual style voice-over commentary to explicitly justify the war. According to the commentary, Aidid had obstructed the efforts of the multinational UN peacekeeping force to deliver food and Delta Force was deployed 'with the sole purpose of capturing Aidid'. 'Capturing the tyrant', it says, will protect the weak United Nations and allow them deliver humanitarian aid. The visuals include a close shot of an American soldier and a smiling Somali boy (shot 11) as well as a series of shots demonstrating the combat skills of the elite soldiers (shots 20–7), accompanied by stirring music. It is worth transcribing the sequence in full:

1 NOVALOGIC presents	*Mournful string music with 'Eastern' feel*
2 VLS Dusty Mogadishu street, camera tracking forwards. Super title: 1991	*Music continues as voice-over starts*: Somalia is reeling from years of famine and constant fighting . . .
3 MS High Angle. Women filling food bowls from large pot	. . . between clans
4 LS Woman walking on deserted country road with basket	*Voice-over*: 300,000 are reported dead
5 MLS Woman standing in centre of courtyard with children seated around her. She carries two bowls, hesitates who to give them to	(*music*)
6 LS Street with crowd of people walking towards camera	*Voice-over*: There is no central government
7 VLS Camera pans along with army plane on runway. Super title: 19 December 1992	*Voice-over*: The US Army 10th Mountain Division deploys . . .
8 MLS Two US soldiers, one carrying a bag of rice, the other a gun, camera tracking with them as they move L–R	. . . to the region as part of a multinational peacekeeping force
9 VLS Truck as bags of rice are loaded from ship into truck	(*music*)
10 MLS Two Somali porters carrying bags of rice via gangplank	(*music*)

11 MCS American soldier and smiling Somali boy. Zoom in	(*music*)
12 CS Aidid addressing crowd. Super title: 5 June 1993	*Voice-over:* Mohammed Farah Aidid, militia leader of the Habr Gadir clan orders an attack . . .
13 VLS High Angle. Somali people running for cover. Zoom in	. . . on a UN relief shipment, killing . . .
14 MLS Masked militia man with gun sitting atop pile of bags of rice	24 Pakistani soldiers . . .
15 MS Militia man swivelling rocket launcher around	. . . In response to the . . .
16 LS Militia man with gun	. . . continued Habr Gadir threat . . .
17 MLS Militia man with rifle mounted on car. Car reverses	. . . task force rangers . . .
18 MLS Militia man on car with rifle. He waves	. . . enter Mogadishu . . .
19 MS Militia man on car. He waves	. . . with the sole purpose of capturing Aidid
20 VLS Black Hawk helicopters flying over desert. Super title: 26 August 1993	(*music*)
21 MLS Two US soldiers about to crash in door	(*music*)
22 LS Two US soldiers crouched on street, signalling to each other	(*music*)
23 MLS (side view) group of soldiers aiming rifles	(*music*)
24 MLS Two US soldiers lying down with guns aimed	*Voice-over:* This force is comprised . . .
25 MLS Two US soldiers moving forward	. . . of US Army Rangers and . . .
26 LS US soldiers crossing road and moving towards building	. . . operators from the First Special Forces . . .
27a LS Humvee driving towards camera. Camera tilts up to	. . . operational Detachment Delta, an elite fighting unit also known as . . .
27b LS Black Hawk helicopter overhead	. . . Delta Force

The movie of *Black Hawk Down* also has a documentary style introduction, but it uses reconstructed rather than authentic footage. Blue-tinted monochrome images provide a documentary 'feel', and factual titles, rather than a voice-over commentary, tell the story. The wailing music establishes a sense of sad desolation as we view famine victims, but changes to an energetic drum roll as the first Black Hawk helicopter comes into shot. The story, as conveyed by the superimposed titles, is almost identical to that of the documentary introduction of the game. Again, the role of the Red Cross, and its relation to the Somali clans, is omitted – but this time only in the words, because the images show a ramshackle truck with a Red Cross flag (shot 7) and, later, a tattered Red Cross flag on a dilapidated building in the background. The Red Cross is clearly depicted as ineffective in fighting the famine and in as much of a state of disrepair as Somalia as a whole. Although we do see the consequences of the famine, we never learn how and why it came about. The sequence as a whole is shown below:

1 Title on black: 'Based on actual events.'
   Mournful music enters mixed in with 'wind' sound.
2 Title on black: 'Only the dead have seen the end of war.' Plato
3 *Blue-tinted black and white images.* Camera tracks over sand towards Medium Shot Somali, seen from behind as he wraps a corpse in a shroud. *Singing voice enters.*
4 Medium Shot Shrouded corpse, tied to chair. Camera tracks back to reveal Long Shot Man squatting in background.
5 Very Long Shot Truck on dusty road, driving towards camera. Superimposed title: 'Somalia, East Africa, 1992.'
6 Title on black: 'Years of warfare among rival clans caused famine on a biblical scale.'
7 Long Shot Ancient-looking truck with tattered Red Cross flag, Somali man standing up in the back. Camera tracks with it revealing, first, a Long Shot of a woman pushing a wheelbarrow, then the man wrapping the corpse. Superimposed title: '300,000 civilians died of starvation.'
8 Title on black: 'Mohamed Farrah Aidid, the most powerful of the warlords, rules the capital Mogadishu.'
9 Medium Shot Somali man as he and another man lift the shrouded corpse. Camera tracks with them as they carry it towards the truck. Superimposed title: 'He seizes international food shipments at the ports. Hunger is his weapon.'
   At the end of this shot the singing stops and the music continues instrumentally.
10 Medium Close Shot White man in white shirt giving Somali man a drink. Low angle. Camera cranes down to his feet and tracks with him as he walks away, revealing emaciated corpses. Superimposed title: 'The world responds. Behind a force of 20,000 US Marines, food is delivered and order is restored.'

Camera continues to track past bodies of famine victims lying on the sand. Superimposed title: 'April 1993 Aidid waits until the Marines withdraw, and then declares war on the remaining UN Peacekeepers.'

11 Title on black: 'In June, Aidid's militia ambush and slaughter 24 Pakistani soldiers, and begin targeting American personnel.'

12 Medium Shot Somali man sitting and staring apathetically. A dilapidated building with tattered Red Cross flag can be seen in the background.
Camera tracks past him to reveal a Medium Shot of an equally apathetic woman.

13 Title on black: 'In late August, America's elite soldiers, Delta Force, Army Rangers and the 160th SOAR are sent to Mogadishu to remove Aidid and restore order.'
Sound of helicopter mixes in with music.

14 Camera tracks backwards into a room, revealing a bed, and, through the window, the outskirts of a town, with apartment buildings. Superimposed title: 'The mission was to take three weeks, but six weeks later, Washington was growing impatient.'
Sound of helicopter increases in volume.

15 Title on black: 'BLACK HAWK DOWN'.
Music changes to energetic drum rolls. Helicopter sound continues.

16 *Full colour image.* Aerial shot of helicopter flying over town. Superimposed title: 'Saturday, October 2, 1993.'

17 Close Shot of Sanderson (Josh Hartnett), who will be the main hero, looking down at the scene from helicopter.
(The scene that follows shows a raid on a UN food relief operation, ending with a challenge by the leader of the raid to the Black Hawk helicopter.)

Once the introduction is over, the style shifts from documentary to drama or game. A dialogue between two of the characters in the *Black Hawk Down* movie expresses this shift — a shift which, in different ways, will also be experienced by the movie audience and the game players.

Soldier A: You don't think we should be here?
Soldier B: You know what I think? Doesn't matter what I think. Once that first bullet goes past your head, politics and all that shit goes right out of the window.

But the transition experienced by the movie audience differs from that experienced by the game player. Movie audiences are addressed individually and identify with the heroes in their imagination. As shown in more detail below, the elite soldiers are not only attractive young Hollywood stars, they are also shown as individuals. The film takes time to introduce them as people with a past, with loved ones back home, with feelings, and with individual character traits. Their emotions, especially when their fellow soldiers are hurt, are shown in close-up. We experience the war with and through them. And the war, in this film, is not pretty. Soldiers get horrific injuries and die painful deaths. War is hell.

In the game, on the other hand, players participate vicariously in the war, looking at the game's images along the barrel of their guns, involved, not in an emotive experience, but in adrenaline-rush action. In other words, while the movie exploits the emotions of the audience for propaganda purposes, the game exploits its users' natural pleasure in concentrated, skilled eye-to-hand coordination for the same reason. And although the enemies sometimes gurgle and cough when they get killed, there is a lot less blood on the screen than in the movie.

Representing the participants

In this section we again use 'social actor' analysis (van Leeuwen, 1996, 2000a) to discuss how the main parties involved in the conflict are represented – the US soldiers, Aidid, the Habr Gedir militia and the Somali civilians. We start by introducing a few further categories from 'social actor' theory, besides those we already encountered in Chapter 3.

Deletion

Many stories omit participants who played a role in the actual events, and deletions of this kind can be highly significant for the way the events are portrayed. The *Black Hawk Down* movie and game, for instance, do not recognise that all Somalis belong to one of five clans. There Is only one clan, represented as a rogue force with a despotic leader. All other Somalis are 'civilians'. The important role of the Red Cross is also omitted, except for its brief appearance in the documentary style introduction of the movie.

Individualisation and collectivisation

Participants can be represented as individuals ('individualisation') or as a group ('collectivisation'), and this, too, can make a lot of difference to the way events are portrayed.

Linguistically, 'collectivisation' is typically expressed by plurality or through mass nouns, and nouns denoting a group of people (for example, 'clan', 'militia'). Visually it is expressed through group or crowd shots, and the members of such a group or crowd can be 'homogenised' to different degrees, for instance by wearing the same clothes, striking the same poses, or performing the same actions (cf. Figure 5.1).

'Individualisation' is linguistically expressed by singularity, and visually by shots that show only one person. Visual individualisation is a matter of degree. It can be diminished by distance, because distance makes individual traits less easy to observe, or by not representing or obscuring individual traits and focusing on the generic features that make people into 'types' rather than individuals, as for instance in the generic representations of 'terrorists' in computer games (cf. Figure 5.2).

Figure 5.1   A group of Special Force soldiers from the introduction to the *Black Hawk Down* game (*Black Hawk Down* © Revolution Studios Distribution Company LLC and Jerry Bruckheimer Inc. All rights reserved. Courtesy of Columbia Pictures)

US soldiers are initially represented as a collective, both in the movie and in the game, and both linguistically (through terms like 'a force of 20,000 marines', 'task force rangers', etc.) and visually (through group shots like Figure 5.1). In the movie, they are then also individualised, and named, but not as Chuck Norris-style individual heroes. The aim of the individualisation is to humanise them, to represent them as people with families, personal characteristics, individual talents and skills, and so on. Once the action starts, however, they are always collectivised, shown as a team. In other words, they have to be at once individuals, so we can empathise with them, and members of a team, because, as we shall see, team spirit is one of the essential aspects of the Special Operations discourse of war.

In the game, the introduction is followed by a change from third person to addressing the player directly (for example, 'Protect the convoy and escort it to its destination') and first-person camera work. But here, too, teamwork is empha-

Figure 5.2 A generic terrorist from the *Black Hawk Down* game

sised. Even in 'single play', there is constant dialogue with an invisible voice that commands, issues warnings, or gives admonitions, compliments, and so on.

The enemy is also collectivised, but for a different reason – because they do not matter as individuals. They are just a motley collection of rebels. Aidid, on the other hand, is always individualised, both in the movie and in the game, and both linguistically and visually, through demonising close-ups (cf. Figure 5.3). However, in the game he appears only in the introduction, and after that the enemy becomes an anonymous, de-personalised collective. Given that the enemy has a tyrannical leader, it might be expected that the Americans have the opposite – an idealised heroic leader – but this is not the case. War is represented as a job of work for a professional team. In the film, the role of high military command is played down, and in the game it is absent altogether.

Civilians are initially statistics, faces in the crowd. In the film there are just a very few fleeting moments in which they can be seen individually, but in the main they remain distant and do not acquire specific, individual characteristics, just as is the case in the 'professional Western', where, in contrast to the 'classic Western',

This food is the property of Mohamed Farrah Aidid!

Figure 5.3   Demonised image of Aidid from the *Black Hawk Down* movie

the 'society' protected by the heroes is increasingly backgrounded, to the point where it becomes little more than a backdrop (Wright, 1975). The same applies to the group the elite soldiers are supposedly protecting, the UN Peacekeepers, who are represented as weak and unable to defend themselves. What is foregrounded is the elite soldiers' fight against 'rebels', and their superior skill, superior coordination, and, above all, spirit of teamwork and concern for each other. As one of the soldiers says in the film: 'They won't understand why we did it. They won't understand it is about the man next to you. That's all it is.'

Names and titles

Who is named, and who remains anonymous? This, too, can be revealing. In *Black Hawk Down*, the pattern is simple. US soldiers and Aidid are named, both in the movie and in the documentary introduction to the game. Somalis other than Aidid remain anonymous members of the crowd.

Categorisation

Chapter 3 discussed the role of 'categorisation' in identity discourses. Here, too, we could ask: which participants in this discourse are categorised, and how? The two types of linguistic categorisation that are most important here are classification (representing people by reference to what they, supposedly, 'are') and functionalisation (representing people by reference to what they *do*). Visual categorisation, as described in Chapter 3, is either 'cultural' or 'biological' (the two may also be combined). Cultural categorisation is expressed through standard attributes of dress, hairstyle, body adornment, etc. Biological categorisation is expressed through stereotyped physical characteristics.

In both the film and the game, US soldiers are frequently functionalised, linguistically through terms such as 'elite soldiers', 'operators', etc., and visually through the attributes of their role as soldiers. In the game they are, in addition, 'biologically' characterised, through their 'Action Man'-style square jaws and solid build. In the documentary introductions, Aidid is also functionalised, as a 'militia leader' and 'warlord'. The demonic militia leader who, in the film, shoots at civilians during a Red Cross food relief operation (it is not clear whether he is meant to be Aidid or one of his henchmen), is also 'biologically' categorised, as a burly black man who fits traditional racist stereotypes (cf. Nederveen Pieterse, 1992).

The militia men are linguistically functionalised, but visually categorised, not so much by specific attributes as by the lack of the attributes that characterise a regular army. They differ from the civilians, who wear traditional dress (and who include older people, women and children) by wearing Western clothes, so that they are not 'authentic' locals. And they differ from US soldiers by being badly dressed, badly armed, and without order and discipline – a motley collection of individuals. Both differences play an important role in the contemporary justification of war. As Colin Powell has said, in relation to the Iraq war, 'We have not been attacked by an army, but by rebel groups that do not represent the people of Iraq' (*Le Monde*, 2003). The civilians, therefore, *do* represent the people on whose behalf the war is fought, however much they remain in the background, both in the film and the game. They are represented as 'authentic' Somalis who, in happier times, would dutifully add *couleur locale* for visiting tourists.

The special operations discourse

The discourse schema that organises how the movie and the game conceptualise war differs from that discussed in Chapter 4. It is a 'quest' type of schema, a schema in which the key participants pursue a set goal, face various setbacks on the way to achieving it, and are helped by the tools of technology. It is quite similar to the schema of the 'professional Western' as described by Wright (1975), which features a band of hardened men 'doing a job' to protect a weak 'society', relying on superior 'professional' skills, and motivated more by their loyalty towards each other than by concern for those they are protecting. It is striking that it was Reagan, with his background as an actor in Hollywood westerns, who played a key role in moving this fictional scenario into the arena of real warfare, as discussed in more detail below. Figure 5.4 shows the basic schema for the film.

Figure 5.5 shows the basic schema for the game, which is almost identical, bar one significant difference.

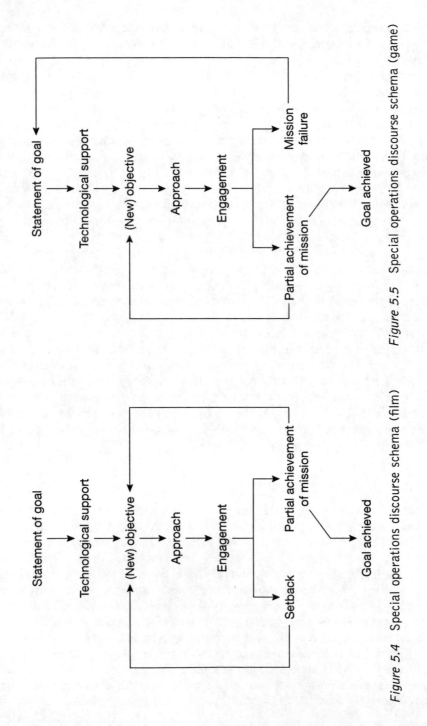

Figure 5.4 Special operations discourse schema (film)

Figure 5.5 Special operations discourse schema (game)

The elements of this schema can be described as follows:

Statement of goal

A 'special operation' always has a specific, circumscribed goal, such as rescuing hostages, capturing (or killing) a specific individual, destroying a specific building, and so on. Typically this takes the form of a 'mission briefing'. In the film this is realised by a scene in which General Garrison explains the mission to the soldiers, complete with map and photos of 'the men we're after'. A detailed scenario for the operation is provided: '15.45 Force Delta will infiltrate the target building. Rope in at 15.46. Extraction . . .', and the soldiers are reminded of the 'rules of engagement': 'Make no mistake. You are in a completely hostile neighbourhood. Remember the rules of engagement. No one fires unless fired upon . . . .'

In the game the mission briefing is a specific screen:

Mission 1

Marka Breakdown
Date: February 16, 1993, 1530 hours
Location: Marka Village, Jubba Valley

Situation:
A UN Convoy carrying food and supplies has broken down in the valley just north of Marka. It is suspected the militia might try to raise the convoy and take the shipment for themselves. Board the waiting Humvee and proceed to their location. Protect the convoy and escort it to its destination.

Technological support

'Technological support' refers to the technological means for the operation, and is an indispensable element of the discourse. In the film it is realised by a scene in which the soldiers test and pack their equipment, in the game by an illustrated menu allowing players to select a 'primary weapon', a 'secondary weapon' and an 'accessory' (for example, a hand grenade).

Objectives

The operation itself is divided into stages with specific objectives – the bracketed sections in the schemas (Objective – Approach – Engagement – Outcome) indicate such a stage and can be repeated any number of times. All stages contribute towards the achievement of the overall goal of the operation. In the film a new stage may be triggered by an enemy action such as the downing of a helicopter, which may require a revision of the action plan, and a new objective, a new directive from HQ

('I want ground force to move and secure a new perimeter round that crash site'). The film story, therefore, exhibits a kind of narrative causality, while the game is more episodic and procedural – all the enemy can do is kill you, in which case you will have to start from scratch (although some games attempt to build in other obstacles and allow the enemy a modicum of strategic planning).

Approach

The approach is that of the heroes towards the location where engagement (for example, exchange of fire) will take place.

Engagement

This is the exchange of fire, the taking of a room, a rescue, or some other key stage of the operation.

Setback/partial achievement of mission/achievement of goal

The engagement may result in the achievement of a particular stage of the operation, or of the operation as a whole. In the former case, a new objective will be formulated, in the latter the operation as a whole has succeeded, or not succeeded, as the case may be. In the film, this leads to a new objective, as shown above, a counter-move to regain the upper hand. In the game it signals the end of a game, and the player will have to start from scratch.

The key element of this discourse is its stress on the qualities of the elite forces: high combat skills, superior technology and teamwork, the absolute priority of looking after wounded members of the team, and a stress on the speed, the meticulous timing, of the operation and the quick and efficient 'insertion' and 'extraction' of the force. The enemy, meanwhile, is represented differently, as being under the sway of a despotic warlord, tyrant or super-terrorist, and as ill-disciplined and ill-equipped by comparison to the US soldiers.

The origins of this discourse lie in the history of counterinsurgency generally, and in Reagan's doctrine of the quick, effective operation and creation of 'Delta Force' specifically. Special Forces, or what we now think of as elite soldiers, are nothing new. They came into their own during the Second World War, for guerrilla warfare behind enemy lines. Much was made of the heroics of the SAS, even though their overall contribution to the war was relatively minor. SAS soldiers were portrayed as individual heroes, risking all on next to impossible missions (John Newsinger, 1997). After the Second World War, when the League of Nations was replaced by the UN, it became less easy for countries to use open military action in other countries. But this did not end war. Throughout the 1950s and 1960s the USA carried out secret operations, especially in Latin America, in order to bring about regime change, using the experience gained in the Second World War counterinsurgency and guerrilla warfare. The Green Berets and the Seals were created for precisely this purpose. Mostly only small numbers of US personnel were involved, to train and arm much larger groups of indigenous people. Throughout the 1960s this counterinsurgency warfare, remaining largely hidden from the American people, and, some argue, to a degree from the President himself, became a kind of science, elaborated in manuals which can now be accessed, for instance, in the Kennedy Presidential Library. A document titled 'US Department of the Army, Operations Against Irregular Forces' FM 31–15 (May 1961: 6–7), for instance, lists the following activities as appropriate strategies: (a) meeting engagements, (b) attacks, (c) defence, (d) ambushes, (e) raids, (f) pursuit actions, (g) interception actions, and . . . (h) terror operations. The same manual lists procedures such as:

> terror by assassination, bombing, armed robbery, torture, mutilation and kidnapping; provocation of incidents, reprisals, and holding of hostages; and denial activities, such as arson, flooding, demolition, use of chemical or biological agents . . . sabotage . . . assassination, extortion, black mail, theft, counterfeiting, and identifying individuals for terroristic attack.

In a manual from 1969, called 'Civil Affairs Operations' FM 41–10 (Cited Statecraft), we read:

> The murder of a village chief or a tax collector can serve the insurgent cause in several ways. First, it demonstrates its power to kill selected individuals of its choice, which may help to persuade people that safety lies with adherence to the insurgent cause. Second, each such act weakens the government . . . Third, it causes fear in other functionaries . . . Mass terror is used to demonstrate the weakness of the government, its inability to protect its people.

Already in the 1960s the American people were familiar with the idea of miscellaneous evildoers around the world being portrayed as their enemies. Kennedy had spoken of free world security 'being slowly nibbled away at the periphery' by world terrorists and subversion (Barber and Neale Ronning, 1963: 31), and said that 'we are opposed around the world by a monolithic and ruthless conspiracy that relies primarily on covert means for expanding its sphere of influence' (McConnell, 2001). In due course, this discourse would become second nature to American political thinking, for instance in the justification of 'Operation Restore Hope', or in the Bush administration's post-9/11 document 'National Strategy for Combating Terrorism', which lays out a vision for a new world order based on the need to keep an eye on the 'enemies of freedom'.

In the 1970s President Carter had wanted to make human rights central to US foreign policy. His 1974 Human Rights Amendment to the Foreign Assistance Act 1961 (Section 502B) stated that no assistance was to be provided to countries whose government grossly violated human rights. But later events allowed Carter's policies to be portrayed as weakness. His failure to resolve the Iranian hostage crisis of 1980 allowed Ronald Reagan to proclaim the need for America to be strong again in the face of the world threat, and to pump money into the defence budget, much of it going to Special Forces (apart, of course, from the massive amount spent on nuclear weapons). What Reagan had in mind was not an all-out war, such as in Vietnam, but 'low-intensity wars', such as those in Afghanistan, Angola, Chad and Nicaragua, in which Special Forces would play a major role. On 3 April 1984 he signed the National Security Decision Directive 138 approving pre-emptive attacks on terrorists – a term by now indiscriminately used to refer to political protesters, drug traffickers and home-grown psychopaths alike.

Yet counterinsurgency did not acquire a fully overt and legitimate public face until after a succession of events in the 1980s – the bombing of US embassies in Lebanon and Kuwait, leading to the deaths of hundreds of Americans, and, later, the two Trade Tower bombings (McClintock, 2002). The response? A renewed emphasis on the rhetoric of a 'strong America' and new elite units such as Delta Force to carry out raids on terrorist groups. In his acceptance speech as Republican leader, Reagan declared, 'I would regard my election as proof that we have renewed our resolve to preserve world peace and freedom. This nation will once again be strong enough to do that' (www.rightwingnews.com/speeches/destiny.php).

We are now used to the idea that this is a reasonable account of events and people in the world. The USA not only sells arms and knows how to carry out this kind of warfare all around the planet, it also sells the discourses that lay out the rules of the game and provide its justification. But real wars do not necessarily happen in the way in which they are represented here. The role of aerial bombardment is excluded or backgrounded, for instance, and so are the civilian casualties involved. As we have seen, the role of the Special Forces is not necessarily as vital as we are made to believe, and the idea of the 'quick fix' does not always work in the way it is presented here. As for the evil motives of the 'rebels', Maren (1994) has noted that when he returned to Somalia, visiting some of the areas where the most aggressive fighting had taken place, he found that former fighters from different clans were now farming and trading with each other. When there is no 'foreign assistance' of the kind the USA gave to Barre, he concluded, peace returns.

Symbolic anchorage in a Hezbollah game

We have seen that American computer war games tend to open with documentary or quasi-documentary footage that relates them to the real events on which they are based. According to *Delta Force* creator Mark Long, this creates a 'narrative setting' and 'adds to the experience'. Here is another example of such an introduction, this time to a game titled *Delta Force*:

Typewritten title unfolds as it is written: NOVALOGIC presents	Distant clashing noises, soft typewriting sound
Terrain map of Africa. ('Satellite') zoom on to Sudan area	Music begins – military snare rolls combined with mournful horns
Two interlocking lines with longitude and latitude degrees pinpoint Sudan	'Gentlemen, what's the status?'
Typewritten text: 0500 Hours. Jabal Abyad Plateau Sudan. Objective: destroy terrorist weapon shipment	'Sir, the 3103 carrying weapons has just touched down in the Sudan to refill. We have a team standing by'. 'Game Six to . . .
LS (very high angle) Airfield with watchtower, guards and refuelling plane. Camera moves in to MS aeroplane	'. . . Gas Can, what is your position?' 'By the target, say the word.' 'You have two minutes until the perimeter patrol returns.'
CS Soldier looking to right of frame. He puts on night-vision helmet and waves forward	'Move out. You heard the man . . .'
CS Overshoulder Soldier. Three Soldiers run past him. Camera pans with them	'. . . let's go.'
MS (low angle) Three Soldiers, eyes lit by night vision, moving towards and over camera, silhouetted by bright helicopter light	Gentle noise of helicopter. Music continues in background – tension rolls and mournful horns
MS Soldier cutting Guard's throat. Two more soldiers enter frame, running	'Gurgle'. 'Game Six, Snake Bite, perimeter clear.'
CS Sniper lying in bushes, aiming	'Long Bow, we got a guard by the bay door.'
MS Guard (through sniper sight)	'Roger that, I'm on him.'
VCS Finger pulling trigger	Music
MS Guard falling dead (through sniper sight)	Soft, sharp shooting sound, impact and gasp. 'Clear.'
LS Bay of plane. A Soldier enters, two more cover him	'Cover me.' 'Hurry up there we got company.'

VCS Hand pressing button on timer of explosives	'Just a few seconds . . . there.' Music building to triumphant crescendo – bass drum, more brass
LS (low angle) Soldiers run past camera from exploding plane	Indistinct shouting and explosion. Music stops
The light from the explosion expands to form Delta Force motif	'Game Six, Gas Can, target destroyed, Whooyeah!' 'Good work, Black Widow is on the way.'

Although the action of this game is set in Sudan, visually the scene does not depict a specific location. It could be anywhere. Three things are emphasised: the skill of the soldiers and the superiority of their weapons; the individuality and camaraderie of the soldiers; and a sense of adventure. The voice-over indexes the tight, machine-like level of organisation and efficiency, as does the cool professionalism of the sniper, taking out a sentry in a classic silent kill. Precision, accuracy and deliberateness pervade the action, and the sequence showcases the technology, for instance the night-vision and silent weaponry. At the same time the soldiers are humanised. The dialogue emphasises their tight teamwork and their faces are shown in individualising close-ups, while the enemy is shown in long shot, or facing away from camera. Finally, there is a sense of adventure: at the end of the sequence one of the soldiers shouts 'Whooyeah' as the target explodes. All this is reminiscent of classic Hollywood narrative. As Bordwell (1985: 157) has said, 'the reliance upon character-centred causality and the definition of the action as the attempt to achieve a goal are both salient features of the canonic format'. In other words, this sequence uses well-worn and well-known features of Hollywood narrative to make viewers identify with the elite soldiers.

Compare this now to the introduction of *Special Force*, the Hezbollah game:

A bright shining star of light bursts in from the left corner as the planet Earth spins away to rest in the centre of the frame, mid-distance, placed within the brilliant shining Hezbollah logo. Title below the logo, in brilliant gold: 'Hezbollah is everywhere.' Underneath that, in brilliant blue: 'Central Internet Department of Development and Programming'.	Solemn, hymn-like music, powerful, proud and optimistic, with rapid military snare drum rolls
As Earth comes to rest in its central position, the star on its left moves in slightly, as in many television news opening sequences; the viewer is positioned 'in orbit', watching events from space.	
The remainder of the sequence is one continuous shot.	Music stops
Camera moves down in between two rows of columns painted with military camouflage; brilliant light reflects off the lens.	Music: distant horns and military snare roll (sense of something about to happen)
As the camera moves down in between two rows of columns, a Mirkava tank appears from left, in medium shot. On its side is a large, bright blue Star of David.	Loud sound of rolling tank enters (tracks and engine), increasing in intensity in a way that is disproportionate to the size of the tank
The tank stops in the middle of the row of columns. A gun comes into view, in close shot, almost pointing towards camera, after which the camera moves back to medium shot.	Sound of rocket
Glorious bright light comes from the right corner of the image, hitting the tank. We see debris from the tank even though the tank remains intact.	Sound of explosion; music returns to proud hymn with military snare rolls

The camera rotates upwards to an aerial medium shot of the tank and the columns, then out to a long shot, which reveals that the column behind the tank is the Hezbollah logo, and, as it moves out further, that the columns form the words 'Islamic Resistance' and 'Special Force'. The tank remains between the columns but now appears tiny; a searchlight comes to rest on the words 'Special Force'.	
The screen goes blank and the game logo appears, rotating to reveal the title in English – the words 'Special Force' appear below a gun with sights and the letter 'O' in 'Force' is a crosshairs.	
The screen goes blank.	Music stops
Home page address of Genesis3D, the graphics engine producers, appears.	Music returns to distant horns and military snare rolls
Menu appears.	

In this sequence, the Mirkava tank is a symbol of Israel's technological superiority over the Palestinians. Before it is blown up, the music and the diffused, magical light that reflects off the columns indicate that something very special is about to happen. Then, just as the tank seems about to strike, it is taken out by a rocket-propelled grenade (although we only see another 'heavenly' flash). Finally, as it rotates upwards to an aerial view, the camera reveals that the Special Force is everywhere, surrounding the tank on all sides. While the mission is loading, a banner announces: 'We are coming.' It is a quotation from the Koran, where the full text is 'We are coming to Jerusalem', in the context of worship. But here the phrase is used to mean that the resistance is coming for the Zionists.

Like *Delta Force*, *Special Force* emphasises covert operations. But it does not humanise and individualise the soldiers, or stress superior skill and technology. Unlike American ideology, Hezbollah ideology foregrounds sacrifice, as part of the Islamic struggle. Strength comes, not from technology, but from God, as symbolised by heavenly light. The more powerful the adversary in terms of technology, the stronger would be the will of the resistance (cf. Figure 5.6).

Overall, this sequence appears much less realistic. It is dominated by magic, flickering lights and an 'unreal', symbolic landscape (although elsewhere in the game we find more attention to realistic detail). The intention is not to be 'realistic', but to represent the *reality* of the resistance 'being all around', 'everywhere', an almost invisible challenge to the powerful, arrogant enemy. By contrast, the introduction to the American game appears more realistic. Even though the actions it shows do not portray an actual historical event, its surface realism is greater. The realism of the Arab movie thus adheres to the reality criterion of socialist realism illustrated by this quote from Bertolt Brecht:

> Less than at any time does a simple reproduction of reality tell us anything about reality. A photograph of the Krupp works or GEC yields almost nothing about these institutions. Therefore something has actually to be constructed, something artificial, something set up.
>
> (quoted in Benjamin, 1972: 24)

Figure 5.6 Game menu in the Hezbollah game

The realism of the American game, on the other hand, is the surface realism that confronts us daily in gritty realistic news bulletins from war zones, showing journalists bravely reporting amidst explosions and gunfire. Yet in the end, how much do such bulletins tell us about the actual nature and causes of the events (Carruthers, 2000)?

Different ways of representing the participants and the environment, identical discourses

In *Delta Force*, the American game, the main participants are represented in much the same way as in *Black Hawk Down*. US forces are represented both as a collective and as individuals. Linguistically they are referred to as 'Special Forces', 'CIA', 'Delta Team', or 'Marine Force Recon Squad'. Visual collectivisation is realised by uniforms, equipment and actions, which are similar for all soldiers. Yet the US soldiers are also humanised and individualised, linguistically through their nicknames (for example, 'Gas Can'), and visually through individual characteristics such as beards, personalised items of clothing (for example, bandanas) and personal choice of weapons. Bordwell (1995) has written of the way Hollywood movies use simple motifs to stand for complex character traits. Audiences are, therefore, schooled in recognising these forms of individual characterisation.

The enemy, on the other hand, is always collectivised, and linguistically referred to as 'various terrorist groups' and 'a militant terrorist group', and through the names of the groups (for example, 'The Hand of Justice'), which suggests fanaticism. Visually, all enemies look identical, facially and in their (non-military) clothing. A game designer we interviewed explained that this was to save time and money. Soldiers were 'sprites', he said, units which can be used repeatedly. But if the reason for this lack of differentiation is economical rather than political, we asked, why is so much time and money expended on the individual and highly realistic detail of the different weapons? He was unable to answer this question. Clearly these are ideological choices. For *Delta Force* designers it is more important to spend time and money on the representation of technological superiority than on the humanity and individuality of the enemy. And from a propagandistic point of view it is important to make terrorists appear as a nondescript and all-pervasive threat.

The Special Forces of the Arab game, on the other hand, are not individualised but always collectivised, except at the end of the game which features the names and photographs of actual resistance martyrs. Linguistically this is realised by terms such as 'Resistance', 'knights' and 'heroes' (Hezbollah itself is not mentioned). Visually it is realised by group shots in which all soldiers have beards and wear the same clothes. Close shots are not used, except in the logo, which depicts a single soldier in determined pose. In the video at the end, individual fighters are shown during manoeuvres, displaying a sense of solidarity, simplicity and frugality, but still all looking the same. This is unlike the classic, individual Hollywood hero, and much more like the collective heroes of Soviet movies of the 1920s such as Eisenstein's

Potemkin (1925), in which the hero is a collective struggling against adversaries, and triumph a matter, not of achieving individual glory, but of effecting social and political change.

The enemy of the Arab game is also collectivised. Linguistically this is realised through terms such as 'Israeli', 'Zionist enemy' and 'defeated army', and through 'instrumentalisations' (van Leeuwen, 1996: 59) which metonymically refer to the enemy in terms of their technology – 'tanks', 'helicopters', 'machine guns'. Visually all enemies look and move the same (cf. Figure 5.7), and are only seen in close shot when they are dead.

The soldiers in *Delta Force*, the American game, are predominantly functionalised, represented in terms of what they do, linguistically through terms like 'soldier' and 'sniper', and visually by means of the technological attributes (night vision, satellite feeds, intercoms, high-tech weapons) which emphasise their skill and deadly efficiency. Visually, however, they are also classified – 'biologically' through their chiselled jaws and muscular bodies, and 'culturally' through a mixture of high-tech uniforms and individual 'rebel' touches such as bandanas.

Figure 5.7 Enemy in the Hezbollah game

The *Delta Force* enemies, too, are *linguistically* functionalised, primarily by means of the key term 'terrorist', and *visually* classified – 'biologically' through their stereotyped Middle-Eastern features, and 'culturally' through their beards and black jumpers, and through the way they raise their weapons in undisciplined poses, which then contrasts with the US soldiers' efficiency and economy of movement.

Unlike the American game, the Arab game does not use functionalisation. Its Special Force soldiers are always classified as 'Islamic', both linguistically and visually (through Islamic attributes such as the Koran). Weaponry plays less of a role in the depiction. Special Force soldiers are, for instance, shown with very rudimentary weapons such as the Kalashnikov automatic rifle, whereas in reality many Hezbollah fighters used US M-16s. This suggests that these weapons have a symbolic function, demonstrating that Hezbollah soldiers fight with their will, rather than with technology.

The enemies of the Arab game are linguistically categorised as 'defeated enemies', and visually through exaggeratedly large blue Stars of David on their breast pockets. They are depicted as dehumanised robots, their faces hidden by masks. When high-tech weapons and night-vision helmets are shown, they connote this 'inhuman' quality, rather than their skills as elite soldiers, as in the American game. Clearly, the two games represent the principal parties in the conflict very differently, in ways that are profoundly influenced by their different interests and ideologies.

The same applies to the way the environment is represented. Linguistically, the American game denotes locations by means of military code words – a village, for instance, is called 'Objective Cell'. This turns a specific, real place, where real people carry out their daily lives, into a non-specific territory for military operations. Little does it matter whether the enemy is in South Lebanon or Sudan. All terrorists are alike and all terrorist locations are alike: havens for terrorists. The reality of the environment is thrown out of focus, just as in many Hollywood movies, where long lenses focus on the actors and the drama of their interactions, and de-emphasise the setting in which the action takes place. This hides the detail of the location just as the names of American military operations hide the detail of what these names really stand for, and of the histories behind them: 'Operation Desert Storm' was in fact a large-scale bombing and obliteration of an vastly inferior enemy, 'Operation Restore Hope' in Somalia, a US Special Forces promotion which hid two decades of the USA feeding arms into the country in return for military bases on the Horn of Africa.

Visually, *Delta Force* locations all look alike, whether they are set in Sudan or South America. The precise details of towns and roads are not represented. The landscape is hilly and little else. At best, small details, such as flat-roofed houses, index a generic African or Mediterranean/Arab environment.

The Arab game treats locations very differently. Here the action takes place in named places that actually exist, and these places are represented in specific detail, so that you would recognise them if you knew them. Instead of zooming into 'Sudan', the map of South Lebanon zooms into a detailed map of the roads in the area surrounding a particular village, Maidoun village. Visually the map zooms from a map of Lebanon to a map of the roads in the surrounding area of this village. Mission details, written in red and yellow on a black background, are correlated to a map with gridlines, suggesting that, while the soldiers may be shown as poorly armed, there is good intelligence and organisation behind the operation. The terrain is accurately modelled from photographs, with much detail in the stone brick walls of the buildings and the rocky hillsides (cf. Figure 5.8). Unlike the American game, this game looks as if it is shot with a wide-angle lens that keeps the background in focus and anchors people and events in concrete and specific settings. It is real terrain that is contested here, not a generalised space for American heroism and camaraderie.

Both games, then, represent some aspects in specific and authentic detail and others generically, but they do so differently. In the Arab game it is the *environment* of the action, in the American game it is the *technology* that is depicted in accurate detail. Such differences reveal what is considered relevant and important in each case. American game designers work from the assumption that the setting is not important to players, although they do feel that basing games on actual missions

Figure 5.8   Representing the setting in the Hezbollah game

provides a compelling narrative for the action. Essentially, however, all the locations in which American Special Forces operate are treated as near-identical. In the Arab game, on the other hand, authenticity does not serve to spice up the drama, and location is crucial, because the fight is about location, about territory, as has been attested by many commentators on Arab movies (Khatib, 2004; Said, 1978).

Clearly, there are significant differences between the ways the American and the Arab game represent the participants, the settings and the tools of the discourse. But when we turn to the action structure, we find that the Arab game uses exactly the same discourse schema as the American ones. Its 'mission statement', for instance, closely follows the format of games like *Delta Force* and *Black Hawk Down*:

> Maidoun village is considered one of the frontline positions confronting the Zionist enemy, and is one of the strategic points that monitor and paralyze any advancing operation by the Zionist enemy. With this data the Zionist enemy conducted an operation towards the village, with a selection of army, tanks and helicopters in order to terminate the positions of Islamic resistance. You must oppose, confront and destroy the machines of the Zionist enemy and remind them that entering Lebanese villages is not a stroll.

Although the technology is simpler in the Arab game, because victory must be seen to come from the will to fight, rather than from the power of technology, choosing your weapons remains a key part of the script, and the 'Technology Support' stage of the game is again near-identical to that of *Black Hawk Down*, as is the rest of the structure of the game. In the way they represent participants, weapons and settings, the two games realise distinctly different, 'local' interests and distinctly different political and ideological positions. But from the point of view of their *format* the games realise the same discourse of war, a discourse that is, as we have seen, American in its origin, and now increasingly global.

This format, we have argued, is not a neutral container for diverse and local content. It embodies an ideology which, because of its immense economic and technological power, is becoming increasingly dominant across the globe. The Arab designers of *Special Forces* had played many US Special Forces games before designing their own game, and felt that this format, with its First-person Shooter technology and its small units of elite soldiers moving stealthily through an area to accomplish a basic mission, could be successfully adapted for their quite different purposes. But the designer of another Arab game, *Underash*, was concerned about reproducing the American format and told us he had tried to place more emphasis on the consequences of settlement by the Israelis rather than only on straightforward shooting.

Can we imagine a computer game which resolves conflict step by step, through subtle diplomacy? Or are we moving towards a future in which every interest will have its own elite forces wipe out its own evil-looking enemies and in which the shooting gallery will become the dominant, the only and inescapable model of conflict resolution?

Realism and the players

We have already discussed how *Delta Force* producer Mark Long stresses the importance of 'authentic' detail and the realism of the 'look and feel', and shies away from making connections between computer war games and real wars. His criterion for realism is a 'naturalistic' one (Kress and van Leeuwen, 1996: 168). What matters is accuracy, 'getting the detail right', 'bringing more realism' and increasing the sophistication of the action. Here he is talking about *Task Force Dagger*:

> The story covers the globe. You'll be fighting guerrillas, terrorists, army irregulars and even foreign rogue special forces in some situations. The enemies are created from real world cyber-scanned people to bring more realism to the game. And each type of enemy will speak its native language in the game. In spite of the effort we're making to get the look and feel of *Task Force Dagger* right, you have to remember this is just a game – any similarity ends there. We'll leave the politics to the Department of Defence.

The same criteria can of course also be used to criticise games as unrealistic, as in this quote from Rod, a 22-year-old shop worker from Wales – note the 'expert' terminology:

> I think all of the guns used in AAO are unrealistic. You just won't stand up after a sawburst shooting at you and hitting you 3 or 4 shots. No bloody way! And the same goes for all the guns. I always use the saw and sometimes it takes like 10 shots from a 50–70 shot burst to kill someone who is near you. Come on!

Traditionally, the naturalistic 'reality criterion' is perceptual, and rooted in technologies of audiovisual *reproduction*. The question behind it is: 'How much does what we see here on a screen, and hear here from a speaker, correspond to what we would have seen and heard if we had been there, in reality?' (cf. Kress and van Leeuwen, 1996: 168–71). But for many computer game players naturalism is *experiential* rather than perceptual, based on the question: 'How much do my *actions*, as a player, resemble the actions of a real Special Operations soldier?' And this experiential criterion focuses almost entirely on the self, on *my* actions as a player/soldier and on *my* feelings of accomplishment and pleasure. The lack of specificity ('some place', 'a situation', 'the enemy') and the stress on the superiority of the elite player/soldier and the weakness of the enemy in the following quote from our interview with Paul, a 30-year-old from London, correspond strikingly to our analyses in the preceding sections:

> Yes, *Delta Force* is realistic. You get dumped in some place where you have to deal with a situation. The enemy are less trained and you have to use your stealth to take them out. You feel proud when you do take your time and they don't even know you were there.

Wang, a 23-year-old student from China, expresses a very similar view: 'These games are very realistic. They are very good at showing what being a special soldier is like. They show you how you have to be brave and intelligent to defeat your enemy.'

The critique of games is not always based on the 'naturalistic' criterion. It can also be based on contrasting the 'Special Operations' discourse to other discourses, which are then held to be more real, such as the 'war is hell' discourse that informs many American war movies, including *Black Hawk Down*. Tom, a 25-year-old bank administrator, starts by criticising computer war games as devoid of 'horrific death and injury, mud and rubble', but then reverts to 'experiential naturalism' ('You get the feeling that you are there'):

> Is it realistic? War is shit, war is about men dying. It is about horrific death and injury, mud and rubble. So it isn't realistic, you don't get dirty and you don't die. But you get the feeling that you are there with the games that are more realistic. In *Call of Duty* they are just shooting at you all over the place, and the enemy will hide or grenade you out if you hide. That's realistic. The *Black Hawk Down* games are pretty good as well.

The 'war is hell' discourse focuses on 'what wars are like' in general. Other critiques of the 'Special Operations' version of war contrast it to discourses which focus more specifically on America's contemporary wars, as in the case of Phil, a 27-year-old from America, who sees the USA as 'shooting the fuck out of Arabs' rather than as saving the world from terrorists:

> This is American propaganda. You get to shoot the fuck out of a bunch of Arabs. But I just see it as a game. Is it realistic? Well I would say that's the way it is in the world, the Americans shoot the fuck out of a bunch of Arabs.

Similarly, though less cynically, Maz, a 32-year-old Muslim taxi driver from the UK, sees the Arab game as realistic because it corresponds to 'what really happened', rather than because of experiential naturalism: 'This game is really good. It is about what really happened. You get to see the truth.' When we asked him, 'What about the demonised enemy, all the music and colours?' he replied: 'Well, it is a game. You can't do everything in a game. But it is important as it shows that the Muslims can drive Israelis out of their villages. And the Israelis are monsters.'

Note the contradictions in these views. On the one hand Phil and Maz, like many other players we have interviewed, see the representation of war in these games as realistic, as corresponding to the facts. On the other hand, they distance themselves from the games-as-political-representations: 'it is just a game'. For other players, on the other hand, experiential and political reality coincide seamlessly, for example for Gary, a 15-year-old from a poor Welsh neighbourhood:

These games are just like it is. You have to kill the Arabs. I like killing Arabs. I would like to be able to be a soldier like this and kill Arabs. I hate them. They are real as you can use all your weapons and hide and blow them up. They are too stupid to win. They are Arabs.

Are people like Gary the kind of young men US Sgt Kevin Benderman referred to when, after ten years in the Army and two tours of duty in Iraq, he applied for a discharge as a conscientious objector because 'the young men he commanded ... treated war like bumping off targets in a video game' (*The Guardian*, 19 March 2005: 19)?

We end with the views of Sa, a 35-year-old Vietnamese musician. Talking about war movies, she rejects the 'war is hell' discourse as superficial, concerned only with naturalism, and unable to reveal the causes and consequences of war: 'The American films about my country are simply lies. They only show American soldiers suffering, or some pretty young girl. You find nothing about the imperialism that put them there in the first place.' But, when we showed her the games, she perceived the power of the experience they offer. Where many of our interviewees could not resolve, or even perceive, the contradiction between the experiential reality of computer games and the political reality of the events they represent, Sa realised that the reality of computer games ultimately lies, neither in the visual veracity of its representations, nor even in the factuality of its political events, but in the real bodily engagement they offer, in the way they hijack real action and real human pleasure in skilled hand-to-eye coordination for political ends: 'They *are* realistic. I think this is a bad thing. Young boys are playing these games. It is bad that they should be able to play at being a soldier. They don't understand what this means.'

Questions

1 Find a comic strip in which an action hero fights terrorists and use 'social actor' analysis to analyse how the hero, the terrorists and, if applicable, the 'civilians' are portrayed. Is the action based on specific historical events?
2 Contemporary toy guns have moved away from the iconography of the Western and the gangster movie. Look at modern toy guns and their packaging and identify how they draw on the 'Special Operations' discourse we have described in this chapter.
3 Study the way that Bush justified war in his 2001 'War on Terror' speech and compare it to the way war is justified in a recent American war movie or computer war game of your choice.
4 Interview two teenagers from different backgrounds who regularly play computer war games. Ask them whether they think the games simulate war realistically. Also ask them whether they would like to be soldiers, and if not, why not.

Note

1 This chapter is based on two earlier publications: Machin and van Leeuwen (2005b) and Machin and Suleiman (2006). Usama Suleiman's help in translating and researching the Hezbollah game and its background has been invaluable.

PART III

Language and image

The three chapters in this section deal with the forms and formats of global media communication. But the distinction between form and content is not watertight. The forms and formats of today's global media are not neutral. They shape and limit what they contain. Global media genres such as news, soap opera, movies and adverts, and their linguistic and visual styles, communicate values and identities, not just through their content but through their structure, and through the way they address us. And while content is often localised, media forms and formats tend to be global, addressing people in much the same way the world over, whatever their nationality or cultural background. It is, therefore, all the more important to pay close attention, not just to the content, but also to the genres of global media, and to their visual and verbal styles.

The first chapter in this section (Chapter 6) looks at genre through the example of the women's magazine *Cosmopolitan*. We show how the same genre of communication is used for the domains of work, sex, relationships and fashion, favouring particular ways of acting and particular kinds of identity, and blurring the differences between these spheres of life. The particular genre we look at allows the magazine to claim that it empowers women. But this empowerment can only be achieved through the consumption of global goods and services, and although these goods and services may be localised to some degree, their underlying global sameness always remains visible.

Chapter 7 deals with language styles. Local versions of global formats may contain localised English, but always in ways that suit the requirements of the global formats. Conversely, global media may produce versions of their product in local languages, but these languages will have to learn to adapt to the requirements of global media formats. We examine first the English-language version of a Vietnamese newspaper, and then the linguistic style of the Indian, Chinese, Spanish and Dutch versions of *Cosmopolitan*.

Chapter 8 deals with the global visual language. Due to economies of scale and lack of global regulation, large corporations now provide media outlets around the world with cheap and easily accessible photographs. Again, it is not just the content, but also, and especially, the form which matters. These images are designed to look good on the page, to harmonise with advertising and to be reusable. For this reason they rarely depict specific people, places and events, but work instead with a limited repertoire of symbolic motifs to communicate the kind of concepts and values global media may seek to illustrate.

6   Global genres[1]

Genre

Global media of the kind discussed in this book follow a strategy not unlike that of McDonalds. McDonalds may sell 'sushiburgers' in Japan and 'curryburgers' in India, but burgers remain burgers, and it is in their 'burger-ness' that the essence of their global cultural significance must be looked for. Like burgers, media formats are not value-free, not mere containers, but key technologies for the dissemination of global values and lifestyles. Two such 'burger'-like constants in the 48 international versions of *Cosmopolitan* are the modality of the photography and the generic structure of the 'hot tips' problem–solution genre. Both can readily accommodate local content, yet look the same the world over. Both appear neutral, mere carriers of content, but in fact convey a message of their own.

Our principal methodological tools for investigating these formats in this chapter are genre analysis and modality analysis. The former derives from systemic-functional discourse analysis (Martin, 1992), the latter from social semiotic visual analysis (Kress and van Leeuwen, 1996). Both methodologies form part of the 'media discourse' approach that has been elaborated both in sociolinguistics (for example, Bell, 1991; Bell and Garrett, 1998) and in critical discourse analysis (for example, Fowler, 1991; Fairclough, 1995).

The kind of genre analysis we adopt here focuses on spoken and written text as communicative action. It tries to bring out, step by step, how this action unfolds, regardless of whether it obeys explicit prescriptions or rules, follows a habitual pattern, or uses generic resources in a creative response to the exigencies of a particular communicative situation. A genre analysis of an advertisement such as the one below, taken from the Dutch *Cosmopolitan* of November 2001, brings out a habitual *format* of communicative action – the 'problem–solution' format – a format which can of course be combined with a wide range of contents. Note that there is a difference between a problem–solution format and a problem–solution discourse schema. A problem–solution discourse schema can underlie texts in many different genres. It is a construction of the *issues* at stake. A problem–solution genre constructs a particular kind of communicative interaction in which a problem is explicitly formulated, and an answer provided, in that order (see Table 6.1).

The overall aim of advertisements of this kind is to persuade people to use a product or service. Different strategies for doing so have developed in the course of the history of persuasive communication – this particular one presents the services of the Health Diet Clinic as the solution to the reader's problem, a strategy which

Text	Genre analysis
Skin problems?	**Problem 1** ⇓
Recuperating from a crash diet and unable to achieve the right weight?	**Problem 2**
With our personal dietary advice and guidance (day and night) most problems can be prevented and remedied	**Solution** ⇓
Beautiful Skin for a lifetime	**Result** ⇓
Our Skin Care System keeps your skin young and healthy and repairs ageing skin, acne, scars, striae and pigment problems	**Elaboration of** **solution** **and result** ⇓
Health Diet Clinic (address, telephone nr.)	Contact details

Table 6.1

is by no means restricted to this particular service, or even to advertisements, and can be used whenever we want to persuade people to do something. In other words, although it is represented here as the format of a particular text, the problem–solution genre is a general format that can be applied to many different problems and many different solutions – and it is also a relatively flexible format, a format that allows for variation. There may, for instance, be one or several problems, or one or several solutions, and there may also be additional elements, for instance one or more sentences praising the product or service. Still, if it is to enact the problem–solution strategy, there must be, at the very least, one problem and one solution.

The moves or 'stages' in the genre will tend towards certain linguistic realisations. For instance, the 'problem' stage will typically be expressed as a question and contain, or imply, direct address ('Do *you* suffer from skin problems?'). It also needs a reference to something that is recognised as a problem in the given context (as are skin blemishes and weight problems in women's magazines). The 'solution' will tend to be a statement (the answer to the question), which presents the solution either as the agent ('*our system* keeps your skin young') or as the means ('*with our system* the problem can be remedied ...') of the action that prevents or remedies the problem. But note that these stages can be expressed in other ways, and need not even be expressed verbally. The 'problem' might be expressed by a picture of a blemished skin, the 'solution' by a picture of the product, the 'result' by a picture of an unblemished skin, for instance, or some stages may be realised visually and others verbally. Genres are multimodal.

The approach to genre analysis discussed so far has been designed for linear texts. However, magazine texts are not necessarily linear. There is also a spatial element to their organisation, through the use of layout. Kress and van Leeuwen (1996: 181ff.) recognise three key principles, which can be combined in various ways. First, information may be organised along a horizontal axis, with one element (for example, a picture) on the left, and another (for example, text) on the right. The left element is then presented as 'Given', that is, positioned as something already known to the reader or viewer, while the information on the right is presented as 'New', as something not yet known to the reader or viewer, and hence as something to which attention must be paid, and which is, at least in principle, negotiable or contestable in the larger communicative context.

Second, if information is organised vertically, with two different elements positioned one above the other, the information on top is presented as 'Ideal', that is, as the more abstract or generalised essence of the message, and the information below as 'Real', that is, as more down to earth and practical, and/or more detailed and specific. Finally, information can be organised concentrically. In that case the 'Centre' contains the information that is presented as the core, and the 'Margins' contain information that is presented as in some sense subservient or complementary to the Centre, and deriving its identity and meaning from it. Combinations of the three principles are also possible.

Kress and van Leeuwen also describe two other aspects of the spatial organisation of information, the *salience* of the different elements, which can be realised by the size of the elements, or, for instance, by means of conspicuous colouring or tonal contrast, and the *framing* of the different elements, which signifies the degree to which they are meant to be read as separate items or as 'belonging together', and which can be realised, for instance, by frame lines, or by the use of colour which can either make distinct elements cohere (for example, through recurring colours), or contrast (for example, through contrasting colours).

As mentioned, a given genre can accommodate many different contents. The problem–solution genre, for instance, can accommodate many different kinds of problem and many different kinds of solution. It is easily transferred from one context to another. But, again, that does not mean that it is a neutral container. It embodies the suggestion that we do things, *not*, for instance, to follow parental example or cultural tradition or religious prescription, but because they are practical solutions to common human problems. For many people the choice of what to eat is strongly dependent on cultural tradition and religious prescription. The kind of diets proposed by advertisements such as the above, however, are not presented as an alternative cultural tradition or religious prescription, but as 'value-free' solutions, oriented purely to the prevention and remedying of health problems and, as such, transcending cultural difference, and legitimately 'global'. Clearly, it is here the containers rather than the content which most effectively fulfil the cultural mission of globalisation. To understand globalisation we, therefore, need to understand the cultural meanings of genres, and we need to find out what genres they supplant or now exist side by side with, how their meanings sit together with those of the already available genres, and what kind of cultural influence they exert on them.

The same applies to layout. A 'Given and New' layout, for instance, is read the way it is because of the left-to-right and top-to-bottom tradition of Western writing. But is this aspect of textual organisation localised by magazines such as *Cosmopolitan*? And if it is not, does it influence already available forms of the spatial organisation of information? Concentric layout, for instance, makes it possible to bring a range of 'marginal' elements in harmony with each other, by stressing that they all share the same relation to a common Centre, while Given–New layout polarises elements into binary oppositions. Kress and van Leeuwen (1996: 203) noted a tendency to favour concentric layout in the work of Singapore design students. How is this potential contradiction negotiated?

Modality

Our second methodological tool is modality analysis. The term 'modality' refers to semiotic resources for indicating how true or how real communication content is to be taken. In this chapter we deal primarily with the modality of images, the question of how images signify their status as factual or fictional, truth or fantasy, and so on.

For an initial example, think again of advertising images. In many single-page magazine advertisements, the top part of the page shows the 'promise' of the product – how beautiful or glamorous or successful you will become if you buy the product, or how cool or soft or luxurious it will feel or taste or smell. The bottom part then provides factual detail and/or a picture of the product itself. In such advertisements the modality value of the two parts of the advertisement tend to differ. The top (Ideal) usually shows what you *might* be or *could* be (relatively low modality), the bottom (Real) what *is*, what you can *actually* buy right now in the shop if you want to (high modality). This is then expressed through subtle differences in the way certain means of visual expression are used. The top part may feature a photo in a sepia-tinted black and white, the bottom part a photo of the product in full colour. The picture showing the 'promise of the product' may have soft focus, the photo in the bottom part may show the product in sharp detail. This illustrates how visual modality works. Increases or decreases in the degree to which certain means of visual expression are used (colour, sharpness, etc.) express increases or decreases in 'as how real' the image is meant to be taken.

According to Kress and van Leeuwen (1996), the following means of visual expression are involved in judgements of visual modality:

- Degrees of the *articulation of detail* form a scale which runs from the simplest line drawing to the sharpest and most finely grained representation.
- Degrees of the *articulation of the background* range from zero articulation, as when something is shown against a white or black background, via lightly sketched in- or out-of-focus backgrounds, to maximally sharp and detailed backgrounds.

- Degrees of *colour saturation* range from the absence of saturation (black and white) to the use of maximally saturated colours.
- Degrees of *colour modulation* range from the use of flat, unmodulated colour to the representation of all the fine nuances and colour modulations of a given colour (for example, skin colour or the colour of grass).
- Degrees of *colour differentiation* range from monochrome to the use of a full palette of diverse colours.
- Degrees of *depth articulation* range from the absence of any representation of depth to maximally deep perspective, with various other possibilities in between (for example, simple overlapping without perspectival foreshortening).
- Degrees of the *articulation of light and shadow* range from zero to the articulation of the maximum number of degrees of 'depth' of shade, with options such as simple hatching in between.
- Degrees of the *articulation of tone* range from just two shades of tonal gradation, black and white (or a light and dark version of another colour) to maximal tonal gradation.

All these means of visual expression are graded. They allow the relevant dimension of articulation to be increased or reduced. And what is more, the different parameters may be amplified or reduced to different degrees, resulting in many possible modality configurations. These configurations cue viewers' judgements of modality, of 'as how real' images (or parts of images) are to be taken. Newspaper cartoons, for instance, tend to have reduced articulation of detail, background, depth, and light and shade, and no articulation of colour and tonal gradation. By comparison, the articulation of these same parameters in news photographs is much amplified. This corresponds to their modality value: cartoons are taken as visual 'opinions' and hence as less factual than news photographs, which are held to provide reliable, documentary information.

It is not the case, however, that modality always decreases as articulation is reduced. If this were so, simple line diagrams would always have low modality and be judged as 'not real'. But despite the fact that their articulation is usually greatly reduced, scientific line diagrams are clearly to be read as images with high truth value, and not as fictions or fantasies. This means that there is no fixed correspondence between modality judgements and points on the scales of articulation described above. Instead the modality value of a given configuration depends on the kind of visual truth which is preferred in the given context.

In many contexts *naturalistic* truth remains dominant. Its modality criterion is more or less as follows: the more an image of something resembles the way we would see it in reality, from a specific viewpoint, and under specific conditions of illumination, the higher its modality. This, at least, is the theory, for in reality naturalistic modality judgements depend very much on the way in which the currently dominant naturalistic imaging resources represent the visual world. When black and white was the norm, colour was regarded as 'more than real'. In films it was used for fantasy sequences (for example, *The Wizard of Oz*) or for relatively unrealistic genres such as musicals and Westerns, and serious contemporary realist drama was done in black and white. Today colour is the norm and black and white tends to be lower in modality, used for representing the past, dreams, fantasies.

In *abstract modality*, common in scientific visuals and modern art, visual truth is abstract truth. The more an image represents the deeper 'essence' of what it depicts, or the more it represents the general pattern underlying superficially different specific instances, the higher its modality from the point of view of the abstract truth. This is expressed by reduced articulation. Specifics of illumination, nuances of colour, the details that create individual differences are all irrelevant from the point of view of the essential or general truth. This is seen, for instance, when naturalistic and abstract visuals are combined. Children's books about dinosaurs have detailed naturalistic pictures of dinosaurs in primeval landscapes to excite the imagination, and simple line drawings to help them recognise the essential attributes of different kinds of dinosaur.

In *technological modality*, visual truth is based on the practical usefulness of the image. The more an image can be used as a blueprint or aid for action, the higher its modality. Many maps are of this kind, and so are patterns for dressmaking, architectural drawings, and the assembly instructions of do-it-yourself kits. The corresponding modality configurations will tend towards strongly decreased articulation. Perspective, for instance, will be reduced to zero, as foreshortening would make it difficult to take measurements from the image.

In *sensory modality*, finally, visual truth is based on the effect of pleasure or displeasure created by visuals, and realised by a degree of articulation which is amplified beyond the point of naturalism, so that sharpness, colour, depth, the play of light and shade, etc. become (from the point of view of naturalistic modality) 'more than real'. Sensory modality is, therefore, used in contexts where pleasure matters: in food photography and perfume ads, for instance, or in contexts which try to create an intensity of experience akin to that of the dream or the hallucination (for example, in certain kinds of surrealist art, or in horror films).

We have specific reasons for using modality as a methodological tool in investigating a global medium like *Cosmopolitan*. We assume that *Cosmopolitan* seeks to communicate certain truths (for example, those of the various experts on which it relies and the truths that go with certain forms of social, and especially sexual, behaviour) and seeks to extend these truths and these behaviours globally. But we also assume that the use of modality in *Cosmopolitan* is complex. As we have already seen, many cultures communicate cultural truths and culturally endorsed courses of action, not through factual but through fictional texts, stories set in a distant past rather than in the present, and played out among 'others', rather than among 'us'. Today's global media are no different. Movie audiences are able to accept all manner of coincidences and absurdities as they are trained to follow movie causality in terms of its own logic. Advertisements, despite their pragmatic, persuasive goals, often have low modality, showing fantasies and daydreams rather than realities, and impossibly beautiful and glamorous supermodels rather than real people.

Many analysts of these types of social communication (for example, Bettelheim, 1976; Durand, 1983; Williamson, 1979) have rightly drawn on psychoanalysis to point out that such stories are the way they are in order to allow us to by-pass the 'censorship' between our conscious and unconscious thought, and to connect with desires that transgress social norms. This applies not only in advertisements, with their appeals to envy and sexual desire, but also in fairytales, which may, as we have seen, even allow children to fantasise their parents as cruelly abandoning them (Hansel and Gretel, in Bettelheim, 1976). Even irony and sarcasm need not necessarily signify that the speaker does not believe in what he or she is saying. They may also be used as defence mechanisms, to deflect attention from deeper attractions and identifications that are not permitted by the norms that prevail in the given cultural context. We, therefore, expect that the modality of magazines such as *Cosmopolitan* will be lower the greater the distance between the overt, real mores of a 'market' (especially the sexual mores, and the real position and role of women in society), and the mores propagated by *Cosmopolitan*, with its 'fun, fearless female' ethos.

Case study: women's work in the Dutch version of Cosmopolitan

As we have already seen, every issue of every *Cosmopolitan* contains a section related to work. In the Dutch *Cosmopolitan* of November 2001, this section is entitled *Werk en Reizen* ('Work and Travel'). Only two of the five items in it deal with work. A page titled 'Career' has five mixed items (among them the one shown in Figure 6.1), and a five-page feature has interviews with young Dutch women working in PR for, respectively, a fashion house, a theatre company, a zoo and a beauty products manufacturer. But work also appears in many other contexts. An article on gossip contains a section 'gossip at work', and an article on dealing with anger uses many work-related examples – always set in unspecified office environments. Profiles of actresses and singers also deal with work-related issues, for example stress. The agony column includes a letter from a woman who cannot choose between her job (she is given a chance to work abroad) and her boyfriend, and the astrology column contains many references to work ('Book a holiday for the 14th because there will many conflicts in the office that day'). Finally, although the vast majority of the 62 advertisements are for perfumes, shampoo and other beauty products, and lingerie, there are five work-related advertisements, four of them for internet job search sites. One of them ('A Career in Fashion Looks Good on You') in fact masquerades as a lingerie advertisement, with the copy in white lettering on a bluish photograph of a bra.

The text in Figure 6.1 is from the Dutch 'Career' page.

Omgaan met de Euro

Het schijnt dat we allemaal een aantal prijzen van producten uit ons hoofd kennen. De prijs van een liter melk bijvoorbeeld, of een concertkaartje. Om erachter te komen of iets duur of goedkoop is, vergelijken we prijzen met die in ons hoofd. Met de komst van **de Euro** zijn deze gulden-bedragen niet meer bruikbaar. Om meteen lekker met de Euro te kunnen rekenen, raadt het Nibud aan om een lijstje van zo'n tien zeer verschillende producten te maken en het ergens op te hangen waar je het dagelijks ziet. Op de site van het Nibud vind je een test waarmee je je eigen Euro-lijst kunt samenstellen. Kijk op www.nibud.nl

Après-vakantie stress?

Er zijn van die banen waarin het werk zich na je vakantie enorm heeft opgestapeld. Voor je het weet ben je je mooie reis op dag één door de stress alweer vergeten.

Met deze tips gebeurt dat niet:
● Moet je iets bewaren, stop het in een dossier-map.
● Reserveer voordat je op vakantie gaat ruimte in je agenda om de 'rotzooi' te kunnen opruimen als je terug bent.
● Zorg dat je op de ochtend van je eerste werk-dag geen afspraken hebt. Dan heb je even kans om ongestoord de dingen door te nemen die zich op je bureau hebben opgestapeld.
● Zijn er werkzaamheden, noteer die dan op een doe-lijstje.
● En heb je iets niet meer nodig: gooi het weg!
● Meer lezen? Kijk in het boek 'Tijdmanagement voor Dummies', door Jeffrey J. Mayer, ISBN: 906789981 X

Carrière
DOOR VIOLA ROBBEMONDT

Plat en draadloos

Je kunt 'm zelfs in bed gebruiken: dit nieuwe draadloze toetsenbord Cordless Desktop Optical ƒ349/€158,37 van Logitech. Dit super-dunne ontwerp is ook goed nieuws voor RSI-patiënten, want het zorgt ervoor dat je polsen tijdens het typen in een neutrale positie blijven waardoor je ze minimaal hoeft te bewegen. De optische muis, Cordless MouseMan Optical ƒ179/€81,23 genaamd, heeft geen balle-tje waardoor je 'm zelfs op een zachte ondergrond kunt gebruiken. *Meer info, kijk op www.logitech.nl*

Lettertype verraadt je karakter

Volgens psycholoog Aric Sigman vertelt het lettertype dat je op je computer kiest voor het schrijven van een brief boekdelen over je persoonlijkheid.

Courier New = tikkeltje ouderwets
Georgia = je hebt flair
Hevetica = modern
Times New Roman = wekt vertrouwen
Universal = anoniem
Comic Sans = aandacht trekkend
Verdana = professioneel

Bij het schrijven van bijvoorbeeld een sollicitatiebrief, kun je volgens Sigman het beste deze twee regels aanhouden:
1. Een kleiner lettertype, bijvoorbeeld 10 of 11 punts straalt meer zelfvertrouwen en gewichtigheid uit dan een groter. Minder is meer.
2. Stem je lettertype af op de bood-schap. Gebruik Times als je sollici-teert bij een traditioneel bedrijf en Verdana bij een modern. Schrijf je een ontslagbrief, wees dan profes-sioneel en gebruik courier new voor de noodzakelijke afstandelijkheid.

De secretaresse van Oprah Winfrey weigerde bij de talkshowqueen in dienst te blijven. Ze vond de tol - 24 uur per dag klaar staan - te hoog. Ze moest zelfs klaar-staan met een handdoek, als Oprah mee-deed aan een hardloopwedstrijd. Het salaris waar deze secretaresse 'nee' tegen zei? 1,8 miljoen dollar per jaar. 75

Figure 6.1 'Career' page (*Cosmopolitan NL,* November 2001, p. 75)

It translates as follows[2]:

Post-holiday stress?

> There are jobs in which the jobs pile up while you're on holiday. It takes less than a day before stress makes you forget your beautiful trip.

> **With these tips, that won't happen:**

> *   If you need to keep something put it in a folder.
> *   Before you go on holiday, reserve time to clear the 'rubbish' when you come back.
> *   Make sure you have no appointments on your first morning back. This will give you a chance to look through the stuff that has piled up on your desk.
> *   If there are any jobs waiting for you, put them on a to-do list.
> *   And throw out anything you don't need any more!
> *   Want to read more? Look in the book *Time Management for Dummies* by Jeffrey J. Mayer, ISBN: 906789981 X.

Below we discuss three key characteristics of this item:

The photograph has relatively low naturalistic modality and depicts 'women at work' as glamorous, but also as vulnerable and not fully in control

The picture shows an attractive model standing near a row of files. Although it illustrates a factual item, it has the sensory qualities of highly produced fashion and advertising photographs. There is an emphasis on the shimmering slinky clingy fabrics of the model's dress and on her loose and lavish hair. The background is reduced, perhaps suggesting the photographer's studio rather than a real office location. The files in front of her only hint at a work setting. This is typical for *Cosmopolitan* work images (and for the work images in many advertisements and fashion shots): a few attributes – a computer, a pen, files, a plant – stand for work, in an abstracted, stylised way. Equally typical is the way the woman relates to – or rather, does not relate to – this attribute of work. Her position in relation to the files, and her way of touching them, do not clearly show her as actually searching for something. She is merely using the files as a support for her pose. And she is looking away, at something we cannot see, something left open for the viewer to fill in, or to supply from the context. Is she looking back, at the past, remembering that holiday? Frequently such wistful looks at something unseen are used of vulnerable people – refugees, victims of famines and other calamities, people who are no longer in control of their destinies. Here, then, we see a woman at work, glamorous, but also vulnerable, almost helpless, in a picture with a distinct air of unreality.

The text has high modality and uses a 'hot tips' problem–solution genre

The text, on the other hand, is relatively straightforward. It fits Hodge and Kress's description of high modality: 'emphatic, without qualifications . . . we know that we are being asked to believe that it is true' (1988: 121). It directly addresses the reader, first describing a familiar enough problem and then providing the solution in the form of a relatively unordered list of 'tips', which, as it happens, do not envisage the possibility that stress at work may derive from structural problems, and displace it to the level of minor organisational problems, suggesting that problems will go away when you get yourself organised.

Problem–solution genres pervade magazines like *Cosmopolitan*. Articles on subjects such as 'gossip', 'anger', 'embarrassing moments', etc. may be interrupted by tips, or contain tips in boxes, and profiles of stars may go quite deeply into the details of how such stars deal with stress, or keep themselves looking young and fit. A feature on the 'negative sides of autumn and winter' (*Cosmopolitan NL*, November 2001: 5) starts with a problem and then offers the solution ('boost our resistance'), a solution worked out in sections on 'eating with more energy', vitamin pills, exercise and the 'power nap' and boxes on aromatherapy and an 'instant energy' lamp:

> You tire more easily, you have problems concentrating, you are irritable, you feel listless and you have difficulty sleeping. Sounds like diminished resistance. In this condition you're more likely to catch a cold or some other disease. Time to boost your resistance.

The issue also contains tips on how to calm down when you are overwhelmed with anger, how to keep your cool in the traffic, how to be hip without losing your own personality, and how to apply make-up and yet look 'natural'. The latter belongs to a slightly different category, however, as the 'tips', the direct 'what to do' instructions, are ordered sequentially, as in a recipe, while the tips in a 'hot tips' problem–solution text can appear in any order. In problem–solution advertisements, finally, there is only one solution, buy the product or obtain the service, even though there may of course be several problems – the more problems a product can solve, the better. There are, therefore, at least three problem–solution genres: a 'single solution' genre; a 'hot tips' multiple solution genre (unordered list of 'instructions'); and a 'procedure' multiple solution genre (time-ordered list of 'instructions').

The picture is the Ideal and the text is the Real

The photograph and the text are spatially organised in terms of an Ideal-Real syntagm. The enticingly glamorous but also vulnerable and somewhat helpless *Cosmopolitan* woman is positioned as the idealised essence of the message, which not only emphasises the problem (lack of control) over the solution (regaining a sense of control by getting organised), but also creates contradictions between the fantasy of pleasurable glamour and the reality of the reader's life and work.

Cosmopolitan also includes texts which claim to be about real people doing real jobs. The images that accompany the profiles of women working in public relations in the Dutch version are higher in modality and less glamorous. In the image that accompanied the text below, Linda Teeling is seen slightly from above and smiling at the camera, somewhat self-consciously, perhaps. The picture is clearly taken on location and the colours do not have the enhanced saturation and texture of those in Figure 6.1. High naturalistic, but lower sensory modality, therefore – the look of a snapshot, of a record of a real person in a real environment. But the image is still softened, and it still has the slightly blurred setting and the sense of high key lighting that are also characteristic of stock images.

Although starting like a narrative, the text follows the genre of the testimonial. The first stage describes the 'conversion', the way in which Linda became involved with the Kuyichi brand. In the next stage Linda describes the brand identity, the Kuyichi message. Next she describes her own role in disseminating the message, her mission, and finally she gives an account of her identification with that role, first in a more specific way, and then again, by means of an analogy in which she talks of her work as a personal relationship, in terms that are very compatible with the *Cosmopolitan* 'philosophy'. What is excluded here is as interesting as what is included: there are no managers telling Linda what to do, no other employees in fact, except through the 'we's' and the 'ours' of the 'message' stage. Everything she does stems from her own initiative and her own total commitment to, and personal identification with, the brand. As far as the article is concerned, she has no boyfriend, no friends, no family, no hobbies – her work for the company is everything (see Table 6.2).

This testimonial has all the hallmarks of a religious testimonial: it tells a story of looking for the truth and finding it, and then testifies to that truth, and to the speaker's unstinting, personal and all-inclusive devotion to its dissemination.

As for the spatial organisation of the page, this time it is horizontal. The picture is Given and the text New. We, therefore, think of the girl as someone 'already known', perhaps as someone just like us, the real Dutch readers of *Cosmopolitan*, who do not necessarily look like supermodels. The New is her devotion to a fashion brand and to the kind of total and quasi-religious devotion which many contemporary corporations require of their employees, and which, it is suggested here, combines fun, looking good, hard work and – important in a Dutch context – 'good works', charity.

Case study: women's work in the Indian version of Cosmopolitan

The 'Cosmo Careers' section of the same month's Indian issue of *Cosmopolitan* contains four items. '4 Ways to Win them Over' aims to help managers to improve their communication skills. 'My Brilliant Career' is a short profile of the Senior Vice-President of a cable TV company. And then there are 'I lied on my CV – should I come clean with my boss?' and a quote from the 'president of Indian business and professional women': 'The successful women in technology I know don't believe in

Text	Genre analysis
I already worked here during the last few months of my studies. For my final project I did a communications plan for Kuyichi, and after I graduated I could start with them straightaway. Some parts from my plan are now actually implemented, but that's still a secret.	'Conversion' ⇓
What we have already done is send woollen socks with the invitation to the press to introduce the Fair Trade aspect in a humorous way. Kuyichi is a new fun brand with a story.	Brand message
Our jeans are made in accordance with Fair Trade practices: better working conditions, no child labour, that kind of thing. They cost the same as the competition but part of the profit goes to the people in Peru.	⇓
As marketing and PR worker I have to promote the brand in the right way, through promotions and advertisements. I have to ensure that the brand radiates to others what we feel for it here.	Mission ⇓
At the moment I have only got one pair of Kuyichi jeans. I always wear them at work. Soon we'll be getting more stock in and I can choose whatever I want. They are special fun clothes which I would have chosen myself anyway. That's why I identify with the brand and that's just as well. It would be hard to promote something you didn't believe in.	Identification with role (1) ⇓
You have to relate to people to be able to do this work. I see the brand as a relationship: you put a lot of energy in it. Some things go well, some don't. You feel that immediately and you've got to keep working at it.	Identification with role (2)

Table 6.2

a glass ceiling.' Clearly, this magazine does not address the same kind of reader as the Dutch version. It sees its readers as an elite of managers and bosses, while in European versions women's work almost always means office work, and the problem is not how to relate to your subordinates, but how to relate to your boss. In India, the message of *Cosmopolitan* is, for the time being, only for an elite of taste-makers and trendsetters; in Europe it is has already filtered through to a much larger section of the population.

In the index of the Indian *Cosmopolitan*, this 'Careers' page is listed under the heading 'Life and Work'. The articles included in this section all apply the same ideas to work and life (love life, that is, for in the world of the 'fun, fearless female' there is only love and work). The article, '9 Ways to Be a Bad Chick' gives tongue-in-cheek advice on love ('get down and dirty to snag your man') as well as work ('cuss out a pushy boss'). 'Great Advice for 30 Somethings' counsels the 30-something reader to 'stop job-hopping' and 'find someone who wants a commitment'. In 'Live your Dream Destiny', 'bad-vibe backlash' catches up with a woman who 'hooked up with her friend's guy' as well as with a woman who 'secretly went after a job her friend had applied for'. And 'How to Change Your Life for the Better' profiles four women who overcame obstacles and realised their dreams – of getting a steady boyfriend, recuperating from depression, slimming down, and making a career in fashion. Some of the articles in the other sections also mix work life and intimate life in this way, for example 'Hit the Big Time', the 'Cosmo Quiz' ('How independent are you?') and the profile of the 'fun, fearless female' of the month.

In the case of the Indian 'Cosmo Careers', like its Dutch counterpart, there is a similar layout and a similar generic structure of the items included. Again, a 'hot tips' item is prominently featured (see Table 6.3).

4 Ways to Win them Over	Goal
	⇓
Arindham Caudhuri author of *Count Your Chickens Before they Hatch* shares his mantras of *effective communication.*	Restatement of Goal
	⇓
Be audience-friendly. Follow the KISS (keep it short and simple) principle while addressing and audience. Get a wee bit of clarity in the way you speak and watch it make a difference in what people around you perceive.	Tip 1
	⇓
Be polite and polished. The fact is that what you say fades over time, but how you felt during that conversation remains with you for a long time. Politeness is a virtue because it creates lasting impressions.	Tip 2
	⇓
Bring on the humour. Managers who use wit in their presentations come across as more approachable. So if you manage a lot of people, maintain their morale by showing that you have a funny bone.	Tip 3
	⇓
Don't forget the LAW. Looks, action and words all matter. You don't have to be born with Aishwarya's looks to be a good communicator. What you need is a pleasing, smiling personality that endears you to everyone around you. So work at it.	Tip 4

Table 6.3

An analysis of this item brings out further similarities:

The photograph has relatively low naturalistic modality and shows women
as glamorous, but not as being in control of a situation or activity

The picture shows two models standing in front of a desk. As in the Dutch version, the models are attractive, with lavish hair and radiant smiles, but not strikingly beautiful. The modality is both abstract and sensory. It is abstract, and hence slightly unreal from a naturalistic point of view, because of the reduced colour differentiation (an overall emphasis on blue) and the reduced background, with its use of just a few props (computer, files) to suggest an office setting. During the 1970s and 1980s *Cosmopolitan* still included photographs taken in actual work settings and contemporary magazines from other Asian countries, for example Vietnam's *Woman's World* (Figure 6.2) still do. On the other hand the picture is sensory, and reminiscent of advertising and fashion photography in its use of very vivid, sensual colour. *Cosmopolitan* photographer Michael Wray told us that the magazine prefers photos that 'look great', and are 'joyful', but also blend into the design of the page. People should forget them instantly and not even be directly drawn towards them, he said.

And why, when the item addresses women who 'manage a lot of people', do we see two women smiling blankly (and not particularly confidently) at each other over a cup of tea? Why are they not actually shown in their role as managers?

Figure 6.2 Women in the workplace (from *Woman's World*, Vietnam)

The text has high modality and uses a 'hot tips' problem–solution genre

As in the Dutch version the text uses a 'hot tips' format and is relatively straight-forward, lacking the air of unreality of the photograph. The format is graphically realised by having the underlined words in large blue font and the tips bullet-pointed in a box, and it is expanded by using 'maxims', pieces of expert wisdom such as 'the fact is that what you say fades over time', to lend authority to the directives. Typically the tips start with a directive (for example, 'be audience friendly') and then link this to a maxim, for example:

Bring on the humour.	Directive
	⇓
Managers who use wit in their presentations come across as more approachable.	Maxim
	⇓
So if you manage a lot of people, maintain their morale by showing that you have a funny bone.	Elaboration of directive

The same format is found elsewhere, for example in the already mentioned '9 Ways to Be a Bad Chick'

Smoke a cigar.	Directive
	⇓
Leave the ultrathins to the wuss.	Directive
	⇓
Nothing's worse than a girl with a mean cigar tucked between her teeth.	Maxim
	⇓
Wrap your scarlet pouters around a Habano and blow smoke rings as you discuss the stock market with your contemporaries.	Elaboration of Directive

In longer versions tips may be endorsed by expert opinions and/or illustrated with case stories. Such variations and expansions of the 'hot tips' genre form a key aspect of *Cosmopolitan* writing – even articles which at first sight seem to deal with an issue or to tell a story, turn out to be 'hot tips' format in disguise. Thus the magazine positions itself as expert and friend, drawing in case stories to give a sense of real women and common interests.

The picture is the Ideal and the text is the Real

As in the Dutch version, fantasy and reality are ambiguously juxtaposed. The somewhat unreal picture, showing woman as glamorous but not 'in control' is positioned as the idealised essence of the message, and the more straightforward text, seeking to help women to gain greater control over a specific aspect of their reality, is positioned as the Real.

'My Brilliant Career', taken from the same page as '4 Ways to Win them Over', can be compared with the 'real woman' profile in the Dutch version. Here, too, the 'passport photo' image has higher modality, to indicate a real person. The lighting is realistic and what little can be seen of the background is highly articulated. *Cosmopolitan* photographers have spoken to us of the way make-up and hair have to be modified to give the sense of a real person (Romilly Lockyer) and of the need for higher colour modulation in photographs of this kind (Michael Wray).

Text	Genre Analysis
We find out how 32-year-old Monica Tata keeps television buffs glued to their couches	problem (narrativised) ⇓
Tata started out as a summer trainee with Aron Advertising at Rs 2,500 per month in 1989, and then moved on to space selling. She joined Star India Pt Ltd in 1992 as a sales executive and for eight years, sold ad time for the channels.	tip (career history) ⇓
Tata moved from ad sales to programming in 2000 and is currently senior vice president, Star Gold Channel.	
Tips for a programmer: Know the USP of your Channel. 'Star Gold is dedicated to the nostalgia Genre, so all programming is done keeping this in mind,' she says. So, no baby Roshan on this Channel, but daddy does take a bow off and on.	tip ⇓
Motto: I am going to make a difference.	directive (career attitudes) ⇓
My get-ahead-traits: Risk taking, can-do attitude, competitive aggressiveness.	directive (maxim) ⇓
Pearl of wisdom: Work hard, play hard!	directive (maxim)

Table 6.4

Like the Dutch text, this text indicates total support for, and total dedication to, work and its values. But unlike Linda, Tata is a boss, and she is in it for herself. If she adheres to the 'mission' of the channel she works for, she does so in the first place to further her own career, and the Dutch emphasis on *believing* in that mission is lacking. Linda, the employee, is happy to 'serve'. She seeks job satisfaction ('it's like a relationship') rather than career advancement. Tata, the boss, on the other hand, aggressively seeks career advancement and success.

As for the genre, although it is, in principle, a story, a 'how to' element has been worked into both the title and the body of the article (the tip). In fact, the whole story can be seen as a tip, a model for how to succeed in the commercial world. The final part of the text has intertextual affinities with the Q&A genre in that the introductions to each 'career attitude' could be seen as questions (for example, 'What is your motto?') and also with CVs, those documents in which we must narrativise ourselves in such a way that companies will 'buy'.

Conclusion

Different versions of *Cosmopolitan* construct women's work in different, 'local' ways. The Dutch version is oriented towards employees taking personal responsibility for their work and working for the sake of job satisfaction rather than material rewards (perhaps not totally unsurprising in a country with a Calvinist tradition). The Indian version is oriented towards employers and managers working for status and material rewards, rather than for moral satisfaction. Other versions are different again. In the Spanish and Greek versions women tend to be office workers with male bosses. They fear unemployment and are preoccupied with keeping the boss happy and leaving a good impression when moving on. Such versions reflect differences in the *Cosmopolitan* readership in these countries and their cultural and economical background.

However, all these versions are presented in very much the same format, and in all of them the sphere of work, as it has taken shape in the neo-capitalist global order, becomes indistinguishably mixed up with the sphere of women's libidinal and personal lives, and with fantasies of glamour which, at the same time, perpetuate women's traditional vulnerability and lack of control. And they are presented, not as ideological constructs, but as practical solutions to common problems, endorsed by expert psychological truths about human nature and, therefore, as transcending cultural difference and as legitimately 'global'. The 'local' is reduced to a kind of adornment or decoration embedded in a basic architecture of the global, and in the process it is transformed, though never to the extent that it ceases to be recognisable as local.

The term 'glocalisation' has been proposed to capture this process of merging. But the way in which it has been defined has usually failed to recognise that globalisation deliberately and strategically embeds the local in Western/capitalist models. As for the audiences, structural anthropologists like Leach (1954, 1969) and Lévi-Strauss (1978a, 1978b) argued that it is not so much the immediate surface part of a story, the characters, locations, etc., but the deeper structure that carries its core ideas about agency, roles and social organisation. This analysis applies equally to the stories of contemporary corporate storytellers. Global corporate media may set their stories in different locations and populate them with different characters, but the fundamental reasons for the behaviour of these characters, for what they want and how they seek to attain it, follows one and the same logic wherever these stories are told.

Questions

1   Find a problem–solution advertisement and use the approach to genre analysis introduced in this chapter to analyse it. How does its format differ from that of the 'hot tips' items discussed in this chapter, and why?
2   Find three magazine pages or advertisements that contain contrasts in visual modality (for example, one picture in black and white and another in colour, or a drawing as well as a photograph). Use modality analysis to interpret why these different modalities have been used.
3   Using concepts introduced in this chapter, analyse the layout of the home pages of three of the localised websites of a global company. What is the same about them and what different?
4   Find (or construct) a 'single solution' and a 'hot tips' text relating to the same problem. Show the two versions to women from two generations or two different backgrounds and ask them which of the two they prefer and why.

Notes

1   This chapter is a version of an earlier publication (Machin and van Leeuwen, 2004).
2   The Dutch translations are by Theo van Leeuwen.

7 Global language(s)

Global and local languages

Linguistic globalisation has stirred up much the same issues as media globalisation. Phillipson (1992: 1) condemns the 'linguistic imperialism' of English. 'The British Empire has given way to the Empire of English', he says, and the global ELT profession 'promotes both the "rules of English" and the "rule of English"' (cf. also Skuttnab-Kangas and Phillipson, 1994). It is not hard to find facts and figures to support his view. English is not only the mother tongue of some 400 million people, it is the second language of another 430 million, while 750 million speak it reasonably well as a foreign language and as many as a billion are learning (Crystal, 2003: 67–9): 'In 1959 everyone in China was carrying a book of the thoughts of Chairman Mao, today everyone is carrying a book of elementary English' (Crystal, 1996: 360). English is the official language of over 60 countries and 85 per cent of international organisations. It is without doubt the dominant language in the areas of entertainment and information (at present 80 per cent of electronically stored information is in English), economics and management, and science and technology.

Two-thirds of the world's scientists write in English, and most journals have shifted from other languages to English. In Germany, for instance, not only 98 per cent of physicists and 81 per cent of biologists, but also 72 per cent of sociologists and 50 per cent of philosophers use English as their main working language, and even two-thirds of France's scientific publications are in English (Graddol, 1998: 9). Many have related the rise of English directly to the decline and death of other languages (cf. Crystal, 2000; Nettle and Romaine, 2000). An average of two languages dies each month, and with them die 'sagas, folk songs, rituals, proverbs, and many other practices [that] provide us with a unique view of our world' (Crystal, 2003: 20). Although some have denied such a direct connection between the rise of English and language death, there can be no doubt that the dominance of language is, and always has been, directly related to other forms of dominance, in the past mostly military, and now also economic and technological.

Other linguists disagree with the 'linguistic imperialism' thesis (for example, Graddol, 1998), pointing at a number of other developments:

The rise of other languages

Spanish, for example, is also a global language, with some 400 million speakers and a growing popularity as a second language, so much so that the USA, with its large numbers of Spanish-speaking immigrants, has introduced a law to declare English the official language, and abolished bilingual education in California (Mar-Molinero, 2000). Chinese, Arabic and Hindi/Urdu are also spreading their wings across the globe.

Localisation

From the 1980s onwards, global corporations have made increasing use of 'local' languages in their global communication, not only in the media, as we have already seen, but also in many other areas. Technical information, for instance, is now routinely translated increasingly in many different languages (Strunk, 2000), and as a result many 'local' languages have to change, to accommodate domains of communication that were formerly only associated with English.

World Englishes

As it spreads across the world, English itself also changes – hence the plural 'World Englishes'. 'Post-colonial' literatures in English have played an important role in this development, and some of its authors have expressed the need for new 'Englishes', for instance, the Indian author Raja Rao (quoted in Crystal, 2003: 184–5):

> English is not really an alien language to us. It is the language of our intellectual make-up – like Sanskrit and Persian was before – but not of our emotional make-up . . . We cannot write like the English. We should not. We cannot write only as Indians. We have grown to look at the large world as part of us. Our method of expression has to be a dialect which will some day prove to be as distinctive and colourful as the Irish or the American.

The regeneration of minority languages

And finally, quite a few minority languages may actually get a new lease of life as a result of globalisation. The European Union officially only recognises the languages of nation states, but it has a regional policy that has contributed much to the regeneration of languages like Welsh and Catalan. The French Canadians, a minority which had long fought an uphill battle for its linguistic rights, suddenly found that the rise of new global industries such as call centres and heritage tourism gave them an advantage in the job market (Heller, 2003). Former minority languages in the Baltic states and former Yugoslavia became national languages again after the fall of Communism in 1989 (Busch *et al.*, 2001). In Croatia, for instance, the government appointed linguists to purify Croatian from Serbian influences and test the competence of journalists in the new state's language, with the result that 60 per cent of journalists employed by Croatian State Television lost their job – lack of fluency in the new national language was held to signify being oppositional and 'non-Croatian', just as had been the case in France two hundred years earlier, when French (at that time spoken by less than half the population) became the official language of the Revolution: 'Federalism and superstition speak Breton, emigration and hatred for the Republic speak German, the contra-revolution speaks Italian, and fanatism speaks Basque', Barère had said in 1794 (quoted in Busch *et al.*, 2001: 147). In all these cases the media play a key role. They propagate the new regimes and develop nationalist 'identity designs' for the people, as Busch puts it.

But all this complexity did not mean the disappearance of 'linguistic imperialism'. The Voice of America, for instance, which had started in 1942 for purposes of war propaganda, continues to beam its messages across the world, using its 'Special English', a simplified and standardised English of its own concoction which uses only 1,500 'simple words that describe objects, actions or emotions', 'is written in short, simple sentences that contain only one idea', eschews idioms, and is 'spoken at a slower pace, about two-thirds the speed of standard English' (www.manythings. org/voa/voa.htm). Its purpose is not just the spread of English, it is also political: 'Today's stable nations may be tomorrow's terrorist havens, drug producers or arenas of civil war', and, therefore, 'we must be flexible and mobile . . . able to respond rapidly to crises, as we did in Kosovo' (Sanford Ungar, former Director of VOA, quoted in Busch, 2001: 170).

In this chapter we explore two case studies. The one is an example of the local adoption of English, the other a case of localisation into languages other than English. In both cases the question is not just what language is used, but also and especially how the languages are used, and how they mix the global (English) and the local (non-English languages), or not. In other words, we are trying to document some instances of linguistic change. Linguists still tend to speak of linguistic change as some kind of autonomous process. According to Crystal (2003: 142), the spread of English demonstrates that language is 'open to the winds of change in totally unpredictable ways'. In the case of global media discourses, however, linguistic change results from quite deliberate policies and practices, regardless of whether these policies and practices are implemented locally, as in our first example, or imposed by the headquarters of a global corporation, as in the second. As Jan Blommaert has said (2003: 608), 'we need to move from languages to language varieties and repertoires':

> What is globalized is not an abstract Language, but specific speech forms, genres, styles, and forms of literacy practice. And the way in which such globalized varieties enter into local environments is by a reordering of the locally available repertoires and the relative hierarchical relations between ingredients in the hierarchy.

The global language of the journalism of information[1]

The *Vietnam News* is a 28-page English-language, tabloid-size newspaper published every day in Hanoi. It features translations of selected articles from the Vietnamese press, together with English-language stories from the international wire services and occasional reports by Vietnamese journalists written directly in English. It was started in June 1991 by the Ministry of Culture and Information as part of Vietnam's *doi moi,* Vietnam's drive to become part of the global market economy. It aims at foreign readers in Vietnam (tourists, potential investors, expatriates, etc.), though Vietnamese learners of English also use it. But it has another readership as well, the diplomatic community and the newspaper's ministerial overseers. Front-page coverage is skewed towards diplomatic 'handshake' stories which send coded messages to the embassies. At the Ministry of Culture and Information, the newspaper is carefully re-read the next day, and deviations from the party line are brought to the editor's attention in no uncertain terms.

The staff of the *Vietnam News* consists of some 40 translators who double as proofreaders and occasionally write their own stories as well. They work together with six to eight British and Australian sub-editors who correct the translated English and write headlines and captions. The policies and practices of these sub-editors rest on their own interpretation of how Western journalistic practices should be adapted for the purposes of the *Vietnam News,* and on continuing negotiation with, on the one hand, the editor-in-chief and, on the other hand, the Vietnamese translator/reporters. Just as global news agencies have done since the nineteenth century, these sub-editors try to teach their Vietnamese colleagues the values of the Western 'journalism of information' – and sometimes these values clash with those of the Vietnamese journalists. Western journalism likes dramatic headlines, for instance, but in Vietnam positive news is important and should be published on the front page: 'Today's journalists are not struggling for the country's liberty, but for its development, for its people's good' (Tran Lam, quoted in *Vietnam News,* 28 December 2001).

We discuss the English of the *Vietnam News* in three steps. First we will look at its grammar and vocabulary, then at its journalistic style, and finally at the discourses, the ways in which the events and issues covered by the paper are represented.

A new variety of English?

The excerpt below shows how an Australian sub-editor changed the work of a Vietnamese translator/reporter. The original version is on the left, the corrected one on the right.

Some of the changes correct grammatical mistakes, for instance the lack of the definite article 'the' in 'This was the government's effort to help young generation understand . . .' (paragraph 4a). The grammar of Vietnamese has interfered here with the grammar of English. Vietnamese has no articles. It uses 'one' where English

(1a) Overall planning should be developed nationwide not only in major cities.	(1b) The government will thus have to look at the bigger picture.
(2a) The government has decided to established the Tay Bac University in the north, and the medical and teachers' training universities in the south and widen the Tay Nguyen (the Central Highlands) University.	(2b) including setting up the Tay Bac University in the north, building new medical and teacher training colleges in the south, and expanding the Tay Nguyen (Central Highlands) University.
(3a) He said more than 500 young nurseries and doctors have been sent to remote mountainous areas with VND5 billion from the State budget.	(3b) Khiem said more than 500 young nurses and doctors had been sent to remote mountainous areas, backed by VND5 billion from the State budget.
(4a) This was the government's effort to help young generation understand their duties to people in mountainous areas.	(4b) This programme would not only benefit the target regions, he suggested, but also help young people remember their obligations towards the less well-off. **Fighting social evils**
(5a) The Deputy Prime Minister said that the fight against drug and prostitution is taking place very complicated making new challenges not only in Vietnam, but also the region and the world.	(5b) The Deputy PM said the fight against drugs and prostitution required sophisticated strategies for dealing with a complex and evolving set of challenges.
(6a) The fight must be constant. It's not a seasonal campaign. Co-ordination is not close enough among relevant organisations in the fight and it leads to inefficient results.	(6b) He affirmed that the campaign should be constant, and required close co-ordination between relevant bodies and organisations.

uses the indefinite article, and demonstratives ('this' and 'that') where English uses the definite article. In the absence of such determiners, reference will be generic, referring to a 'class' or 'type' of people, places and things, rather than to specific people, places or things. But there is also a difference in what counts as generic. To give just one example, uncountable nouns are considered to be generic – hence the translation 'young generation' instead of 'the young generation'.

Other grammatical mistakes are not hard to find, for instance the sentence 'the fight . . . is taking place very complicated making new challenges not only in Vietnam . . .' (paragraph 5a). The Vietnamese translator/reporters also have trouble with English suffixes, sometimes with unintended comic effect – for example, 'nurseries' instead of 'nurses', 'air conditional system', 'more than half of the rural people will be accessible to safe water', 'the Vietnamese footballers started the match confidentially'. This is because in Vietnamese the meanings of suffixes and prefixes are not integrated within words (for example, instead of 'confidentially', Vietnamese would say 'in a confidential manner'). All these mistakes are corrected by the sub-editors in the name of correct English.

But the question is, are they mistakes? Asian and African linguists have now begun to describe 'new Englishes' such as Malayan English, Pakistani English, Nigerian English, Ghanaian English, and so on, and for them the constructions the *Vietnam News* sub-editors correct are not mistakes but distinctive features of new varieties of English. Baskaran (1994), for instance, sees the omission of definite articles as a regular feature of Malayan English ('There'll be traffic jam'; 'She was given last chance'), and Gyasi (1991) describes words such as 'delayance' and 'costive' (instead of 'costly) as regular forms of Ghanaian English. Crystal (2003) lists many other examples. The sub-editors of the *Vietnam News* and these Asian and African linguists are both professional keepers of the rules of language, language arbiters. But they make rather different decisions.

Many of the 'mistakes' of the Vietnamese journalists result from a keen interest in wordplay, and a genuine attempt to sound authentic and idiomatic, sometimes, again, with unintended comic effect: '"To occupy the market-share of the lion, Vietnam businesses must compete drastically", Lan Ahn confessed.'

At other times, however, they bring a little bit of poetry to the language:

Combat to write and write to combat
They did not sign their names in the nation's history. Instead they penned other people's names and victories in the history.
Armed with a rifle plus a pen, or a camera, they fought and recorded moments in time.
Following the same sacred mission, those gone-away were honoured heroes of the heart by the survivors.

From the point of view of the Vietnamese, there are two rules about English: 'don't translate' and 'speak simply'. In their view, the English do not appreciate poetry, flowery language and exotic adjectives. From an English perspective, Vietnamese writing is overly 'florid' and 'rhetorical'. Most foreign sub-editors simply rewrite such passages in their own, simpler style, but some favour retaining something of the 'voice' of the Vietnamese reporter, especially in items such as *Talk Around Town*, a personal opinion column.

Then again, the Vietnamese translator/reporters are not necessarily appreciative of this. Many prefer to see their thoughts rendered in good 'global' English, even if that entails some loss of voice and thereby perhaps also of meaning. Good, global English means being able to compete globally, and that is important in Asia. It was for this reason, for instance, that Prime Minister Goh Chok Tong of Singapore devoted part of his 1999 National Day speech to an attempt to persuade Singaporeans to speak Standard English rather than Singlish (a mixture of English, Chinese and Malay). Clearly, two points of view compete here, global English as economically empowering, local English as expressing local cultural identity.

Journalistic style

Vietnamese journalists often load up the front of the story with background and statistics, where Western 'leads', as we saw in Chapter 1, should 'stand as a self-contained story, complete with source if the subject is contentious' (Palmer, 1998: 187) and be no longer than 20 or 30 words. The excerpt below shows how *Vietnam News* sub-editors correct such leads. The long list of names of VIPS with which the piece opens is moved to lower down in the story, and the lead is made more 'newsy'. However, in deference to party etiquette, such changes may later be reversed by the editor-in-chief, especially in front-page stories.

(1a) The 10th session of the National Assembly heard major socio-economic targets for next year delivered by the government on its opening day yesterday.	(1b) Economic restructuring, export promotion and the search for investment capital are among the key planks of next year's socio-economic plan, Prime Minister Phan Van Khai revealed yesterday.
(2a) The year end session of the National Assembly was attended by Party General Secretary Nong Duc Manh; President Tran Duc Luong; Prime Minister Phan Van Khai, and National Assembly Chairman Nguyen Van An.	(2b) He told the opening day of the National Assembly's 10th session that the plan's top priorities were to maintain the tempo of economic growth, sharpen the country's competitive edge, streamline State-owned enterprises and resolve pressing social problems.

(3a) Former advisors to the Party Central Committee Do Muoi and Le Duc Anh and former Party General Secretary Le Kha Phieu were also present on the opening day of the session.	(3b) The PM outlined the plan to the assembled NA deputies and top national leaders including Party General Secretary Nong Duc Manh, President Tran Duc Luong and National Assembly Chairman Nguyen Van An.
(4a) Prime Minister Phan Van Khai read a report mapping out major socio-economic targets for next year.	*(23 further paragraphs)*
(5a) They are: • To maintain a high and sustainable economic growth rate • To sharpen competitive edge • Production restructuring • To streamlining, developing and raising the efficiency of state owned enterprises • To effectively settle a number of urgent social problems • Firmly ensure security and national defence in all circumstances (etc.)	(27b) Former advisors to the Party Central Committee Do Muoi and Le Duc Anh and former Party General Secretary Le Kha Phieu were also present at the NA session yesterday.

The example also illustrates a further point of cultural difference. The poetic impulse we signalled above corresponds to an equally strong tendency towards dry bureaucratic prose as if the two, public information and private self-expression, are further apart here than we are accustomed to in our Western world of government advertising and edutainment. Many of the translated stories sound like official documents, aid organisation reports or diplomatic communiqués. Such stories often contain long lists, whether in the form of bullet points, as in the example above, or in the form of the extremely long sentences in which the Vietnamese language seems to specialise.

Attribution

The foreign sub-editors recommend the use of quotes to liven up stories. But this causes problems when the quotes are translated from Vietnamese – how far can they be changed? It is a sanctified rule of journalism that one never interferes with direct quotes. But because the quotes already lose their exact meaning in translation, the foreign sub-editors tend to tidy them up and make them sound like someone might actually have said them.

However, in stories involving important officials (the Party Leader, Prime Minister, President and Deputy Prime Ministers), there is a danger that this will distort the exact meanings that the leaders are trying to convey. For this reason such stories cannot contain direct quotes and must rely on reported speech, and that creates stylistic problems. Without direct quotes it is hard to avoid starting each sentence with, 'He said that . . .'. There are various options. One can write out a sentence from the statement, then put '. . . he said' at the end. One can vary the saying verb ('urged', 'called on', 'noted', etc.) but verbs like 'claim' and 'assert' can introduce comment where neutral reporting is most urgently required. One can swap pronouns for variety ('Khai', 'he', 'the PM') or use passive voice to make the subject of the PM's sentence into the subject of the news sentence ('Social evils would be tackled in several ways, including higher fines and new supervision procedures'). Tense then becomes the only, rather implicit, marker of attribution.

In the eyes of Western journalists, this makes stories of this kind quite unreadable. Vietnamese journalists are less bothered. To them, stories like this are designed with only one reader in mind, the Ideology Commission of the Ministry of Information who will read it with a fine-tooth comb the next day for any signs of deviance, and, if there is an embassy involved, the political attaché who will read the story to glean official party policy towards their country or that issue.

One of the hardest things for Vietnamese journalists to learn is feature writing. As explained by the *Vietnam News* sub-editors in their training course for the Vietnamese translator/reporters, features must 'interest the reader', and to this end they must lead with a 'theme', the 'idea or point you want to explain in your story' (note the term 'explain'). In *Vietnam News* features, the to-be-interested reader is of course a foreign reader, so the Vietnamese translator/reporters must take into account both the Western way of leading a 'story' with an 'explanation' and the foreign reader's interests. In the example below the Vietnamese writer has used an entirely narrative, explanation-free approach to the beginning of the story – the kind of 'scene setting' introduction that was also common in early nineteenth-century English and American journalism but disappeared with the rise of the 'journalism of information'. But the sub-editor changed this, so that the story would lead with a more general theme, 'respect for teachers', no doubt on the basis of the assumption that this is part of the ideas Westerners have about the 'Orient'.

(1a) We came to visit the old teacher Bui Van Huyen, at Dong Thai Commune, Ba Vi District, Ha Tay Province. It was a small straw house with a newly built portico bearing the Chinese character 'Heart'.

(2a) The class room was a 20 sq.m. house with beaten earth walls on which were hung many pictures of leaders and Dong Ho paintings.

(3a) Everything in the house was made of wood and bamboo. The most precious assets were an old TV set and a radio transistor.

(4a) Though already 84 years old the teacher was still alert. He moved through the desks to give instruction to one pupil or to help another write properly. The pupils' pens were made of bamboo, because the teacher did not want his pupils to use ball pens.

(5a) I asked him: 'Do you teach every day?' He answered: 'Yes, for already 30 years, since 1971.'

(6a) Then he told me his story.

(1b) Vietnam is a country that respects and admires its teachers. But some teachers deserve that admiration in especially generous doses.

(2b) Bui Van Huyen, 84, lives in a humble abode in Dong Thai Commune, located in Ha Tay Province's Ba Vi District.

(3b) Not only has he devoted his whole life to teaching, but for the last three decades his work has been entirely voluntary.

(4b) Physically frail and sight-impaired, nothing has stood in the way of his determination to bring literacy to underprivileged children.

(5b) These days, he teaches in his 20 sq. m. hut with beaten earth walls, on which are hung many pictures of leaders and Dong Ho paintings.

(6b) Everything in the classroom is made of wood and bamboo – there is nothing more valuable than an old TV set and a radio transistor.

(7b) He may be old, but he is still firm of purpose, moving along the desks to offer advice to his pupils or help them with their writing technique.

(8b) The students all use pens made of bamboo, which he prefers to ball-point.

Discursive adaptation

Translating Vietnamese journalistic discourse involves not only language correction and stylistic adaptation, but also a 'repositioning' of the reader. The foreign sub-editors play a crucial role in this process, acting as cultural interpreters, and changing a local perspective on events to an outsider's perspective. This not only means unpacking Vietnamese concepts and terminology (for instance, the Vietnamese use of 'equitisation' instead of 'privatisation'), but also backgrounding or deleting Communist terminology. 'Cadres' become 'officials', 'the fight' becomes 'a campaign', 'State control' becomes 'supervision', 'being enlightened' becomes 'being converted to the Communist cause', and so on. The fact that Vietnam, market reform notwith-standing, is still a Communist country is watered down for foreign consumption, but not hidden. Enough Communist terms (for example, 'revisionists', 'social evils', 'a firm political orientation', 'tendencies contrary to Party guidelines') remain to provide *couleur locale* in this respect. The following example is fairly typical:

Trong told them that he shared his sympathy at losses caused by the Michelle storm to Cuban people and expressed his admiration toward the Cuban people's hard work and firm revolutionary spirit so as to step by step leading their country overcome the special period, obtaining an economic growth and brokening the enemy's scheme to stifle their revolutionary fruits.	During the talks, Trong conveyed his country's sympathies over the losses Cuba suffered during the severe hurricane *Michelle*, and expressed his admiration for the Cuban people's hard work and firm revolutionary spirit.

Feature leads are crucial in this process of cultural adaptation. As we have seen, it is the function of leads to 'create interest', and this is best done by reference to something with which the reader is already familiar. This means that the Vietnamese journalists must learn to distance themselves from themselves, to explain things that would normally go without saying, to see interest in things they would normally take for granted, and to refer to themselves as 'others' (for example, 'the Vietnamese people' , as in 1b, p. 136). Quite a few stories start with a Vietnamese saying, introduced as new information, for example, 'In Vietnam, it is said that because one weds only once, the wedding should give no cause for regret or complaint.'

Preconceptions about Vietnam, or more generally the 'Orient' (as in the example of the admired teacher above), are one kind of theme considered familiar and interesting to the reader. Comparisons between Vietnamese and Western traditions or practices are another. The example below explicitly envisages the global readership

('Ascot to Melbourne, Hong Kong to Dubai') and contains information that would be unnecessary for Vietnamese readers (for example, the region where the ethnic minorities mentioned live). Specific cultural detail is deleted or generalised, although a few details are retained for the sake of *couleur locale*, in a judicious mixture of the exotic and the familiar (and, as it happens, also the local and the global):

	(1b) Ask most Vietnamese people what their favourite sport is, and the answer is sure to be football – it's a national passion, almost a religion, and nobody is immune.
	(2b) But just because Vietnam's number one sport is the 'global game' doesn't mean the country doesn't have a few national sports of its own.
	(3b) They may not have the high profile of soccer, tennis or the martial arts, but they are still considered an integral part of the nation's traditional culture.
	(4b) Unsurprisingly, these sports aren't totally unfamiliar. Most sports all round the world tend to use bats, balls, boats or animals, and they basically either pit people against each other in a race, or in a head-to-head skills contest.
	(5b) But it's the local flavour that makes each country's version of these games unique.
(1a) Horse racing has become the festivity of many ethnic groups such as Taa, Dao, Mong.	(6b) Take horse racing, for example. It's practised everywhere from Ascot to Melbourne, Hong Kong to Dubai.
(2a) When there is news about a horse racing the village is filled with pleasure.	(7b) But head up into the northern mountains of Vietnam, and you'll find the Taa, Dao and Mong doing it, too.

(3a) The girls from Mong and Dao ethnic minorities prepare their best clothes for the occasion. (4a) The young men prepare good young grass for their horses. (5a) They even give their horses earth jingsen and other herbs to drink. (6a) They are massaged according to the traditional method so that they can gallop well in the competition.	(8b) A whole village will hum with excitement when a horse race is in the offing. The younger villagers can hardly conceal their joy, and preparations are frenzied. (9b) The girls from the Mong and Dao ethnic minorities prepare their best clothes for the occasion. (10b) The young men prepare top-notch fodder for their horses. They even give their horses ginseng and other herbs to drink and traditional massages to improve their performance.

In the example below the description of a landscape is rewritten to bring it closer to Western travel journalism in both style and content. Note how the deletion of the 'house roofs' and the 'fishing hamlet' removes the local inhabitants and makes the landscape more 'unspoilt' and Edenic:

Amidst the deep blue colour of the sea and sky, a dazzling white sand belt comes into sight with a coconut-tree grove interspersed with house roofs while by the sea-side lie nonchalantly a dozen of boats belonging to a quiet fishing hamlet nearby. Lang Co is really a precious nature-given gift!	It's everything you've ever imagined of paradise: coconut trees and the sound of water lapping at the hulls of small fishing boats.

Apart from the Vietnamese proverbs, four kinds of themes are favoured in *Vietnam News* feature leads:

1   *themes oriented to tourism*, such as ancient monuments, 'sun, surf and sand' locations (as in the example above), local festivals, and local crafts, music and dance;

2   *themes oriented to business and technology*: for example, the internet, mobile phones, branding, courses in business English, women entrepreneurs, and stories of enterprising individuals working their way up;

3   *Western perceptions of the Orient, and developing countries generally*: positive themes of this kind include respect for teachers and reaching extremely high age due to a healthy village life in an unspoilt part of the world. Negative themes include poverty and HIV-Aids orphans; and

4   *universal themes*, for example sport as a universal human pastime (see the example above), weddings, and simple everyday things like deciding what to eat today.

As part of Vietnam's move to enter the global market, the *Vietnam News* must adopt English, and the global 'journalism of information'. Young Vietnamese journalists are aware of the advantages this will bring them, and grateful for the help they get from the foreign sub-editors, some of whom stay in touch long after they have left Vietnam and continue to mentor their careers. But all this comes at a price. Local traditions and local values are backgrounded, becoming an exotic backdrop for global business and tourism, and some of the local tone of voice, with its playful poetry, is lost.

In one way, however, the *Vietnam News* remains very different from Western newspapers. It is run by the State. The Ministry of Information is in charge. As we have seen, this leaves its mark on the way language is used, despite the sub-editors' best efforts. So in this sense the English of the *Vietnam News* is perhaps a local variety of journalistic English after all.

Localisation[2]

For our second case study we return to *Cosmopolitan*, whose distinct writing style can be described as a composite of five styles:

1   the style of advertising;
2   the style of the fashion caption;
3   the style of expert discourse;
4   street style, the slang of the trendy and the young; and
5   conversational style.

In Chapter 3 we argued that lifestyles are expressed through 'composites of connotations', using dress as an example. The writing style of *Cosmopolitan* follows the same principle. It expresses the magazine's identity as a composite of the values connoted by:

•   advertising (connotation: consumer goods as associated with glamour, success, hedonism, sensuality, sexuality, etc.);

- fashion (connotation: fashion, glamour, attractiveness);
- expert discourse (connotation: reliable and trustworthy information);
- street language (connotation: young, up to date on the latest trends, a touch provocative); and
- conversational style (connotation: the way you talk with your friends).

All versions of the magazine must adopt this style, and all editors of local versions must go to New York to be trained by the Hearst Corporation. But in the end, it is the local editors who must somehow translate the *Cosmo* style into their own languages. They do so in many different ways, calquing the kind of neologisms American copywriters have developed, putting local genres of writing to new purposes, using focus groups to learn about the language of the local young and trendy people, arranging surveys to see which English words are known to their readers, and so on. And in developing a local adaptation of the *Cosmo* style, they are inevitably influenced by local language attitudes and local views of what is and what is not stylistically appropriate in women's magazines. In this section we describe the local *Cosmo* styles of four versions of the magazine, the Dutch, Spanish, Chinese and Indian versions. Of these only the Indian version is in English, and the others are in the 'local' languages.

Advertising style

Advertising style developed, not just to sell products and services, but also to model the identities and values of consumer society. It was the first 'corporate' language variety, and it played a key role in what Fairclough (1993) has called the 'marketisation' of discourse. Now that consumer society is coming into its own, so is advertising style. It is rapidly spreading beyond the confines of actual advertisements and infiltrating other genres, for instance the 'advertorials' of magazines and the burgeoning lifestyle sections of the print media. Displaced from its original function, advertising style connotes a preoccupation with consumer goods and their meanings and attractions, and with specific identities and values. We discuss three aspects of this style in a little more detail: direct address, evaluative adjectives and poetic devices.

Direct address

Advertising style uses direct address for both ideological and practical reasons. Ideologically, it has always sought to address *you*, personally and individually, and so to transcend its nature as a mass medium. Practically, advertisements need to persuade readers and viewers to do or think certain things, and hence they are replete with imperatives (which also address readers and viewers directly). This excerpt from Indian *Cosmopolitan* (October 2001) is not an advertisement, yet it is full of imperatives and instances of 'second person' address, even though there are also remnants of 'proper' magazine reporting style (for example, attributed statements such as 'Too many accessories can kill your style . . .', says hairstylist Jojo').

SUPERSLEEK STRANDS

'Too many accessories can kill *your* style. Sleek hair that is off *your* face looks really glamorous,' says hairstylist Jojo. *Fake* a poker straight mane with this simple tip from him. 'Before styling, *use* a good conditioner on *your* hair. *Blow-dry your* mane using a round brush. Then *spray* an anti-frizz product on *your* dry hair. *Divide your* tresses into sections and *run* a straightening iron through the whole length. *Finish* with a spritz of a shine enhancing product,' he suggests. Jojo likes L'Oreal Professionel's Tec-ni-Art Liss Control+, RS 339, Tec-ni-Art Spray Fixant Anti-Fizz, RS 399, and Tec-ni-Art Gloss Shine & Hold Spray, ES 399.

The Indian *Cosmopolitan* is published in English, but the same advertising-like features occur in non-English versions, for instance in the Dutch version (October 2001)[3]: '*Gebruik in plaats van een vloeibare eyeliner een potlood of oogschaduw die je mooi uitwerkt*' (literal translation: '*Use* instead of mascara an eye pencil or eye shadow which *you* apply beautifully'). Or in the Spanish version (October 2001): '*Aprovecha para exfoliar tu piel y recuperar su luz*' (literal translation: '*Take* advantage to exfoliate *your* skin and recuperate its glow'). Or in the Chinese version (October 2001): '*Fu yu pi fu tan xing, gai shan song chi qu xian*' (literal translation: '*Give your* skin elasticity, *tighten* those loose curves').

Adjectives

Adjectives play a key role in advertising style because many adjectives can apply both to the advertised product (the signifier) and to the values it signifies. For instance, in the US version (October 2001): 'Dramatic, passion-inspiring purple is the season's hottest hue. To instantly make any outfit feel more "fall 2002", just add a taste of plum.'

Here 'dramatic' and 'passionate' can both be seen as a description of the colour (the signifier) and as a 'mood' or 'personality trait' that the reader can express by means of the colour. Similarly in the Dutch version of the magazine (October 2001):

Heerlijk warme, zachte stoffen, lieve bloemen en zoete pastels in combinatie met wit. Zo wordt je huis een op-en-top winterpaleis, voor het ultieme prinsessengevoel.

('Deliciously warm, soft fabrics, darling flowers and sweet pastels in combination with white. That's how your house becomes a winterpalace, for the ultimate princess-feeling.')

Clearly adjectives like 'warm', 'darling' and 'sweet' can apply to the fabrics as well as to the reader who chooses them to decorate her home, that is, the 'princess' in her 'winterpalace'. This ambiguity gives the adjective a key role in adverting. It welds together the signifier (the colour) and the signified (the personality traits of the user), making them seem like two sides of the same coin. Cook (1992: 162) has commented in some detail on the referential ambiguity of adjectives in advertising.

Poetic devices

Advertising style also makes abundant use of poetic devices. Here is another example from the Indian *Cosmopolitan* (November 2001):

> **Flaunt that gorgeous body:**
> A sure shot way of upping your sinister sister image is showing off that bold bod – the right way. Give up the tedious treadmill at the gym for a sexy stretchy session of yoga to attract attention to all the right places.

Note the alliterations and half rhymes: 'sinister sister image', 'bold bod', 'tedious treadmill', 'sexy stretchy session'.

This use of poetic devices has again both a practical and an ideological function. 'Recall' is a major practical problem in advertising, and a major theme in its trade and research journals. How can we make sure that people will remember the brand, the product, the message? Poetic devices (and music) can help. In societies without alphabetic writing, knowledge had to be stored in memory and, therefore, often took the form of epic poems, with standard meters and an abundance of poetic devices (Ong, 1982). We can see this mnemonic function of poetic devices in the few traditional proverbs and sayings we still remember, for example in the parallelisms and repetitions in 'Red in the morning, shepherd's warning, red in the night, shepherd's delight.' Advertising has revitalised the tradition with its ear-catching language and musical jingles.

But poetic devices also make advertising style more entertaining and pleasurable than, for instance, technical descriptions of products, or instruction manuals. Advertising style pioneered 'edutainment', the combination of instruction (for instance, on how to make yourself beautiful or how to keep your teeth white) and pleasure, thereby undermining the traditional split between the serious and the popular, between high art and low art – and between the higher and lower classes and their different tastes (think also of the way advertising has incorporated high art, classical music, etc.). Advertising's emphasis on pleasure is, therefore, not just expressed through the pleasurable activities it portrays or alludes to, but also through its linguistic style.

This theme is closely related to another aspect of advertising, its *transgressive* nature. Advertising is deliberately unconventional, deliberately bent on breaking rules and defying taboos, as in the above quote where women are encouraged to flaunt their femininity unashamedly. Again this is not just a matter of content, but also of style. Advertising style also breaks rules of spelling (*'Mudd. Pure Inddulgence'*), grammar (*'B&Q it'*), and vocabulary – by concocting often punning neologisms: examples from the October 2001 US *Cosmopolitan* include *'bootylicious'* and *'denim-ite'*. The Chinese version of the magazine delights in creating such neologisms, such as:

> *yan yi zhen wo mei li.*
> ('Show me real charm.')

> *mi mei du zhu.*
> ('Gamble on glam.')

> *yi tou hu mei de jon se juan fa ji yi shuang lan bao shi ban de yan tong*
> ('foxy-charming curly hair and diamond-blue pupils').

And so does the Dutch version. One of us grew up in the Netherlands and can remember how neologistic compounds such as *winterbleek* ('winter-pale'), *natuurzacht* ('nature-soft'), and superlatives such as *krachtproteïne* ('power-protein') and *superlicht* ('super-light') were first introduced when commercials began to appear on Dutch television in the 1960s. He was not the only one who felt it forced the Dutch language and sounded alien – but in time that perception has paled.

This breaking of rules is always tongue-in-cheek, so that we can at once enjoy the transgression and dismiss it as 'not serious', 'only a joke', 'ironical'. The message is at once received and denied. Many lifestyle sociologists and cultural analysts see irony and self-parodying as a key feature of modern lifestyle identities, characteristic of postmodernity. In advertising they have played an important role for a long time, traditionally to allow advertisers to appeal quite openly to the consumer's greed, envy and lust – and get away with it.

But in this respect there are differences between the localised versions of the magazine. The Indian version takes the tongue-in-cheek approach to extremes, as if to make it absolutely clear that it's only a game, accompanied by much nervous laughter and giggling. Compared to the USA and Western Europe, India is still very much a man's world, where the gospel of *Cosmopolitan* has by no means been fully accepted. The Spanish version, on the other hand, is more subdued and serious. The use of rhyme and alliteration is for the most part restricted to the headlines, and the body of the texts uses a more formal style. The subtitle of the magazine, for instance, is not 'Fun Fearless Female' as in the USA and the UK, but 'The Woman who is Changing the World'. In Spain there is still a reluctance to mix information and entertainment. There are, for instance, no tabloid newspapers, and attempts to introduce them failed within a few weeks (Papatheodorou and Machin, 2003). And there are also well-patrolled boundaries between high culture and popular culture. Members of the editorial staff of the magazine stress that they seek to take the business of women's status in society seriously as Spain is still quite sexist, and the magazine often carries items on further education for women and women's rights which would never appear in the US or UK versions. This seriousness is not only a matter of content, but also of style. In Spain it is very important to show your level of culture and education through the way you speak and write. Introducing elements of 'street language' in your speech is not done.

The Chinese version, on the other hand, has adopted the *Cosmo* style with enthusiasm: 'Let's compete to see who is more joyfully casual.' There are economic reasons for this, because they see it as a style that will attract advertisers. At the same time, in creating a Chinese version of *Cosmo* 'poetics' they draw on classical Chinese styles, such as the symmetrical arrangements of words in the 'antithetical couplet', rather than on Western poetic devices. Apparently market reform has been accompanied by a revitalisation of traditional forms in China, for instance a return of traditional characters (Scollon and Scollon, 1998), even in popular culture texts imported from the USA, Hong Kong and Japan (Nakano, 2002).

> *Yue guang zhi wen, mi zi zhi lian*
> ('Moon light's kiss, mi zi's love')

> *Zai sheng huo zhong, mei li de xiao, you ya de chou*
> ('In life, beautifully smile, gracefully worry')

The style of the fashion caption

The style of the fashion caption has much in common with advertising style, including the use of direct address, adjectives and poetic devices, yet it is instantly recognisable as a style of its own (the examples are from the October 2002 US version).

> Dramatic passion-inspiring purple is the season's hottest hue. To instantly make any outfit feel more 'fall 2002', just add a taste of plum.

> Check out these stellar deals on faux fur – the season must-have that'll keep you feeling cosy and looking foxy as hell.

> A sweet peasant skirt and sexy tank look lovely on a low-key date at the movies or a dive bar.

As Barthes (1983) has shown, the fashion caption is a 'metalinguistic' statement, an entry in an ongoing, constantly changing and playfully written dictionary of fashion. It links a signifier (an outfit, or an item of clothing, or some aspect of it, for example a colour) to a signified, in this case, to either or both of two kinds of signified: first, the simple assertion 'this is in fashion', which can be phrased in a myriad of ways (for example, 'the season's hottest', 'feel fall 2002', 'the season must-have'); and/or second, a meaning which either indicates, for instance, the type of activities or the time of day for which the outfit is suitable ('a low-key date at the movies or a dive bar'), and/or a 'mood' or 'personality trait' ('dramatic', 'passionate', feeling cosy', 'foxy', 'sweet', 'sexy', lovely'). It does so in a way which is 'imperative' ('must have') and inescapable, an edict that must be followed, yet at the same time playful and pleasurable ('hottest hue', 'feel fall', 'look lovely on a low-key . . .'), so that the fashion caption, like advertising style, is a proto-form of 'edutainment', of learning what to do in a playful, pleasurable and entertaining way. Originally confined to actual fashion spreads, the style of the fashion caption, with its function of introducing people to the latest symbolic meanings of consumption goods, has now infiltrated many other domains, so as to connote, wherever it goes, the overriding importance of being in fashion and up to date.

The style of the expert

Cosmopolitan style is shot through with the style of the expert, whether it is that of the psychologist, the beautician, the dietician, or the *trend deskundige* ('trend expert'), for example Hilde Roothart ('from the *Trendslator* company'), who is quoted in the Dutch version of *Cosmopolitan* (October 2001: 74) as distinguishing between people who 'make their own style' and people who 'slavishly follow styles' and who concludes: 'Really cool people are not followers. They are the vanguard. They think of new things and make new combinations. I expect we are at the start of a period which stresses originality, being creative instead of following others.'

Some of the key characteristics of expert style include a more formal vocabulary, with technical terms (for example, 'anger management' and 'inferiority complex'), a preference for abstract and general nouns (for example, 'the phenomenon of gossip' instead of just 'gossip'), a limited vocabulary of verbs (mostly 'be', 'have' and 'mean' and their synonyms) and an objective, third-person form of address which, in magazines like *Cosmopolitan*, often contrasts with the second-person address that derives from advertising and conversational style. Here is an example of a journalist using elements of expert style (Dutch *Cosmopolitan*, October 2001). Note the shift from the 'subjective' second person in the first sentence to the 'objective' third person in the second sentence:

> *We kennen allemaal . . . de buikpijn, het schaamtegevoel en de boosheid als je hoort dat jij degene bent over wie de verhalen gaan. Het fenomeen roddelen heeft een slechte reputatie, het woord an sich heeft dan ook een negative betekenis.* ('We all know . . . the pain, the shame and the anger when finding out that *you* are the butt of the stories. As a result the phenomenon of gossip has a bad reputation, and the term on its own a negative meaning.')

Apart from the style of the psychologist, as in the example above, *Cosmopolitan* also draws on the style of the doctor, the beautician, the dietician, and so on. Here a journalist uses the style of the expert dietician, in the Dutch version (October 2001):

> *Soms sla je in alle haast een maatijd over. En soms is het verlangen naar een vette snack sterker dan het gezonde verstand. Het gevolg: veel Nederlanders krijgen te weinig mineralen en vitaminen binnen. Bijna iedereen mist wel iets, blijkt uit onderzoek van TNO.*
> ('Sometimes you skip a meal. And sometimes your desire for a greasy snack is stronger than your common sense. The result: many Dutch do not consume enough minerals and vitamins. Almost everybody lacks something, according to research by TNO.')

And here is the style of the beautician, in the Spanish version (October 2001):

> *La piel de los labios es muy finita, no tiene glándulas sebáceas, de manera que no produce lípidos o grasa como el resto de la piel y por esa razón se encuentra más desprotegida.*
> ('The skin of the lips is very fine and does not have sweat glands and so does not produce its own oils like the rest of the skin. Therefore it finds itself unprotected.')

In its use of expert style, the Spanish version is again more conservative. It does not like mixing expert style with other styles. This makes the expert information in the magazine more authoritative and 'top down', and again expresses the importance that the Spanish attach to formal knowledge and the use of 'proper' style in information-oriented writing.

The style of the street

Being up to date is an important aspect of lifestyle. Both the consumer goods and the identities and values they express are often short-lived and in need of constant updating. This can be connoted by 'street' vocabulary, by using a sprinkling of the latest slang expressions of the young and the trendy. As mentioned, many editorial teams seek out such expressions by organising focus groups with young and trendy locals.

The US version is full of slang of this kind: 'for a smokin-hot style', 'showing off your gams' (i.e. breasts), 'if you have a good butt', 'mattress-mambo sex', and so on. And, as has already been seen, the Indian version takes it to extremes, with 'vamp varnish' for nail polish, 'mane' for hair, 'smoochers' or 'pouters' for lips, 'chicas', 'sirens', 'vixens', 'babes' and 'chicks' for girls, and so on. In many non-English versions, trendiness is almost synonymous with the English language. The Dutch version, for instance, is full of English words (in the translations we have italicised the words that were in English in the original):

Saaie novembermaanden vragen om een lekker opvallende make-up, die niet ophoudt bij een beetje mascara en gekleurde lippen. Smoky eyes, roze wangen en lippen, en vooral: glamorous glans!
('Dull November months call for a nice eye-catching make-up which doesn't stop at a little mascara and coloured lips. *Smoky eyes*, pink cheeks and lips and above all: *glamorous* gloss!')

Een roze blush op je wangen geeft je winterbleke gezicht een warme gloed. Plaats de blush hoog op de wangen voor het gewenste effect.
('A pink *blush* on your cheeks gives your winter-pale face a warm glow. Place the blush high on the cheeks for the desired effect.')

The Chinese version also makes a lot of use of English – and employs market research to make sure the readers know the English words:

nu ren yu shou dair de guan xi ke yi shi hen ou miao de, si best friend you si fan
('The relation between women and their handbags can be very subtle, like a *best friend* and also like a *fan*.')

ni de mei li Must-Have shi shen me?
('What is your beauty *Must-Have*?')

fei yang shen cai shi party qian shi party hou?
('Glowing with health and radiating vigour, before and after the *party*.')

The Spanish version, on the other hand, avoids slang. Although it occasionally modifies words (for example, 'protagonista' to 'prota') to give a youthful feel, this remains the exception rather than the rule. In the main, the Spanish version prefers a formal, traditional and homogeneous style.

Conversational style

Cosmopolitan also draws on conversational style, to add a sense of informality to the stylistic mix. Conversation is essentially private speech, dialogue between equals. Yet, ever since the 1920s, elements of conversational style have systematically and deliberately been introduced in public communication, where they can give a flavour of equality to forms of communication that are in fact deeply unequal, for instance media communication (where viewers and listeners cannot talk back) and political communication.

David Cardiff (1989) has documented how, during the late 1920s, the BBC quite deliberately developed a conversational style for radio speakers, complete with fully scripted hesitations and errors, so as to sound more 'natural', and to soften the new intrusion of public speech into private living rooms. He also showed how, in the early days of BBC radio, 'vox pops' were fully scripted – and then read in the studio by taxi drivers with Cockney accents – in time 'people-in-the-street' would learn to produce exactly the same kinds of vox pop 'spontaneously', without the need for a script. In the USA the 'spontaneous' reactions in entertainment radio programmes and advertisements were also predesigned, as in this excerpt from a 1920s' script (Barnouw, 1966: 168): 'I am so happy to be here. I do these exercises every morning and I am sure I keep my figure just through these exercises. Thank you [GASP OF RELIEF]. My gawd, I'm glad that's over.'

A decade later, in Nazi Germany, Goebbels would exhort radio speakers to use conversational speech and local dialects so as to 'sound like the listener's best friend' (Leitner, 1980: 26). As noted by Bell and van Leeuwen (1993: 36):

> A new form of public speech developed, a genre which retained the logical structure and advance planning of the formal public monologue speech, but mixed it with elements of informal, private conversation – in a planned and deliberate way, and in order to develop a new mode of social control.

Politicians also started to use the conversational style, as part of an attempt to present themselves to voters as ordinary people, 'just like you and me' – for instance Roosevelt's famous 'fireside chats' of the 1930s. Everywhere the traditional boundary between the public and the private, a boundary intimately connected to style, was erased. In *Cosmopolitan* this is also the case, not just because the magazine uses the same discourses to represent the public life of work and the private life of love, as we saw in Chapter 4, but also by using elements of conversational style. Local versions of the magazine have followed suit. The Chinese version, for instance, makes much use of conversational idioms which formerly would not have been used in writing:

du yi wu er ('the only one in the world')

zong qing xiang shou ('enjoy to one's most')

nong jia cheng zhen ('Let false become true')

The following excerpt from a Dutch *Cosmopolitan* editorial (October 2001), uses a wide range of conversational devices: incomplete sentences, contractions like '*m'n'*, typical conversational fillers like '*je weet wel'* ('you know'), slang words like '*tutten'*, informal spellings like '*friet'* (instead of 'frites', the official, French, spelling), trendy evaluatives like '*onwaarschijnlijk fantastisch'* ('implausibly fantastic'), indications of intonation and timing ('*heeeel'*), and so on. In many ways it sounds just like a trendy contemporary Dutch conversation, but it isn't. It is an editorial in which the writer has cleverly worked in the highlights of the month's issue:

Ben ik raar?
Vorig weekend was ik bij m'n Antwerpse vriendin Linde. Letter tutten samen.
Je weet wel, eerst winkelen, dan mossels met friet lunchen en het hele leven
doornemen. Beetje over de liefde, beetje over de lijn, en heeeel veel over de
nieuwe kleren die we nog willen. En over Cosmo *natuurlijk. Ik raakte helemaal*
op dreef toen ik haar vertelde dat we zo'n onwaarschijnlijk fantastische
Bel&Win-actie hadden gemaakt.

('Am I weird?
Last weekend I was in Antwerp with my friend Linde. Having a nice girly time.
You know, bit of shopping first, then lunch with mussels and chips and discussing
the whole of life. Bit about love, bit about the [waist]line, and looooots about
the new clothes we still want. And about *Cosmo* of course. I really got going
when I told her about this absolutely brilliant Phone&Win action for our lingerie
special.')

To conclude, we have tried to show that *Cosmopolitan* style is a hybrid of different
styles, chosen for the connotations they bring, for the way they help express the
magazine's identity and values. Like the media styles of the 1920s and 1930s, this
style has been quite deliberately designed. And although local versions adopt it in
their own specific ways, overall it is a *global* style. The local languages may differ,
but the identities and values conveyed by the style do not. Like the Bible in the
colonial age, the message is translated into many languages and adapted to the local
circumstances and sensitivities of many different markets, but never to the degree
that the essential global economic and ideological interests behind it are lost from
sight.

Questions

1   Get hold of a newspaper article and an article from a magazine for young people
    in a language other than English. The two articles should be about the same
    topic, and the topic should be of global interest (for example, the internet). List
    the English words in each article. How do they differ in number and kind?
2   Compare the language of the news in three television news programmes: (1)
    a global programme such as CNN; (2) a local commercial channel; and (3) a
    local (national or regional) public channel. Transcribe a few minutes from each
    and list the more formal and the more informal words and grammatical
    constructions in each. How do the programmes differ in the way they mix formal
    and informal language?
3   In the in-flight magazines of their national airlines and their official tourist
    brochures, smaller countries must describe themselves to others in the same
    'distanciating' way as the journalists of the *Vietnam News*. Get hold of an in-
    flight magazine or official tourist brochure from a smaller country and find

examples of writers explaining things that would go without saying for locals, seeing interest in things that locals would take for granted, and so on. Show your examples to someone from that country and ask him or her what he or she thinks of the way they represent his or her country.

4   Many documents that used to be official and bureaucratic are redesigned to become more user-friendly. Find two texts that exemplify this contrast (for example, one job ad starting 'Applications are invited for a Lectureship in the Department of Marketing and Advertising . . .' and one starting 'With our reputation as one of the leading Centres of Excellence in Marketing and Advertising, we're making a lasting impact on the next generation of innovators and business leaders in our field, and you can help . . .'). Identify the main differences in linguistic style. Can the style of the 'user-friendly' text be interpreted as a 'composite of connotations'? If so, what styles does it mix, and what values do you think they connote?

Notes

1   This section reworks an earlier publication (van Leeuwen, 2006). Special thanks must go to Hans van Leeuwen and Emily Pettafor, without whose journalistic experience and knowledge of Vietnam it could not have been written.
2   A version of this section was published earlier as part of Machin and van Leeuwen, 2005a.
3   Translations are by Theo van Leeuwen (Dutch), David Machin (Spanish) and Sally Zhao (Chinese).

8 Global images[1]

Getty images[2]

In March 1995 Getty Communications, a company set up by investment bankers Mark Getty and Jonathan Klein, saw potential in a fragmented world image market. It made its first acquisition by buying the London-based Tony Stone Images, at that time one of the world's leading image agencies. Since then it has taken-over 20 more companies, spending about $1 billion. The company went public on the Nasdaq in 1996.

In 1998 Getty moved into digital imaging with the purchase of PhotoDisc. This revolutionised the use of image banks. When Getty first acquired Stone, image banking meant filing cabinets full of negatives. In the old-style catalogue system of image access, designers would have to search through catalogues to find the right image and then wait for the order to arrive. Or they could contact the image bank to describe what they wanted. A photo researcher would then do a search to find something that fitted the request. If successful, some samples would be sent, by courier, or by mail. If the designer did not like the images, the whole process would have to be repeated. With the Getty digital online service the same thing could be done quickly and cheaply. The industry's main costs, storage and distribution, were eliminated.

In 1999 Getty bought out Eastman Kodak's Image Bank stock for $183 million. In 2000 it spent $220 million to buy the Visual Communications Group, with its $90 million a year in revenue and hold on European markets. This included what, until then, with a collection of ten million images, was the biggest commercial library of images and film clips in the world (Reuters). In addition Getty licenses the National Geographic image collection which contains over ten million images. It now controls about a quarter of the world's $2 billion a year industry – an industry which used to consist of hundreds of small-scale regional and specialist companies. With their superior technological and financial clout and, of course, economy of scale, Getty boasts, there is no reason why they should not be able to move further into the territory of the remaining smaller operators. In some countries their current 25 per cent market share would be considered illegal. But the company is based in the USA where Microsoft has already paved the way, and at the global level there is no regulation for companies monopolising the world market in this way.

The key to Getty's success is a system that allows designers to simply type in search terms such as 'woman' and 'work' and also 'conceptual terms', as Getty describes them, terms like 'freedom' or 'independence'. The search will then take in some 350,000 images. They are mainly contemporary images but will also include some archival images. This will throw up pages of thumbnails of images associated with the search terms. Designers can then download the images to find one that fits in with their design, and pay online for the rights to use it.

While Getty is a North American company based in Seattle, over 40 per cent of its revenue comes from outside North America, where it draws customers from more than 50 countries. The company has websites in ten languages and wholly owned offices and agents in more than 50 countries, including Singapore, the Philippines, Korea, China, Lebanon, New Zealand, Russia, the United Arab Emirates, Europe and Latin America. Their images can increasingly be found all around the planet in adverts, magazines, promotional material, food packaging, newspapers, etc.

The other massive image bank is Bill Gates' Corbis which has about two million images online. However, Corbis deals mainly in news and archival images, while Getty focuses on licensing stock photography to designers and advertisers. Jonathan Klein, one of the founding directors, has said that old pictures do not bring in the same kind of money as stock photography, for example images of business meetings, skylines, or romantic couples. Initially Getty did not produce images, but used the agencies which had increasingly emerged to take advantage of the many images photographers do not use. More recently, however, Getty has started to actively search out images, informing photographers of the kinds of images they look for. Getty images, according to Morrish (2001), must be 'striking, technically superb, yet meaningless', so that they will 'never conflict with the client's message'.

Getty's promotional material reveals that the company 'is a leading force in building the world's visual language, through its innovative creation, sourcing and distribution of imagery, fonts and related services to the communications industry worldwide'. The company claims to produce and distribute images that touch people every day all over the world. If it does indeed have this kind of global reach, and this kind of influence on the images photographers now produce – and there is every indication that it does – we should take their claim seriously: Getty *is* a leading force in changing the world's visual language from one which emphasised the photograph as witness, as record of reality, to one which emphasises photography as a symbolic system and the photograph as an element of layout design, rather than as an image which can stand on its own. These changes in visual language are driven by the needs of global corporations, more specifically by the requirements of the concept of 'branding', as we will show in more detail below. We will now turn to an analysis of the Getty image, by focusing on three aspects:

1   its genericity
2   its 'timelessness', and
3   its low modality.

The generic image

Photographers we interviewed told us that images produced for Getty need to be general rather than specific. An image of a child with a cuddly toy, for example, can be used to illustrate childhood worries and traumas of many kinds and in many contexts – the more uses it has, the more revenue it is likely to generate. Until recently many key theorists of film and photography have argued that photographic images can never be generic. Contrasting photographic images with words, Christian Metz listed five key differences. One of them was that images can never be generic, while words are always generic and can only become specific in a given context: 'The image of a house can never mean "house" but only ever "Here is a house"' (Metz, 1971: 118). Image banks like Getty are changing this. They promote generic photography, photography which no longer captures specific, unrepeatable moments, photography which denotes general classes or types of people, places and things rather than specific people, places and things. They achieve this in three ways:

1   through decontextualisation
2   through the use of attributes, and
3   through the use of generic models and settings.

Decontextualisation

A key characteristic of the vast majority of Getty images is that the background is either out of focus, or eliminated altogether – many of the images are made in the studio, against a flat background. By means of such decontextualisation a photograph is more easily inserted into different contexts, and acquires a 'conceptual' feel. According to Kress and van Leeuwen (1996: 165) 'by being decontextualised, shown in a void, represented participants become generic, a "typical example", rather than particular, and connected with a particular location and a specific moment in time'. As a result, they say, decontextualisation is one of the hallmarks of the 'abstract coding orientation', an approach to image production in which the validity of images lies, not in their resemblance to visible reality, but in their adequacy with respect to the essential or general nature of the things depicted, and this means 'reducing the individual to the general, and the concrete to its essential qualities' (ibid., 170). We return to this in our discussion of the modality of these images.

If a setting *is* shown, it tends to be either a window, or a generic setting. Windows are favourites, especially when the view behind the window is light and out of focus, because they suffuse the image with a feeling of brightness and airiness. Photographers we interviewed said that this provided 'optimism', 'delicacy' and 'beauty'. Clearly the world of the image bank image is the bright and happy world of 'positive thinking' favoured by contemporary corporate ideology. If other settings are shown they tend to be *generic settings*. Generic interiors avoid clutter. Their style is the style of the showroom or the interior in the home decoration magazine, which must allow as many people as possible to imagine the space as their own. Often there is a sense of opulence, as in the airport lounge, or the modern designer shoe shop, or restaurant or media office in New York or London: expansive wooden floors, bright modern lighting, minimalist furniture highlighting perhaps one single, exciting colour. Exteriors also tend to be generic: mountains, the ocean, a nondescript city street that might be anywhere in the world.

Figures 8.1, 8.2 and 8.3 illustrate these features. All of them show ambiguous spaces. Two of them have the typical high lighting key. Figure 8.1 is coded by Getty as being an 'office space', yet it might also be a large studio space. Figure 8.2 is categorised as 'construction', but, apart from the power drill and goggles, not much construction is visible.

Figure 8.1 'Office space' (Getty)

Figure 8.2   'Construction' (Getty)

Attributes

Figures 8.1 and 8.2 also illustrate the importance of props for the generic image. Props are used to connote, not only the setting, but also the identities of the actors and the nature of activities, but in terms of 'types' rather than individual identities. An image might be categorised as 'research, science and technology' and show a woman in a white coat, wearing glasses, working at a computer. Take away the white coat, and the woman might as well be a business woman. In Figure 8.1, it is the computer that signifies 'office'. Since this attribute is so unspecific, a wide range of work settings can be signified by this image, allowing it to be used in articles dealing with frustration at work, relationship issues, competition and teamwork and in success stories as well as stories about people who are bored at work, or suffer stress through overwork. Again, Figure 8.2 is categorised as 'construction', but the only visual indicators of this are the drill and goggles.

Roland Barthes has said that the objects in photographs form a 'code of connotation' (1977: 22–3). He said:

> They constitute excellent elements of signification: on the one hand they are discontinuous and complete in themselves, a physical qualification for a sign, while on the other they refer to clear, familiar signifieds. They are thus the elements of a veritable lexicon, stable to a degree which allows them to be readily constituted into syntax.

To our knowledge, the implicit challenge to try and construct such a lexicon has not been taken up in the academic study of photography. But, as shown below, it has been taken up by Getty, whose code book provides precisely such a lexicon and syntax.

Models as generic people

In fashion, the faces of the models are often striking. In stock images, on the other hand, the models are clearly attractive, but not remarkable, because a striking face, an easily recognisable face, would be less easy to reuse. Not only casting, but also hairstyle, make-up and dress must help create genericity or, in terms of the 'social actor' theory we have used in earlier chapters, 'categorisation' (cf. van Leeuwen, 2000c: 95). As we saw in Chapter 5, visual categorisation is not an either/or matter, but depends on the degree to which cultural attributes and physiognomic stereotypes overwhelm or suppress people's unique, individual features. In Figures 8.1 and 8.2, the models have become interchangeable. Their individuality has been fully 'appropriated' by the type they are intended to represent, as Barthes would say (1973: 118). It is as if we are back in the era of medieval art, where saints and mythological or biblical characters were recognised, not on the basis of their physiognomy, but on the basis of their attributes (Jupiter carrying the thunderbolt, St Catherine carrying the wheel) or on the basis of their dress or hairstyle (for example, St Peter was an old man with hair and beard cut short and wearing a blue tunic and yellow cloak). In Figure 8.2 the model becomes a construction worker because of an attribute. Take off the safety goggles and remove the power tool and she could, with a drawing board, become an architect. Give her a lap-top and she is a business woman.

This use of a limited number of props leads to a highly clichéd vocabulary. In the article from which we have already quoted, Christian Metz also said that, while there is a limited stock of words in a given language, photographic images are infinite in number (1971: 118). But when we look at how the Getty image system represents a given category, for instance 'people' or 'settings', we find that it has a quite limited visual vocabulary. Science is indexed by a white coat, construction by a hard hat or safety goggles, office work by a computer or filing cabinet, and so on. This is particularly important in relation to the representation of women. In the early 1970s women began to be represented in the mass media as part of the corporate world. This corporate world, particularly during the 1980s, was mythologised as a world of innovation, ideas, groundbreaking cut-and-thrust business moves. Advertising and women's magazines often used images of women in formal suits (usually with short skirts) with either a mobile phone or a lap-top to index positions of power in business and the corporate cityscape. While the actual power of the woman and the reality of the world in which she operated were never formulated, the props did their work.

In the Spanish version of *Cosmopolitan* television there is a programme called *Sextot* where presenters talk frankly about sex, equating women's agency to a large degree with their sexuality, as does the magazine itself (Caldas-Coulthard, 1996). In the opening sequence, the camera moves along a digitally generated street towards the studio set. The street is urban, city high-rise. The camera lingers on the people carrying out their lives silhouetted in the windows. Many of them are women sitting at computers. In other words, the *Cosmo* viewer is constructed as an empowered woman through the attributes of open sexuality (which has its own history) and corporate technology.

Above we cited the words of one of Getty's founders who said that his company would have a defining role in the world's visual language. We are beginning to get a glimpse of the elements of this language. Until recently they were used only in restricted fields like advertising, fashion, and to some degree 'art' photography. Today they move out of these fields into the territory that used to belong to photojournalism and documentary photography – while paradoxically some advertising images go the other way (Benetton).

Timelessness

Closely related is the fact that image bank images tend to lose their origin in time and space. The past is reduced to a simple iconography, while the present becomes a symbolic world with a fairly stable global vocabulary.

The Observer of 9 June 2002 carried a Getty image of a woman, wearing a headscarf and holding a child. The image was used to illustrate the conflict in Kashmir which was highly newsworthy at the time – and it came from the *National Geographic* collection which is incorporated in the Getty image bank. As is typical of *National Geographic* images, it is highly stylised, with rich, deep colours and an out-of-focus background. Here it is used to give the reader a sense of the effect of the conflict on ordinary people. It has been argued convincingly (Lutz and Collins, 1993) that *National Geographic* offers a very Western view of the world, always emphasising enduring human values like motherhood, childhood, colourful clothes and always using exotic settings to emphasise the colourfulness of humanity – at the expense of truly revealing difference and political realities. *National Geographic* itself is open about the way it uses photography (Abramson, 1987; Bryan, 2001), yet here all this is concealed, as the image is transformed from being a witness, a record of moments in the world, into a symbolic representation of the vulnerability of the mother and child in conflict. Again, there is in principle nothing wrong with symbolic representations of this kind. We need both the abstract truth of the symbolic representation and the empirical truth of the record. What is problematic is the confusion between the two that characterises the current period of transition from the hegemony of the one to the hegemony of the other.

Frederick Jameson (1984) once described the effect that movies had on the distorted and mythical representation of America in the 1950s, with its small town diner, prom night, sneakers, nerds, etc. A limited number of icons came to represent the whole of a particular time, place and way of life. According to photographer Michael Wray,[3] stock images work this way, and we gradually come to accept them as showing us how the world really is. Professional photographers have no choice but to produce these kinds of images and no others. They receive a list of search categories from the image bank which they use as a guide. The images they produce may or may not carry their own signature. But a less distinguishable image which contains the required generic features will have more chance of re-use than an image which draws attention to itself. Wray suggested that even 'edgy' looking images have become a generic category. For a while perhaps denotation and connotation held each other in balance. Now, it seems, we are moving to a photography in which there is only connotation.

Modality

To explore a further characteristic of image bank images, we return to modality, a topic introduced in Chapter 6. Image bank images lack 'denotative excess'. According to Roland Barthes (1977: 50), it is (but now, perhaps, we need to say, 'was') typical of photographs that connotation can never exhaust them, 'there always remains in the discourse a certain denotation without which, precisely, the discourse would not be possible'. In other words, because photographs reproduce reality, they have an 'ineffable richness' of detail, an 'analogical plenitude' (ibid., 33) which guarantees that the photograph, however much it is a message with a connoted cultural meaning, also always contains a surplus of things that 'are just there', without contributing anything to the cultural meaning, other than that they 'naturalise' it by being there.

Exactly the same phenomenon happens in fiction, where certain realistic details, 'indices', as Barthes calls them (1977: 93), add nothing to the story line or its interpretation but serve only to heighten realism. In image bank images such realistic detail, such denotative excess, is eliminated. Apparently it is not needed any more. Apparently signification can, today, be more overt, and is no longer in need of naturalisation. Indeed, indexes of artifice, of *un*-reality, may be added, such as the emphasis on colour coordination, which gives away that the images are designed rather than 'captured'. In advertising images, such unreality was common already. The difference is that, today, the corporate image and its ideology also pervade the territory formerly held by the documentary photograph.

Kress and van Leeuwen (1996: 161ff.) have pointed out that verisimilitude has never been the only criterion for the truth of images. In scientific images and abstract art, images must be truthful, not in the sense that they resemble what they represent, but in the sense that they correspond to the underlying nature, or 'essence' of what they represent. This is why in scientific illustrations a simplified diagram might be more true than a highly detailed photograph. In such a context a photograph may be seen as showing only the surface, while diagrams can get underneath that surface by representing the structures common to a range of superficially different phenomena. Similarly a sculpture of a woman by Miró represents, not a specific woman, but 'woman' in general (as Miró saw her). In such images a reduction in the use of the means of visual representation signifies higher modality – a line drawing rather than a photograph, a blank background rather than a specific landscape, black and white rather than colour, plain colour rather than modulated colour, and so on.

Another possible validity criterion for images is their emotive resonance. Here what matters is neither the truth of verisimilitude, nor the abstract, 'essential' truth, but emotive, 'sensory' truth. From the point of view of photographic realism such 'sensory' images will be less realistic, but this time not because of a reduction, but because of an increase in the use of the means of visual representation: uncannily fine detail, richer colour, extra deep perspective. Think of Dali – or of food advertisements. And artists may, of course, combine the abstract and the sensory truth, for instance by using simplified forms but intensified colours, as did Miró. The same appears to be happening now with image bank images. They are, it seems, increasingly moving towards the abstract truth and, at the same time, the sensory, emotive truth. In doing so they are also increasingly moving *away* from the naturalistic, empirical truth.

Meaning potential

In the early 1960s, Roland Barthes (1977: 39) said that images are 'polysemous': 'they imply, underlying their signifiers, a "floating chain" of signifieds, the reader able to choose some and ignore others'. Words, he said, are needed to 'fix the floating chain of signifieds' and 'hold the connoted meanings from proliferating', in other words, to control the meaning of images by selecting single specific meanings for them and expressing these meanings verbally in captions. More recent theories have emphasised how readers, rather than captions, anchor the meaning of images and, indeed, verbal texts as well. The texts themselves embody a meaning *potential* (Halliday, 1978), a *set of possible meanings*, and which of these meanings will be actualised depends on the context – on who 'reads', where, when and for what reason. This is also the kind of 'reading', or rather 'using', that image banks cater for. Image bank images are not 'anchored' by a specific caption, but categorised in terms of a range of possible meanings, which are labelled by search words, words being more easily managed in a computer than images. These search words specify the kind of people, places and things shown in the image, and sometimes also the period and the type of photograph. In addition, they provide a connotative meaning potential, categorising the images in conceptual terms, as expressing 'freedom', 'romance', and so on.

The search terms play a key role in the visual language of Getty – and they can also provide a framework for our investigation of it. They allow us to ask, not 'What *does* this image mean?', but 'What, according to Getty, *can* be said with this image, and with the Getty visual language as a whole?' And this of course also allows us to ask: 'What *cannot* be said in the Getty visual language?' Here, for example, is a description of the meaning potential of a Getty image:

> Open Plan, Bending, Computer Equipment, One Woman Only, Businesswoman, Office Equipment, Telephone, Full Length, Profile, Office, Caucasian, One Person, Working, Desk, One Young Woman Only, Upside Down, Casual, 25–30 Years, Using Computer, Contortionist, Lap-top, Business Person, Barefoot, Side View, Indoors, Day, Business, Agility, Office Equipment, Flexibility, Horizontal, Photography, Balance, Uniqueness, Colour, Individuality

What we want to explore here is not these descriptions themselves, but the structure that underlies them, the structure of the Getty 'semantic field' (cf., for example, Lehrer, 1974). Given the size of the image bank, this is a very large task, and we, therefore, limit the exploration to just two issues. First we look at the semantic field of *settings*. Globalisation is often referred to as 'deterritorialisation'. Looking at the kinds of settings included in the image bank's descriptions might help us understand how deterritorialisation is actually realised in visual communication. Second, we will look at the 'conceptual themes' field.

Settings

We have found a total of 90 setting descriptors in the Getty image bank, and initially categorised them in terms of three broad categories: geography, interiors and exteriors. Here follow some observations.

Given the emphasis on generic images, it is perhaps not surprising that *specific* places are not only relatively underrepresented, but also form a highly unsystematic and incomplete list. Most importantly we found that while most major world cities form search categories on the image bank, the images that the terms throw up are mainly generic, in that they could be anywhere, or iconic, such as Mediterranean beaches, Latin American indigenous people with highly coloured clothing, or Paris as indexed by the Eiffel Tower, London as indexed by Big Ben, etc.

When we did our analysis in 2003 we found only the following descriptions for parts of the world or groups of countries: *Europe, Mediterranean countries, Asia, Middle East, North America, Latin America, Caribbean, Oceania,* and the following list of countries: *Senegal, Cameroon, Bali, Indonesia, Denmark, Norway, Canada, China, India, Jordan, Italy, Argentina, Guatemala, Spain, Greece and Russia.* It is clear that whoever designed the codebook did not assume that Getty's clients would be interested in looking for specific locations, and had no particular interest in creating a systematic database in this regard. Precise geographic location is haphazard, a leftover perhaps from the earlier days in which place and data were the key authenticating data of any documentary or news photograph. By and large, setting has, it seems, become irrelevant – with one exception, tourism. Not only are many of the places listed mainly of interest from the point of view of tourism, further investigation shows that typing in such a place name will bring up places of tourist interest, for instance a search for 'London' will bring up Tower Bridge, Buckingham Palace, and so on, as well as archive images of couples kissing and having fun in London's parks and streets, images which in all other respects have all the hallmarks of the generic image.

It should also be noted that many of the images categorised in terms of a particular location only carry generic indicators of that location. Mediterranean countries, for instance, are represented by slightly out of focus beach scenes, with a model posing. Figure 8.3, indexed as hailing from Western Guatemala, shows a mother carrying a baby, the mother only indicated by ethnic colour and the bundle of textiles she carries, and the background an empty sky. Clearly this image is not intended to document anything about Western Guatemala. It is included because of the way it can connote Western notions of childhood.

Other specific geographic search terms yield equally generic images.

More common than geographic search terms are generic terms for interior and exterior spaces. For example, rooms: *gym, living room, conference room, bedroom, office, school*; types of buildings: *swimming pool, temple, church, railway station, subway, delicatessen, market, noodle bar, café, igloo*; means of transport: *recreational boat, nautical vessel, passenger train, car*; city exteriors: *urban scene, city location, street, alley, square, sidewalk, subway platform, harbour, outdoor market, traffic jam*; and country exteriors: *rural scenes, beach, sea, river, water's edge, jetty, underwater, mountain range, field, ploughed field, village, road*. Some locations can be either in the city or the country: *backyard, fishing industry, running tracks*.

The interior spaces included here are all represented in generic form, as abstract spaces with a few props. Buildings, too, are unremarkable and unmemorable, with little in the design denoting their function, except when they are tourist attractions (as in the case of the igloo), when they feature in a period image (as is the case particularly with railway stations), and in the case of markets, where produce is represented in detail and with high modality, like the advertised products in advertisements (cf. Kress and van Leeuwen, 1996: 164). In the exteriors we note the emphasis on water, which is used a great deal to index freedom, relaxation and relationships. Water has a massive number of images in the image bank, often using the diffused high key lighting that is so characteristic of Getty images. Just as the mobile phone and the lap-top index work and business, so water indexes freedom, escapism and romance, as well as freshness and health. We get a sense here of the way corporate visual language incorporates 'new age' ideas. Connotations of serenity,

Figure 8.3 'Western Guatemala' (Getty)

escape and freedom bring a sense of 'philosophy' or even morality into the corporate world of branding and consumerism.

Finally, while the geographic terms form a haphazard collection, here the beginning of systematicity can be felt. Some of the search terms clearly have a hyponymic relation to others. There is, for instance, the distinction between '*indoors*', and '*outdoors*', with the latter again divided into 'urban scenes' and 'rural scenes', and with each allowing further subdivisions. This has the makings of a systematic taxonomy, entirely along generic and global lines, and entirely abstracting away from the specifics of specific places, except in the case of tourism.

Conceptual themes

When we did our analysis, we found a total of 81 'conceptual' search terms, and were able to categorise them in two main categories: mental states, and themes expressing core values associated with the people, places and activities shown. As we have already suggested, it is these which are the true raison d'être of stock images. As image bank contributor photographer Romilly Lockyer told us, the most important thing about image bank images is that they evoke moods and concepts. For this reason it does not matter much that the picture in Figure 8.3 tells us little if anything at all about Western Guatemala. What matters is that it says something about childhood innocence or cheekiness. The fact that it is also categorised as 'Western Guatemala' might help to tell the designer that the image is likely to have some ethnic content (itself usually indexed in the image by patterned, colourful clothing), which can be a useful corporate/consumer tool for bringing a kind of morality to products.

We have analysed conceptual search terms into four groups:

1   goals and motives;
2   positive characteristics of people, places, things and/or activities;
3   negative characteristics of people, places, things and/or activities; and
4   positive mental states and negative mental states.

Goals and motives all express positive moral values. These include social goals: *togetherness, friendship, love, protection*; a desire for knowledge and progress: *exploration, curiosity, innovation, growth, on the move*; states of mental and physical well-being: *spirituality, balance, relaxation, satisfaction, well-being*; and some other less easily classifiable terms: *freedom, fun, world culture, patriotism, tradition*.

It is immediately obvious that we have here a well-organised and systematic catalogue of the moral values of the new capitalism, values which play a key role in the age of branding where product ranges are associated with precisely this kind of values, so that companies no longer sell whisky, but friendship, no longer shampoo, but hope, and so on.

A Getty image of a woman walking along the seashore in a short dress is categorised under 'spirituality' as well as under 'calm people'. This is once again realised through the presence of water and soft, high key lighting. The model appears to be lost in the moment, but there is nevertheless a horizon, a distant goal, in the shot.

Positive characteristics of people, places, things and activities are often task-oriented: *endurance, strength, agility, determination, concentration,* but they may also be aesthetic/moral, for example *simplicity, purity, elegance, harmony, grace,* or focused on mental resources: *creativity, learning, expertise,* which does not mean that *vitality* and *sensuality* are forgotten. Again we see values here that fit in well with the new global corporate ideology, while the negative characteristics included point at the possible risks of this ideology: *greed, vanity, pride, indulgence, escapism, aggression.* Note how many more positive terms there are: positive thinking is itself a crucial moral value in the corporate/consumerist world.

Positive mental states for women include both affective states such as *pensive, shy, affectionate, cheerful, content, exhilarated, ecstatic,* and cognitive ones such as *anticipation, memories, nostalgia, conflict,* while negative ones include *disappointment, fear, loathing, fury, suspicion, hysteria, rejection.*

The pictures that realise these categories focus on behaviours, which are themselves quite systematically categorised. We see women in a range of postures including *sitting, standing, leaning, lying down,* with a range of facial expressions, such as *looking at camera, staring, frowning, sulking, watching, thinking,* and involved in activities such as *kicking* and *jumping.*

Freedom

We end this chapter with a look at some of the images that realise the conceptual theme of 'freedom'. Freedom has been, and still is, a key concept in the history of Western thought, the basis of human rights, including the right of freedom of expression. In the Getty visual language it has a consistent iconography. Figures 8.4, 8.5 and 8.6 are representative of many hundreds of images catalogued as expressing 'freedom'.

The images in Figures 8.4 and 8.5 are clearly stock images with all the hallmarks of the generic image. There is no background apart from the blue sky – in freedom images blue skies are a must. The model is indistinct. If she were given a pair of glasses and a lap-top she could be a businesswoman. The focus is not so much on her as on the fact of her suspension mid-frame. Jumping, or the raising of limbs generally (arms raised to heaven, legs raised on a bicycle) equals freedom, which, therefore, is interpreted as a subjective experience, a *sense* of freedom; the images are also categorised as expressing *vitality* and *exhilaration,* both of which have many of the same indexes in the image bank.

In Figure 8.6 freedom is again expressed through bodily movement, as freedom to *move* – in none of the images is there any sense that freedom might have something to do with political belief or ideology. A woman is walking through meadows, jumping,

Figure 8.4   'Freedom' (Getty)

spinning, waving her arms. Again there are the blue skies, and the sea – both often co-categorised with 'freedom', 'serenity', 'relaxation' and 'spirituality'. Freedom in other images also equates freedom with the freedom to move but by using images of highways and classic US sports cars, motorbikes, drawing on the Hollywood road movie romance of get-up-and-go, or cycles being ridden down hills with the legs of the rider raised.

In the Getty visual language, concepts like 'freedom' and 'exhilaration' are overwhelmingly realised through the energetic physical activities of individuals, although there are also many American flags and Statues of Liberty with or without war planes flying overhead. American freedom is a mood, a passing feeling, expressed

Figure 8.5 'Freedom' (Getty)

by jumping or other physical activities, and a concept drawing on 'new age' ideas of serenity and simplicity. An important part of the way branding works is by associating a product or company with morally loaded values. As a result, there is a market for the visual expression of such concepts, whereas there is less of a market now for visuals that provide concrete and specific descriptions, the visual of an earlier era of photography and of a time in which products were sold on the basis of their use value.

The semantics of the Getty visual language is a world of morality as 'mood', where freedom equals jumping and independence is a fashion statement. Needless to say, 'capitalism' is not a search term, and 'globalisation' throws up romantic

Figure 8.6 'Freedom' (Getty)

images of global business. There is no category 'welfare state' and 'poverty' is only reflected in black and white archive images, so that an article on poverty has little choice but to use 1950s' images in their layout, which effectively helps create a cushion against the reality of poverty. Spanish *Cosmopolitan* editor Sarah Glattstein Franco told us that image bank symbolic images, as she called them, can 'lift even the most depressing article'. By way of example she showed us an article on what happens in Spain when you need an abortion. Accompanying the text were two images, both generic image bank images. They showed young models in underwear, against blank backgrounds with high key lighting, looking thoughtful.

Global visual language

Images of this kind are globally distributed and used. As a result visual language becomes demonstrably more homogenised, generic and limited in its iconography. Will we still be able to recognise 'work' without the lap-top, 'freedom' without someone jumping, 'ethnicity' without bright and multicoloured clothing? Image banks like Eye-Wire, incorporated into Getty, offer designer categories like 'world family' where beautiful young healthy people smile and leap about in multi-ethnic colourful groups; 'women on top' where women in white-light diffused abstracted rooms speak on telephones or laugh with other women while pointing at computer screens; 'young at heart', where 60+ people cycle along beaches or spray each other with garden hoses; 'attitude', where young 'happening people' in grunge fashion skateboard with shades in front of fluorescent psychedelic backgrounds – in short, a world organised into consumer categories and easy clichés.

   Photographers and art directors told us that the role of the image has changed. Photographs used to be much more descriptive. They would show the viewer details of places, people and activities. Further information would be given in the accompanying text. In contemporary publishing there is a tendency for the photograph to be used as part of the page layout alongside fonts, colours and borders. Headings on texts may use the same colour as the clothing or lips in the photograph. This will be true for ads, features and fashion alike. The image will be used symbolically to represent the essential message of article, but this does not necessarily mean that the photographic message is the same as that of the verbal text. Vietnam's *Woman's World* contained an article on checking for mouth cancer. It was illustrated with an image of the face of a young woman lightly touching her lips, smiling excitedly, against a background suffused with white light. For such an article one might have expected a more serious image. But this was a page for health promotions, which contained several such abstract image bank images. It had to symbolise health, beauty and the exhilaration of life. And the images had to be colour coordinated with the rest of the layout. As a result, the page looked very attractive. The world of consumer health products is a very pleasant one. Even mouth cancer, showing the magazine's serious role, is lifted into controllability in this world. Glamour, health, fun, energy, control and consumerism all become features of the same landscape.

At first glance the image bank seems to offer an unlimited vocabulary with their several hundred thousand online images. Further exploration quickly led us to realise its limitations. The image bank is an ideologically prestructured world, the categories it uses a catalogue of clichés and marketing categories. Phenomena which lie outside of this are excluded. All this calls to mind the critique of standardisation referred to in Chapter 2, when we discussed the work of Adorno (1941, 1991). Adorno was terrified by the way the culture industry, due to the logic of economics and economies of scale, fostered homogenisation and reproduced easily recognisable and easily digestible patterns. And he realised the importance of predictability. He realised that the culture industry needs predictability as it needs to predict the market, and that it can increase predictability by presenting the audience with a preset conceptual space that will allow them to recognise the product. All this in turn would remove the possibility for creativity and innovation.

In this chapter we have seen how image banks transform visual language along the logic of economies of scale, and how the images that sell best accord with existing consumer categories ('world family', 'women on top', etc.). Photographers, in order to make a living, have no choice but to produce images that fit in with these categories. We should be concerned about the effect of this increasingly stylised and predictable world on audience expectations of what the visual representation of the world should look like. We should be concerned about the fact that we no longer flinch when we see a posed, processed, stylised, colour-enhanced *National Geographic* image of a woman and child taken from Getty and placed on a page in *The Guardian* for a documentary feature on the Kashmir conflict.

Machin (2002) argued that we can think of society as a kind of conversation about the world and about life. There have been many ways of doing this – a vast range of conversations. The anthropological archive can be seen as a celebration of this. Today's mass media – and with it the Getty images – form a key part of this conversation. It is clearly in the interest of the global corporations that there should be one conversation only, with one shared language. Should we commend Getty for uniting humanity in this way? At the end of this book the questions with which we opened are as urgent as they were at the beginning.

Notes

1   An earlier version of this chapter was published as Machin (2004).
2   The information in this section relies on Dorfman (2002), an interview with photographer Allen Tannenbaum, and on Getty publicity and the Getty website.
3   Interview with the authors.

Conclusion

Are the media ushering in a global culture, and is it an American/Western culture? This is the question that has dominated the literature. It is not an easy question to answer, as it involves issues of 'diversity' and definitions of culture. Cultures have always been subject to processes of historical change. How do we defend local 'diversity' when it seems to imply, on the one hand, that cultures must remain static, but on the other hand that everyone, whatever their cultural background, should be able to take part in the advantages offered by consumer society? Are 'localism' and 'diversity' among the Western values disseminated everywhere by global media?

Equally complex is the question of the media's part in all this. Research has shown that large media conglomerates such as Disney can and do send their products around the planet, but also that some regional conglomerates rival the US giants. Does this mean that there is no single set of global values, as some have argued? The problem with this approach is that it does not address the precise nature of the products themselves and their take-up in different locations – how their formats shape the kinds of values they can transmit, and how local inflections can challenge the values embodied by global media.

The studies in this book set out to address questions of this kind, to ask where the transmission of global values happens, or even where it may be hidden. Exactly where does the local get modified? Exactly how can the local resist the global by taking on and adapting global formats? Exactly at what levels can local values and identities coexist with those that arrive when global conglomerates import their products or when local media create their own versions of these? It was our intention to demonstrate an approach through which we can, step by step, increase our understanding of these processes. But although we have only made some steps towards that aim, we feel we travelled far enough to begin to get at least a sense of what our answers might look like.

- There is a trend towards global domination by transnational media conglomerates, which are able to lobby and influence politics. Global trade regulation favours these conglomerates in every way. There is also a trend towards large media conglomerates dominating national and regional media. Much of the regulatory framework that has allowed the creation of these large globally acting corporations was designed in the USA and is related to their missionary view of spreading US culture, values and economic domination.
- Global media formats enter localities through a number of routes. Local media may copy global formats. Transnational corporations may buy up local media,

which will still be run locally but with differing degrees of centralised management. Localisers may be given different amounts of autonomy, depending on the political and economic relations between the producers of global media and the countries or regions for or in which they are localised. Over time, there may be in some regions a tendency towards greater globalisation, in others towards localisation, depending, again, on specific political and economic circumstances.

- Crucially, corporate media are driven by advertising revenue and must present a world that is in harmony with the message of advertising. Even where media might be set up to create alternatives, they soon find themselves short of funding and, therefore, short on quality content. Viewers and purchasers will then switch to higher quality ad-funded alternatives.

- Media genres, formats and technologies are increasingly globalised and homogenised. Such genres, formats and technologies are not neutral containers or distributors of content. They carry meaning and value themselves. Although they may carry local or localised content, the way this content is communicated transforms it and turns it into a surface phenomenon, a local variant of the same global message.

- Some locally originated media are specifically and explicitly conceived as political alternatives to global media (for example, computer war games produced by Hezbollah). They nevertheless use the same formats and technologies as the media they set themselves up against and they are, therefore, at least in part aligned to the values and identities of global media.

- Global media favour particular discourses which feature particular kinds of events, participants and settings, and which are usually in harmony with the interests of consumer capitalism. In the case of *Cosmopolitan* they recontextualise the social identities and practices of women, promising independence and empowerment in ways that are fundamentally linked to the consumption of goods and services in areas such as health, beauty, fashion and lifestyle.

- In global media, realms of life that were previously separate merge and operate by the same rules. Work, leisure and relationships are all dealt with strategically as we act to overcome defined problems with strategic solutions. Life becomes a business project where we must look for an edge in a world of competitors.

- Visual discourses are increasingly global, designed to fit in with the layout of advertisements and other global media messages, and focusing on the symbolic representation of the values and identities of late capitalist consumer society. It is also visually, through self-presentation (dress and other lifestyle attributes), that people can recognise others as belonging to the same dispersed lifestyle or taste communities. This is only one of the ways in which the importance of the visual increases in global media, while the importance of language decreases. Another is the attention to visual design in marketing strategies.

- The linguistic style of global media expresses the values and interests of corporations. Global media corporations enforce the principles of this style but leave its implementation to localisers (though to different degrees), thus allowing local 'accents'. This does not apply to visual style, where economic and technical factors threaten the survival of local production everywhere.

- Global media play a key role in fostering new 'lifestyle' identities through the way in which they align practices and values with the consumption of goods and services. Identity here becomes 'lifestyle identity', a cluster of preferred leisure time activities, attitudes and consumer choices. For the time being, these kinds of identity exist alongside older forms of identity, based on national and social groupings.

The mass media have always been used to create consciousness – in the past mostly by nation states, for purposes of legitimation. More recently the USA began to use media to spread its outlook and economic ambitions across the world. Even where the media are not actually American-owned, they are now deeply influenced by modes of production, formats and technologies that originated in the USA. By now American culture and consciousness is no longer just American. It has transformed itself into a global culture and a global consciousness. And while there are other global languages and cultures, it is, for the time being, the richest, the most powerful and the most pervasive.

So what of the increase of homogeneity and the loss of diversity? In part we still live in the world of national cultures, in which one specific ethnic group was usually dominant. In some parts of the world, global culture is slowly pushing national culture towards the margins, fixing it and hollowing it out, turning it into a surface feature, a tourist attraction and a museum exhibit. In other parts of the world it is still very much alive. But alongside the world of national cultures there is now the new global culture, and it fosters its own kind of diversity – a proliferation of choices and lifestyles that can easily incorporate and transform older, ethnic identities. How deep do these identities go? Can they satisfy the human need for identity and belonging? Or are they too fickle, too much subject to the winds of fashion?

Amidst all this, religious revivals are emerging. Religion is also a global phenomenon and can also allow difference and local variety – so long as its essential genres and formats of behaviour are adhered to. We have argued in this book that genres and formats are not neutral containers, and that they betray the most deep-seated values of cultural formations. It is in these deep-seated values that global consumer culture and religions may differ. Religions may favour submission over independence, obedience over power, serving others over satisfying the self. Such opposites have been coexisting human tendencies through the history of human culture. They need to be in balance with each other if we are to avoid, on the one hand, repression, and, on the other, a free fall into decadence. There are plenty of people on this earth who achieve that, despite everything. But the global media are not giving them much help.

References

Abramson, H.S. (1987) *National Geographic: Behind America's Lens on the World*, New York, Crown

Adorno, T.W. (1941) 'On Popular Music', *Studies in Philosophy and Social Science* IX(I)

Adorno, T.W. (1978 [1938]) 'On the Fetish Character in Music and the Regression of Listening', in A. Arato and E. Gebhardt (eds) *The Essential Frankfurt School Reader*, Oxford, Oxford University Press, pp. 270–99

Adorno, T.W. (1991) *The Culture Industry: Selected Essays on Mass Culture*, London, Routledge

Africa Watch (1990) *Somalia: A Government at War with its Own People: Testimonies about Killings and the Conflict in the North*, London, Africa Watch

Ang, I. (1985) *Watching Dallas – Soap Opera and the Melodramatic Imagination*, London, Methuen

Ang, I. (1994) 'Globalisation and Culture', *Continuum*, 8(2): 323–5

Appadurai, A. (1990) 'Disjunction and Difference in the Global Cultural Economy', *Public Culture* 2(2): 1–24

Barber, W.F. and Neale Ronning, C. (1963) *International Security and Military Power: Counterinsurgency and Civic Action in Latin America*, Columbus, OH, Ohio State University Press

Barnouw, E. (1966) *A Tower of Babel: A History of Broadcasting in the United States from 1953*, New York, Oxford University Press

Barthes, R. (1973) *Mythologies*, London, Fontana

Barthes, R. (1977) *Image, Music, Text*, London, Fontana

Barthes, R. (1983) *The Fashion System*, Berkeley, CA, University of California Press

Baskaran, L. (1994) 'The Malaysian English Mosaic', *English Today*, 37: 27–32

Beckham, D. (2000) *Beckham: My World*, London, Hodder and Stoughton

Bell, A. (1991) *The Language of News Media*, Oxford, Blackwell

Bell, A. and Garrett, P. (1998) *Approaches to Media Discourse*, Oxford, Blackwell

Bell, P. (1982) *Headlining Drugs: An Analysis of Newspaper Reports of Drug-Related Issues in the NSW Press, 1980–1981*, Sydney, NSW Drug and Alcohol Education and Information Centre

Bell, P. and van Leeuwen, T. (1993) *The Media Interview – Confession, Contest, Conversation*, Sydney, University of New South Wales Press

Benjamin, W. (1980) 'Der Erzähler', in *Illuminationen*, Frankfurt am Main, Suhrkamp Verlag

Berlo, D.K. (1960) *The Process of Communication*, New York, Holt, Rinehart and Winston.

Bernstein, B. (1990) *The Structuring of Pedagogic Discourse*, London, Routledge

Bettelheim, B. (1976) *The Uses of Enchantment: The Meaning and Importance of Fairy Tales*, London, Thames and Hudson

Bhabha, H. (1990) 'The Third Space in Identity', in J. Rutherford (ed.) *Community, Culture, Difference*, London, Laurence and Wishart

Blommaert, J. (2003) 'Commentary: A Sociolinguistics of Globalization', *Journal of Sociolinguistics* 7(2): 607–23

Bordwell, D. (1985) *Narration in the Fiction Film*, London, Methuen

Boyd-Barrett, O. and Rantanen, T. (eds) (1998) *The Globalization of News*, London, Sage

Bramstedt, E.K. (1965) *Goebbels and National-Socialist Propaganda 1925–1945*, East Lansing, MI, Michigan State University Press

Bruner, J. (1990) *Acts of Meaning*, Cambridge, MA, Harvard University Press

Bryan, C.D.B. (2001) *The National Geographic Society: 100 Years of Adventure and Discovery*, New York, Abradale Press

Busch, B., Hipfl, B. and Robins, K. (eds) (2001) *Bewegte Identitäten – Medien in transkulturellen Kontexten*, Klagenfurt, Drava Verlag

Burke, K. (1944/1971) *A Grammar of Motives*, New York, Prentice Hall

Butcher, M. (2003) *Transnational Television, Cultural Identity and Change: When*, London, Sage

Caldas-Coulthard, C.R. (1996) '"Women Who Pay For Sex. And Enjoy It." Transgression Versus Morality in Women's Magazines', in C.R. Caldas-Coulthard and M. Coulthard (eds) *Texts and Practices: Readings in Critical Discourse Analysis*, London, Routledge, pp. 250–70

Cameron, D. (2000) *Good to Talk? Living and Working in a Communication Culture*, London, Sage

Canning, P. (1996) *American Dreamers – The Wallaces and Reader's Digest*, New York, Simon and Schuster

Cardiff, D. (1989) 'The Serious and the Popular: Aspects of the Evolution of Style in the Radio Talk 1928–1939', *Media, Culture and Society*, 2: 31

Carruthers, S.L. (2000) *The Media at War*, London, Palgrave

Cels, S. (1999) *Grrrls! Jonge vrouwen in de jaren negentig*, Amsterdam, Prometheus

Chaney, D. (1996) *Lifestyles*, London, Routledge

Cook, G. (1992) *The Discourse of Advertising*, London, Routledge

Crystal, D. (1996) *The Cambridge Encyclopaedia of English*, 2nd edition, Cambridge, Cambridge University Press

Crystal, D. (2000) *Language Death*, Cambridge, Cambridge University Press

Crystal, D. (2003) *English as a Global Language*, Cambridge, Cambridge University Press

Dallal, J.A. (2001) 'Hizbollah's Virtual Society', *Television and New Media* 2: 367–72

Derrida, J. (1990) 'Faith and Knowledge', in J. Derrida and G. Vattimo (eds) *Religion: Cultural Memory in the Present*, Stanford, CA, Stanford University Press

De Swaan, A. (1991) *Perron Nederland*, Amsterdam, Meulenhoff

Dorfman, A. (1983) *The Empire's Old Clothes*, London, Pluto Press

Dorfman, A. and Mattelart, M. (1984) *How to Read Donald Duck – Imperialist Ideology in the Disney Comic*, 2nd edition, New York, International General

Douglas, A. and Malti-Douglas, F. (1994) *Arab Comic Strips – Politics of an Emerging Mass Culture*, Bloomington, IN, Indiana University Press

Drotner, K. (2001) 'Donald Seems So Danish: Disney and the Formation of Cultural Identity', in J. Wasko, M. Phillips and E.R. Meehan (eds) *Dazzled by Disney? – The Global Disney Audiences Project*, London, Leicester University Press, pp. 102–120

Durand, P. (1983) 'Rhetoric and the Advertising Image', *Australian Journal of Cultural Studies* 1(2): 29–62

Durkheim, E. (2002) *Suicide*, London, Routledge

Fairclough, N. (1993) 'Critical Discourse Analysis and the Marketization of Public Discourse', *Discourse & Society*, 4(2): 133–69

Fairclough, N. (1995) *Media Discourse*, London, Arnold

Featherstone, M., Lash, S. and Robertson, R. (eds) (1995) *Global Modernities*, London, Sage

Fernhout, J. (2004) *The Dutch Cosmopolitan – The Place of a Glamorous Magazine in a Calvinistic Society*, unpublished research report, Centre for Language and Communication Research, Cardiff University

Fish, S. (1980) *Is There a Text in This Class? The Authority of Interpretive Communities*, Cambridge, MA, Harvard University Press

Foucault, M. (1970) *The Order of Things*, London, Tavistock

Foucault, M. (1972) *The Archaeology of Knowledge*, London, Routledge

Foucault, M. (1981) *A History of Sexuality. Vol 1*, Harmondsworth, Penguin

Fowler, R. (1991) *Language in the News*, London, Routledge

Geertz, C. (1986) 'The Uses of Diversity', *Michigan Quarterly* 25(1)

Giddens, A. (1990) *The Consequences of Modernity*, Cambridge, Polity

Giffard, C.A. (1998) 'Alternative News Agencies', in O. Boyd-Barrett and T. Rantanen (eds) *The Globalization of News*, London, Sage, pp. 191–201

Goebbels, J. (1948) *Diaries 1942–43*, London, Hamish Hamilton

Gorman, R.F. (1981) *Political Conflict on the Horn of Africa*, New York, Praeger

Graddol, D. (1998) *The Future of English?*, London, British Council

Guyot, J. (2001) 'Disney in the Land of Cultural Exception', in J. Wasko, M. Phillips and E.R. Meehan (eds) *Dazzled by Disney? – The Global Disney Audiences Project*, London, Leicester University Press, pp. 121–34

Gyasi, I.K. (1991) 'Aspects of English in Ghana', *English Today* 26: 26–31

Hall, S. (1989) 'Cultural Identity and Diaspora', in J. Rutherford (ed.) *Community, Culture, Difference*, London, Lawrence and Wishart

Halliday, M.A.K. (1978) *Language as Social Semiotic*, London, Arnold

Harvey, D. (1989) *The Condition of Postmodernity*, Oxford, Blackwell

Heller, M. (2003) Globalization, the New Economy, and the Commodification of Language and Identity', *Journal of Sociolinguistics* 7(4): 473–93

Herman, E.S. and Chomsky, N. (1998) *Manufacturing Consent: The Political Economy of the Mass Media*, London, Pantheon

Hermes, J. (1995) *Reading Women's Magazines*, Cambridge, Polity

Hjarvard, S. (1998) 'TV News Exchange', in O. Boyd-Barrett and T. Rantanen (eds) *The Globalization of News*, London, Sage

Hodge, R. and Kress, G. (1988) *Social Semiotics*, Cambridge, Polity

Hollingsworth, M. (1986) *The Press and Political Dissent*, London, Pluto Press

Hymes, D. (1972) 'Models of the Interaction of Language and Social Life', in J. Gumperz and D. Hymes (eds) *Directions in Sociolinguistics – The Ethnography of Communication,* New York, Holt Rinehart and Winston

Jameson, F. (1984) 'Postmodernism or the Cultural Logic of Late Capitalism', *New Left Review*: 146

Kaitatzi-Whitlock, S. and Terzis, G. (1998) 'Disney's Descent on Greece: The Company is the Message', in J. Wasko, M. Phillips and E.R. Meehan (eds) *Dazzled by Disney? – The Global Disney Audiences Project*, London, Leicester University Press, pp. 135–59

Karouny, M. (2003) 'Hizbollah Computer Game Recalls Israeli Battles', Reuters, 18 March, quoted from www.specialforce.net

Katz, E. and Liebes, T. (1986) 'Mutual Aid in the Decoding of Dallas: Notes from a Cross-cultural Study', in P. Drummond and R. Paterson (eds) *Television in Transition*, London, BFI

Kellner, D. (1990) *Television and the Crisis of Democracy*, Boulder, CO, Westview Press

Khatib, L. (2004) 'The Politics of Space: The Spatial Manifestations of Representing Middle Eastern Politics in American and Egyptian Cinema', *Visual Communication* 3: 69–91

Kivikuro, U. (1998) 'From State Socialism to Deregulation', in O. Boyd-Barrett and T. Rantanen (eds) *The Globalization of News*, London, Sage, 137–53

Klein, N. (1999) *No Logo: Taking Aim at the Brand Bullies*, London, Picador

Kool-Smit, J. (1967) 'Het onbehagen van de vrouw', *De Gids*, November

Kress, G. and van Leeuwen, T. (1996) *Reading Images: The Grammar of Visual Design*, London, Routledge

Kress, G. and van Leeuwen, T. (2001) *Multimodal Discourse – The Modes and Media of Contemporary Communication*, London, Arnold

Leach, E.E. (1954) *Political Systems of Highland Burma: A Study of Kachim Social Structure*, London, Houghton Mifflin

Leach, E.E. (1969) *Genesis as Myth*, London, Cape

Lehrer, A. (1974*) Semantic Fields and Lexical Structure*, Amsterdam, North Holland

Leitner, G. (1980) 'BBC English and Deutsche Rundfunksprache: A Comparative and Historical Analysis of the Language of Radio', *International Journal of the Sociology of Language,* 26: 75–100

Le Monde (2003*) Semaine sanglante en Irak,* available at www.LeMonde.fr

Le Page, R. and Tabouret-Keller, A. (1985) *Acts of Identity: Creole-based Approaches to Language and Identity,* Cambridge, Cambridge University Press

Lévi-Strauss, C. (1967) 'The Story of Asdiwal', in E. Leach (ed.) *The Structural Study of Myth and Totemism,* London, Tavistock

Lévi-Strauss, C. (1978a) *Myth and Meaning,* London, Routledge and Kegan Paul

Lévi-Strauss, C. (1978b) *Mythologiques: Introduction to a Science of Mythology,* London, Cape

Lewis, P. (1992) 'Security Council Weighs Role in Somali Civil War', *New York Times,* 18 March: 9

Löfgren, O. (1996) 'The Great Christmas Quarrel: On the Moral Economy of a Family Ritual', in J. Frykman and O. Löfgren (eds) *Force of Habit – Exploring Everyday Culture,* Lund, Lund University Press, pp. 103–19

Lutz, A. and Collins, J.L. (1993) *Reading National Geographic,* Chicago, IL, University of Chicago Press

MacBride, S. and Roach, C. (2000) 'The New International Information Order', in F.J. Lechner and J. Boli (eds) *The Globalization Reader,* Oxford, Blackwell, pp. 286–92

McChesney, R.W. (2004) *The Problem with the Media: US Communication Politics in the 21st Century,* New York: Free Press

McClintock, M. (2002) *Instruments of Statecraft: US Guerrilla Warfare, Counter-insurgency and Counterterrorism 1940–1990,* New York, Pantheon

McConnell, J. (2001) 'The Counter-terrorists at the Fletcher School: The Reagan Administration's New Terrorism Policy', *Boston Review,* October/November

Machin, D. (2002) *Ethnographic Research for Media Studies,* London, Arnold

Machin, D. (2004) 'Building the World's Visual Language: The Increasing Global Importance of Image Banks', *Visual Communication,* 3: 316, 336

Machin, D. and Niblock, S. (2006) *News Production: Theory and Practice,* London, Routledge

Machin, D. and Suleiman, U. (2006) 'Arab and American Computer War Games: The Influence of a Global Technology on Discourse', *Critical Discourse Studies,* 3(1): 1–22

Machin, D. and Thornborrow, J. (2003) 'Branding and Discourse: The Case of *Cosmopolitan*', *Discourse & Society,* 14(4): 453–71

Machin, D. and van Leeuwen, T. (2003) 'Global Schemas and Local Discourses in *Cosmopolitan*', *Journal of Sociolinguistics,* 7(4): 493–513

Machin, D. and van Leeuwen, T. (2004) 'Global Media: Generic Homogeneity and Discursive Diversity', *Continuum,* 18(1): 99–120

Machin, D. and van Leeuwen, T. (2005a) 'Language Style and Lifestyle: the Case of a Global Magazine', *Media, Culture and Society,* 27(4): 577–600

Machin, D. and van Leeuwen, T. (2005b) 'Computer Games as Political Discourse: The Case of Blackhawk Down', *Journal of Language and Politics*, 4: 119–41

McRobbie, A. (1999) *In the Culture Society: Art, Fashion and Popular Music*, London, Routledge

Mak, G. (1999) *The eeuw van mijn vader*, Amsterdam, Atlas

Malik, R. (1992) 'The Global News Agenda', *Intermedia*, 20(1): 8–70

Malinowski, B. (1922) *Argonauts of the Western Pacific*, New York, E.P. Dutton

Malinowski, B. (1935) *Coral Gardens and their Magic*, Vol II, London, Allen and Unwin

Maren, M. (1994) 'Leave Somalia Alone', *New York Times*, 6 July, available at www.netnomad.com/Leave_Somalia.html

Mar-Molinero, C. (2000) *The Politics of Language in the Spanish-Speaking World*, London, Routledge

Martin, J.R. (1992) *English Text – System and Structure*, Amsterdam, Benjamins

Médécins sans Frontières (2002) *Somalia Briefing Document*

Mercer, K. (1990) 'Welcome to the Jungle: Identity and Diversity in Postmodern Politics', in J. Rutherford (ed.) *Community, Culture, Difference*, London, Lawrence and Wishart

Metz, C. (1971) *Essais sur la signification au cinéma*, Tome I, Paris, Klincksieck

Michman, R.D. (1991) *Lifestyle Market Segmentation*, New York, Praeger

Miller, T., Govil, N., McMurray, J. and Maxwell, R. (2000) *Global Hollywood*, London, BFI

Mitchell, A. (1978) *Consumer Values: A Typology*, Menlo Park, CA, Stanford Research Institute

Mitchell, T. (1996) *Popular Music and Local Identity*, Leicester, Leicester University Press

Molina y Vedia, S. (2001) 'Disney in Mexico: Observations on Integrating Global Culture Objects into Everyday Life', in J. Wasko, M. Phillips and E.R. Meehan (eds) *Dazzled by Disney? – The Global Disney Audiences Project*, London, Leicester University Press

Moragas Spa, M. and Lopez, B. (2000) 'Decentralisation Process and 'Proximate' Television in Europe', in G. Wang and J. Servaes (eds) *The New Communications Landscape: Demystifying Media Globalisation*, London, Routledge

Morley, D. (1981) 'Interpreting Television – A Case Study', in *U203 Popular Culture*, Milton Keynes, Open University Press

Morrish, J. (2001) *Business 2.0,* April edition, Seattle, WA, Bizjournals

Nakano, Y. (2002) 'Who Initiates a Global Flow? Japanese Popular Culture in Asia', *Visual Communication*, 1(2): 229–53

Nederveen Pieterse, J. (1992) *White on Black – Images of Africa and Blacks in Western Popular Culture*, New Haven, CT, Yale University Press.

Nederveen Pieterse, J. (1995) 'Globalization as Hybridization', in M. Featherstone, S. Lash and R. Robertson (eds) *Global Modernities*, London, Sage, pp. 45–69

Nettle, D. and Romaine, S. (2000) *Vanishing Voices – The Extinction of the World's Languages*, New York, Oxford University Press

Newsinger, J. (1997) *Dangerous Men: The SAS and Popular Culture*, London, Pluto

Nichols, B. (1981) *Ideology and the Image*, Bloomington, IN, Indiana University Press

Nightingale, V. (2001) 'Disney and the Australian Cultural Imaginary', in J. Wasko, M. Phillip and E.R. Meehan (eds) *Dazzled by Disney? – The Global Disney Audiences Project*, London, Leicester University Press, pp. 65–87

Ong, W.J. (1982) *Orality and Literacy – The Technologizing of the Word*, London, Methuen

Paglia, C. (1992) *Sex, Art and American Culture*, New York, Vintage

Paglia, C. (1994) *Vamps and Tramps*, New York, Vintage

Palmer, M. (1998) 'What Makes News', in O. Boyd-Barrett and T. Rantanen (eds) *The Globalization of News*, London, Sage, pp. 177–90

Papatheodorou, F. and Machin, D. (2003) 'The Umbilical Cord That Was Never Cut: The Post-Dictatorial Intimacy between the Political Elite and the Mass Media in Greece and Spain', *European Journal of Communication*, 18(1): 31–54

Patterson, C. (1998) 'Global Battlefields', in O. Boyd-Barrett and T. Rantanen (eds) *The Globalization of News*, London, Sage, pp. 79–103

Perlez, J. (1992a) 'Armed UN Troops Arrive in Somalia', *New York Times*, 15 September: 10

Perlez, J. (1992b) 'Chaotic Somalia Starves as Strongmen Battle', *New York Times*, 4 October: 1

Perlez, J. (1992c) 'US Says Airlifts Fail Somali Needy', *New York Times*, 31 July: 9

Perlez, J. (1992d) 'Hungry Somalis Still Die but Crops Grow Too', *New York Times*, 23 October: 1

Peterson, S. (2002) 'Black Hawk Down – Good Box Office but Bad History' available at www.telegraph.com

Phillipson, R. (1992) *Linguistic Imperialism*, Oxford, Oxford University Press

Polanyi, M. (1958) *Personal Knowledge: Towards a Post-critical Philosophy*, London, Routledge and Kegan Paul

Post, T. (1992) 'How Do You Spell Relief?' *Newsweek*, 23 November: 38

Propp, V. (1968) *Morphology of the Folktale*, Austin, TX, and London, University of Texas Press

Radway, J. (1987) *Reading the Romance: Women, Patriarchy and Popular Literature*, London, Verso

Radway, J. (1988) 'Reception Study – Ethnography and the Problem of Dispersed Audiences and Nomadic Subjects' *Cultural Studies*, 2(3)

Real, M. (1977) *Mass-mediated Culture*, Englewood Cliffs, NJ, Prentice-Hall

Reis, R. (1998) 'Love it or Hate it: Brazilians' Ambiguous Relationship with Disney, in J. Wasko, M. Phillips and E.R. Meehan (eds) *Dazzled by Disney? – The Global Disney Audiences Project*, London, Leicester University Press, pp. 88–101

Robertson, R. (1995) 'Glocalisation: Time, Space and Homogeneity-heterogeneity', in M. Featherstone, S. Lash and R. Robertson (eds) *Global Modernities*, London, Sage

Robinson, D. (1995) 'The Hollywood Conquest', in *Encyclopaedia Britannica Book of the Year*, Chicago, IL, Encyclopaedia Brittanica, p. 245

Röling, H. (1995) 'Zedelijkheid', in *Nederland in de twintigste eeuw. Een boeiend beeld van een bewogen tijdperk*, Utrecht, Teleac

Romein, J. and Romein, A. (1937) *Erflaters van onze beschaving, deel IV*, Amsterdam, Van Oorschot

Said, E.W. (1980) *The Question of Palestine*, New York, Vintage Books

Schickel, R. (1968) *The Disney Version – The Life, Time, Art and Commerce of Walt Disney*, New York, Simon and Schuster

Schiller, H.I. (1971) *Mass Communication and the American Empire*, Boston, MA, Beacon Press

Schiller, H.I. (1976) *Communication and Cultural Domination*, White Plains, New York, International Arts and Sciences Press

Schraeder, P.J. (1990) The Horn of Africa: US Foreign Policy in an Altered Cold War Environment, *Middle East Journal* 46(4): 573–74

Schulze-Schneider, I. (1998) 'From Dictatorship to Democracy', in O. Boyd-Barrett and T. Rantanen (eds) *The Globalization of News*, London, Sage, pp. 108–24

Sciolino, E. (1993) 'Somalia Puzzle: What Is the American Strategy?', *New York Times*, 5 October: 3

Scollon, R. and Scollon, S.W. (1998) 'Literate Design in the Discourses of Revolution, Reform and Transition: Hong Kong and China', *Written Language and Literacy* 1(1): 1–3

Seung Hyun Kim and Kyung Sook Lee (2001) 'Disney in Korean Mass Culture', in J. Wasko, M. Phillips and E.R. Meehan (eds) *Dazzled by Disney? – The Global Disney Audiences*, London, Leicester University Press, pp. 183–201

Shalom, S.R. (1993) 'Gravy Train: Feeding the Pentagon by Feeding Somalia' *Zmagazine*, February 1993, available at www.zmag.org/zmag/articles/shalom somalia.html

Simmel, G. (1971) *On Individuality and Social Forms* (ed. D. Levine) Chicago, IL, Universisty of Chicago Press

Sinclair, J., Jacka, E. and Cunningham, S. (1996) *New Patterns in Global Television: Peripheral Vision*, Oxford, Oxford University Press

Skuttnab-Kangas, T. and Phillipson, R. (eds) (1994) *Linguistic Human Rights: Overcoming Linguistic Discrimination*, Berlin, Mouton de Gruyter

Snoddy, R. (1996) 'Master of Bits at Home in the Hub', *Financial Times*, 28 May: 18

Strunk, W. (2000) *The Element of Style*, Boston, MA, Allyn and Bacon

Tomlinson, J. (1991) *Cultural Imperialism: A Critical Introduction*, London, Pinter

Tönnies, F. (2001) *Community and Civil Society*, Cambridge, Cambridge University Press

Tunstall, J. (1977) *The Media Are American*, London, Constable

Tunstall, J. and Machin, D. (1999) *The Anglo-American Media Connection*, Oxford, Oxford University Press

UNICEF (1989) *The State of the World's Children*, New York, Oxford University Press

van Leeuwen, T. (1995) 'Representing Social Action', *Discourse and Society*, 6(1): 81–107

van Leeuwen, T. (1996) 'The Representation of Social Actors', in C.R. Caldas-Coulthard and M. Coulthard (eds) *Texts and Practices – Readings in Critical Discourse Analysis*, London, Routledge

van Leeuwen, T. (1999) *Speech, Music, Sound*, London, Macmillan

van Leeuwen, T. (2000a) 'Visual Racism', in M. Reisigl and R. Wodak (eds) *The Semiotics of Racism – Approaches in Critical Discourse Analysis*, Vienna, Passagen Verlag

van Leeuwen, T. (2000b) 'The Construction of Purpose in Discourse', in S. Sarangi and M. Coulthard (eds) *Discourse and Social Life*, London, Longman, pp. 66–82

van Leeuwen, T. (2000c) 'Semiotics and Iconography', in T. van Leeuwen and C. Jewitt (eds) *Handbook of Visual Analysis*, London, Sage, pp. 92–118

van Leeuwen, T. (2006) 'Translation, Adaptation, Globalization: The Vietnam News', *Journalism*, 7(2): 217–37

van Leeuwen, T. and Wodak, R. (1999) 'Legitimizing Immigration Control: A Discourse-Historical Analysis', *Discourse Studies*, 1(1): 83–119

Vegt, R. (2004) 'Vriendinnen van papier. Vrouwentijdschriften tussen 1934 and 2003' in A. Sens (ed.) *Van Zeep tot Soap. Verandering en continuiteit in geillustreerde tijdschriften*, Amsterdam, Persmuseum

von Sturmer, J. (1981) 'Talking with Aborigines', *Australian Institute of Aboriginal Studies Newsletter*, 15: 15–30

Waller, D. (1992) 'Everyone is Sniping at the Marines', *Newsweek*, 29 December: 39

Wallerstein, I. (1984) *The Politics of the World-Economy*, Cambridge, Cambridge University Press

Wasko, J. (1982) *Movies and Money: Financing the American Film Industry*, Norwood, NJ: Ablex

Wasko, J., Phillips, M. and Meehan, E.R. (2001) *Dazzled by Disney? – The Global Disney Audiences Project*, London, Leicester University Press

Wassenaar, I. (1976) *Vrouwenbladen. Spiegels van een mannenmaatschappij*, Amsterdam, Wetenschappelijke Uitgeverij

Weeks, J. (1990) 'The Value Difference in Identity', in J. Rutherford (ed.) *Community, Culture, Difference*, London, Lawrence and Wishart

Wilke, J. (1998) 'The Struggle for Control of Domestic Newsmarkets', in O. Boyd-Barrett and T. Rantanen (eds) *The Globalization of News*, London, Sage, pp. 49–60

Williamson, J. (1979) *Decoding Advertisements*, London, Marion Boyars

Wood, J.P. (1958) *Of Lasting Interest – The Story of The Reader's Digest*, New York, Doubleday

Wright, W. (1975) *Sixguns and Society – A Structural Study of the Western*, Berkeley and Los Angeles, CA, University of California Press

Zablocki, B.D. and Kanter, R.M. (1976) 'The Differentiation of Lifestyles', *Annual Review of Sociology*, 2: 269–98

Index

ROUTLEDGE DISCOURSE

The Discourse Reader

NEW
2ND EDITION

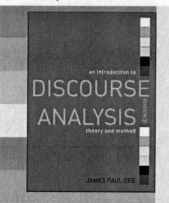

Edited by **Adam Jaworski**, University of Wales, Cardiff, UK
and **Nikolas Coupland**, University of Wales, Cardiff, UK

The Discourse Reader collects in one volume the most
important and influential articles on discourse analysis.
Designed as a structured sourcebook and divided into clear
sections, the book covers the foundations of modern
discourse analysis and represents all of its contemporary
methods and traditions.

The second edition:

• has been revised and updated throughout

• includes six new articles from authors including Teun A.
van Dijk, Judith Butler and Gillian Rose

• includes 'discussion points' to help readers engage with
key issues

• covers the foundations of modern discourse analysis and
represents all of its contemporary methods and traditions.

The new edition of *The Discourse Reader* remains an
essential resource for all students of discourse analysis.

August 2006: 246x174: 592pp
Hb: 0-415-34631-2: **£75.00**
Pb: 0-415-34632-0: **£22.99**

An Introduction to Discourse Analysis
Theory and Method

2ND EDITION

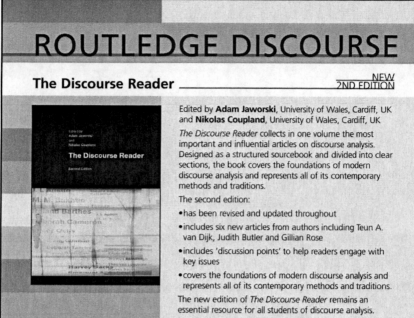

James Paul Gee, University of Madison, Wisconsin, USA

Assuming no prior knowledge of linguistics, the author
presents both a theory of language-in-use and a method
of research. Clearly structured and written in a highly
accessible style, *An Introduction to Discourse Analysis*
incorporates perspectives from a variety of approaches and
disciplines, including applied linguistics, education,
psychology, anthropology and communication to help
students and scholars from a range of backgrounds to
engage in their own discourse analysis.

The second edition has been completely revised and
updated and contains substantial new material and
examples of oral and written language.

2005: 234x156: 224pp
Hb: 0-415-32860-8: **£60.00**
Pb: 0-415-32861-6: **£18.99**

For information on inspection copies please visit www.routledge.com/inspectioncopy.asp
To order online please visit www.routledge.com

www.routledge.com/linguistics

Routledge
Taylor & Francis Group

Forthcoming in 2007

The Language of the News
Martin Conboy

The Language of the News investigates and critiques the conventions of language used in newspapers and provides students with a clear introduction to critical linguistics as a tool for analysis.

Using contemporary examples from UK, US and Australian newspapers, and from TV and radio, this book deals with key themes of representation, from gender and national identity to 'race' and looks at how language is used to construct audiences, to persuade and even to parody. It examines debates in the newspapers themselves about the nature of language including commentary on political correctness, the sensitive use of language and irony as a journalistic weapon.

Featuring chapter openings and summaries, activities, and a wealth of pertinent examples from contemporary news coverage, *The Language of the News* assists students in widening their perceptions of the use of language in the news media and is essential reading for students of Media and Communication, Journalism, and English Language and Linguistics.

Martin Conboy is a reader in Journalism Studies at the University of Sheffield. He is the author of *The Press and Popular Culture, Journalism: A Critical History* and *Tabloid Britain: Constructing a Community Through Language* as well as being the co-editor of a series of books on Journalism Studies.

HB: 978–0–415–37201–5
PB: 978–0–415–37202–2

For more information please go to:
www.routledge.com/linguistics